SACRED HEART
PRAYER BOOK

A COMPLIATION

Compiled and edited by:

Brother James, S.D.B.   (Salesian of Don Bosco)
Saints Peter and Paul Church
666 Filbert Street
San Francisco, California 94133

SACRED HEART PUBLISHERS
861 West San Bruno Avenue
San Bruno, California 94066
(415) 588 - 5673

Imprimi potest: Very Rev. Carmine Vairo, S.D.B.
                 Provincial,
                   Salesians of Saint John Bosco
                   California Province

Nihil obstat: Rev. Joseph Fessio, S.J.
                 University of San Francisco
                 Censor Librorum

Imprimatur: † John R. Quinn
                 Archbishop of San Francisco

                 Feast of St. Mark the Evangelist
                 April 25, 1980

Library of Congress Cataloging in Publication Data

AD JESUM PER MARIAM

TABLE OF CONTENTS

"For all that you give Me, I give you My Heart."

*

"My Heart is a fiery Furnace to which you chosen souls must come to enkindle yours. It belongs to you with all the graces It contains, that you may distribute them to the world, to the many souls who do not know where to seek them, and to so many others who despise them."

1

The Sacred Heart of Jesus

St. Margaret Mary

Once as I was praying before the most Blessed Sacrament, Jesus disclosed to me the marvels of His Love and the inexplicable secrets of His Sacred Heart. He opened to me His Divine Heart.

Jesus: "My Divine Heart is so inflamed with Love for mankind that, being unable any longer to contain within Itself the flames of Its burning Charity, It must be manifested to them in order to enrich them with the precious Treasures which I reveal to you. My Sacred Heart contains all the Graces, Sanctification, and Salvation necessary to withdraw souls from the abyss of hell."

I saw this Divine Heart more brilliant than the sun and transparent as crystal. It has Its adorable Wound and is encircled with a Crown of Thorns which signify the pricks our sins cause It. It was surmounted by a Cross which signifies that from the first moment of the Incarnation, when the Sacred Heart was formed, the Cross was placed in It. From the very first moment this Heart was filled with all the bitterness, humiliations, poverty, sorrow, and contempt which His Sacred Humanity would have to suffer during the whole course of His Life and during His Holy Passion. Our Lord made me understand that the ardent desire He had of being loved by all souls and of rescuing them from the path of perdition into which satan was hurrying them in great numbers, had caused Him to reveal His Sacred Heart to mankind, together with all Its Treasures of Love, Mercy, Grace, Sanctification, and Salvation which It contains.

MORNING PRAYERS

*   *   *   *   *   *   *

Angelus

In the name of the Father, and of the Son, and of the Holy Spirit. Amen.

The Angel of the Lord declared unto Mary, that She would conceive by the Holy Spirit.

Hail Mary, full of Grace, the Lord is with Thee. Blessed art Thou among women, and Blessed is the Fruit of Thy womb, Jesus.
Holy Mary, Mother of God, pray for us sinners, now, and at the hour of our death. Amen.

"Behold the handmaid of the Lord.
Be it done unto me according to your Word."
Hail Mary...

The Word was made flesh,
and dwelt among us.
Hail Mary...

Pray for us O Holy Mother of God,
that we may be made worthy of the promises of Christ.

Eternal Father, fill our hearts with Your Love. By the Virgin Mary's acceptance of the Angel's message, Christ Your Son became Incarnate. By His Passion and Cross, may we accept our cross and be brought to the glory of His Resurrection. We ask this through Jesus our Lord. Amen.

Glory be to the Father...

3

Regina Caeli

In the name of the Father, and of the Son, and of the Holy Spirit. Amen.

Queen of Heaven, rejoice, Alleluia.
For He whom You merited to bear, Alleluia.

Has Risen as He said, Alleluia.
Pray for us to God, Alleluia.

Rejoice and be glad, O Virgin Mary, Alleluia.
Because the Lord is truly Risen, Alleluia.

God our Father, by the Resurrection of Your Son, our Lord Jesus Christ, You gave joy to the world. Through the prayers of His Mother, the Virgin Mary, bring us to the happiness of Eternal Life. We ask this through Christ our Lord. Amen.

Glory be to the Father...
*   *   *
"My beloved, My spouse, come to My Temple. I wish to hear your voice of praise, love, and thanksgiving. I will direct all your actions in the fulfillment of My service and pleasure."
*
I go to Your altar, O God; You are the Joy of my youth.
*
One thing I ask of You, O Lord, this I seek: to dwell in Your House all the days of my life.
*
I love, O God, the beauty of Your House, and the place where Your glory dwells.

My Jesus, my Beloved, I love You. You taught me the Wisdom of Your Heart. I humbly repeat what I have learnt in Your School of Love: I bury myself forever in the Beloved Sepulchre of Your Merciful Heart; There I live to die with You and die to live with You. O Divine Victim, I offer Your Sacred Heart with all Its Love, Merits, and Treasures to the Eternal Father, to forgive the many souls that are ungrateful. I will praise, love, thank, and serve You for all who have not, do not, and will not praise, love, thank, and serve You. I love You on behalf of each one of Your creatures, of each heart that exists. I will spend every instant of this day imploring forgiveness and repairing for sin. I unite my soul to the zeal that consumes Your Sacred Heart, and I will console You. Even in my littleness, I am prepared to repair for the sins mankind commits against You. What a miserable little victim I am.

I place my little heart in the Immaculate Heart of Holy Mary. I offer Her Heart with all Her Love and Treasures to You. Through Her I unite all my thoughts, words, actions, desires, and sufferings to Yours. To Your infinite Love I unite my love.

I offer You my companions: the Angels and Saints, and my brothers and sisters on earth and in purgatory. I offer You all the good they have given You; I renew it with every beat of my heart. I ask them to aid me in fulfilling my duties and my desires toward You. I ask them to pray for me so that I may be able to fulfill Your Holy and Divine Will. To each of them I offer Your Sacred Heart which You have given me; in doing this I do not lose or diminish my Treasure.

Most High and incomprehensible God, my King and my Lord, You are worthy of all glory and reverence. I am dust; as Your creature I love You and adore You. I praise You because of Your infinite Being and Perfection. I give You thanks for regarding my insignificance. By the immensity of Your Divinity You fill all the Heavens and the earth. I, Your servant, desire to fulfill Your Holy Will on all occasions, at all times, and in all places in which Your Providence shall deign to place me. You are my only Good, my Being, and my Life. Toward Your pleasure and satisfaction tend all my thoughts, words, and actions.

*

Who are You, O God, and who am I, that You condescend to look on me who am dust, unworthy of Your Mercy? I behold my lowliness and vileness; I admire Your immensity. I love You, my King and my Lord, and I offer myself as Your slave. Let not my understanding attend to any other object, nor my memory retain any other image, nor my will seek any other pleasure than You, my highest Good, my true and only Love. Let my faculties and senses be attentive only to You and whatever Your Majesty shall direct. You alone are mine, my Beloved, and I will only be Yours, for You are my eternal Good.

*

My dearest King, if You give me any freedom of choice, I wish to choose only suffering unto death in love for You. I beseech You to make of Your slave, a sacrifice and holocaust of suffering acceptable to You. I ask only for Your protection, for You favor the just, stand by those in tribulation, and console the afflicted.

My God, I give You thanks and praise for Your unchangeable Being and infinite Perfections, and for having created me out of nothing. I acknowledge myself as Your creature. I love You, I praise You. I adore You as the supreme Lord and Creator of all that exists. I place my spirit in Your Hands, offering myself with humility and resignation, asking You to dispose of me according to Your Holy Will, today and all the days of my life. Teach me to fulfill whatever is Your pleasure. Receive me as Your slave and supply my deficiency, in order that I may properly serve You. Make me what You desire me to be in Your holy service.

*

O my most Gentle Jesus, compassionate Spouse of my soul, You have called me into this most desirable and delicious solitude, the better to unveil to me the mysteries of Your Love, the inexhaustible treasures of Your infinite Goodness, and the exquisite delicacy of Your Mercy. I come to You with the heart of a spouse, for I expect everything from You, my most Faithful Spouse. I know, O Jesus, that I can bring You only miseries, defects, infidelities, and falls innumerable, but all this does not disturb me, because I know that You are infinitely Good.

Should I say more to You, O Jesus? I will say it, because Your Goodness desires it. I am even glad to be an accumulation of miseries, an abyss of miseries, nothing but misery, because I give more to the action of Your Mercy. O Jesus, be ever to me a Jesus, and grant that I may be ever to You a faithful servant. I trust in You.

*

7

My Jesus, here is my tongue; watch over it; may it utter only what pleases You; may my silence speak to You. Here are my ears; may they listen only to the voice of duty, and to Your Voice. Here are my eyes; may they behold You in every face and in every work.

Here are my hands and my feet. Make them agile. Rivet them to Your service alone, for the execution of Your holy desires. Here are my thoughts; may Your Light illumine them. Here is my heart; may Your Love, O Jesus, reign and rest in it.

*

O Jesus, I am so weak and worthless!

"Then unite yourself to Me, for I am Strength."

How can I do that?

"By remaining in Love! United to Me, you will be stronger than the strong! You must think only of loving Me, and I will think of everything else for you, even to the smallest details!"

*

"My spouse, I Love you. Read these words: 'I Love you,' on the bread you eat, on the water you drink, and on the bed on which you sleep. It is because I Love you that I prepare bread for you; because I Love you, I give you water to drink; because I Love you, I prepare the bed on which you sleep. In everything that happens to you this day, read above all: 'My spouse, I Love you!' "

*

"What I tell one soul, I tell all souls."

8

"Honor My Mother with the Words of Her Son:

O Tender and Loving Mother Mary, most Prudent Virgin, Mother of my Redeemer, I come to salute You today with all the love that I, as a child, can feel for my Mother.

I am Your child, and because I am so helpless I will take the fervor of the Heart of Your Divine Son Jesus; with Him I will salute You as the Purest of creatures, for You were created according to the desires of the all Holy God.

You, Holy Mary, were conceived without sin, exempt from all corruption. You were ever faithful to the impulses of grace, so that Your Soul accumulated such merit, that It was raised above all other creatures.

You were chosen to be the Mother of Jesus, You kept Him in a most Pure Sanctuary; God who came to give Life to souls, Himself took life from You, and received nourishment from You.

O Incomparable Virgin, Immaculate Virgin, You are the Delight of the Blessed Trinity, the Admiration of all the Angels and Saints, the Joy of Heaven. You are the Morning Star, Rose blossoming in springtime, Immaculate Lily, tall and graceful Iris, sweet smelling Violet, Garden enclosed kept for the delight of the King of Heaven. You, Holy Mary, are my Mother, Virgin most Prudent, Ark most precious containing every Virtue. You are my Mother, most Powerful Virgin, Virgin Clement and Faithful. You are my Mother, O Refuge of sinners.

I salute You and I rejoice at the sight of the gifts bestowed on You by the Almighty, and the prerogatives with which He has crowned You.

May You be blest and praised, Mother of my Redeemer, Mother of poor sinners. Have pity on us and cover us with Your motherly protection.

I salute You, Holy Virgin Mary, in the name of my guardian Angel, all the Angels and Saints, the poor souls in purgatory, and my brothers and sisters on earth.

O Holy Mary, would that I could love You with the love and fire of the Seraphim, but as this is too little to satisfy my desire to honor You, and since Jesus has taught me this prayer, I, as a little child, salute and love You with the Love of Your Divine Son, who is my Father, my Redeemer, my Sanctifier, and my Beloved.

I salute You with the Purity of the Holy Spirit and the Sanctity of the Adorable Trinity. Through these Divine Persons I bless You and desire to render You filial homage, constant and pure for all eternity.

O Incomparable Virgin Mary, bless me since I am Your child. Bless all my brothers and sisters. Protect them and pray for them to Jesus my Lord, who is Almighty. He will never refuse to give You whatever You ask.

Adieu, Tender and Sweet Mother Mary; day and night I salute You, in time and for eternity."

* Honor My Mother 2*

Come, O Creator Spirit Blest
And in our souls take up Your rest;
Come with Your grace and heavenly aid,
To fill the hearts which You have made.   Wisdom

O Paraclete, to You we cry,
O Highest Gift of God Most High,
O Fount of Life, O Fire of Love,
And sweet Anointing from above.   Understanding

You in Your sevenfold Gifts are known,
The Finger of God's Hand we own;
The promise of the Father Thou,
Who does the tongue with fire endow.   Science

Our senses kindle from above,
And make our hearts o'erflow with love;
With patience firm and virtue high,
The weakness of our flesh supply.   Fortitude

Drive far from us the foe we dread,
And grant us Your true peace instead;
So shall we not, with You for Guide,
Turn from the path of Life aside.   Counsel

O may Your grace on us bestow,
The Father and the Son to know,
And You through endless times confessed
Of both the Eternal Spirit Blest.   Piety

All Glory while the ages run,
Be to the Father and the Son
Who rose from death; the same to Thee,
O Holy Spirit, eternally. Amen.   Holy Fear of the Lord

Prayer to my Guardian Angel

Angel of God, my guardian dear,
To you God's Love entrusts me here,
Ever this day be at my side,
To light and guard, to rule and guide. Amen.

* * *

Hail, Holy Angel of God, you are the guardian of my soul and body. By the Sweetest Heart of Jesus, the Son of God, take me beneath the shelter of your faithful care. He placed me under your charge on the day of my Baptism. Help me to cross, unharmed and unsullied, the swollen torrent of this life, until I shall be admitted to behold, like you and with you, the beauty of the Supreme King!

O Holy Angel, you were appointed by God to be my guardian. I honor you who assist me, a miserable and worthless creature, with such patient fidelity, and defend me against all the assaults of the devils, our enemies. Blest was the hour in which you were assigned to be my guardian, defender, and patron. Blessed be all your love and care for me, for you do not become weary in furthering my salvation. I give you thanks for all the benefits which you have bestowed on me in body and in soul. In return for all your loving services, I offer you the infinitely Precious and Noble Heart of Jesus, overflowing with all Its Treasures. I beseech you to forgive me for having so often opposed your holy inspirations, and saddened you, my nearest and dearest friend. I firmly resolve to obey you henceforward, and most faithfully to serve my God. Amen.

Prayer to Honor a Saint

O Holy N . . . , I honor and congratulate you with all my heart for all the glory and honor which is rendered to you today, through the boundless supply of the Divine Goodness. I recall to your mind the happiness you had, when you were presented by the Holy Angels to God, to receive your everlasting reward.

For all the benefits and graces which have ever been bestowed on you by the God of Majesty, I adore His unutterable Goodness.

I desire to bind myself to you in a bond of perpetual love, by giving you the Sacred Heart of my Jesus, that Treasure of all good things, together with all the Love and Condescension He has ever shown you upon earth or in Heaven.

With trust, I commend myself to your holy prayers, imploring, that in the hour when my soul shall be separated from my body, you would offer unto the Heart of Jesus, in satisfaction for my many negligences, all the fervor you had on the day you entered Paradise. Amen.

*

Prayer to Honor all the Saints

O Holy Patriarchs and Prophets, I salute you in the Sweetest Heart of Jesus, imploring you to offer to God for me, the ardent desire you had for the Incarnation of Jesus.

O Holy Apostles, I salute you in the Sweetest Heart of Jesus, imploring you to offer to God for me, that faithfulness and constancy which you showed by gathering unto Him a faithful people by your preaching and sacrifices.

O Holy Martyrs, I salute you in the Sweetest Heart of Jesus, imploring you to offer to God for me, that patience with which you shed your blood for His Love.

O Holy Confessors, I salute you in the Sweetest Heart of Jesus, imploring you to offer unto God for me, that sanctity which shone forth in your words and example.

O Holy Virgins, I salute you in the Sweetest Heart of your Divine Spouse, imploring you to offer to God for me, that purity by which you have merited to be so near to Jesus in Heaven.

All you Saints of God, I salute and venerate you in the Sweetest Heart of Jesus our Lord, and through It I render thanks to God for all the good which has ever flowed forth from It for our salvation.

O Saints in Heaven, I ask each of you to offer unto God for me, a miserable sinner, all those virtues and perfections which render you especially pleasing to God. In return, I give to each of you my greatest possession: the Sacred Heart of Jesus.

Honor all the Saints 2*

*

With Jesus, even the Cross is delightful, but without Jesus all delights are but a cross.

*

Jesus, Mary, I love You! Save souls!

14

An Offering of Myself as a Victim of Holocaust to God's Merciful Love.

O my God, most Blessed Trinity, I desire to love You and make You loved, to work for the glory of the Holy Catholic Church, by saving souls on earth and by liberating those souls suffering in purgatory. I desire to accomplish Your Holy Will perfectly, and to reach the degree of glory You have prepared for me in Your Kingdom. I desire, to be a saint, but I feel my helplessness and I beg You, O my God, to be Yourself my Sanctity!

Eternal Father, since You Love me so much as to give me Your only Son as my Savior and my Spouse, the infinite treasures of His Merits are mine. I offer these Merits to You with gladness, begging You to look upon me only in the Face of Jesus, and in His Heart burning with Love.

I offer You, O God of Mercy and Love, all the merits of the Saints in Heaven and on earth, their acts of love, and those of the Holy Angels. I offer You the Love and Merits of the Blessed Virgin Mary, my dearest Mother. It is to Her, my Treasurer, that I abandon my offering, begging Her to present it to You, my God. Her Divine Son Jesus, my Beloved Spouse, told us in the day of His Mortal Life: "Whatever you ask the Father in My Name, He will give it to you!" I am certain then, that You will grant my desires; I know, O my God, that the more You want to give, the more You make us desire! I feel in my heart these desires and it is with confidence that I ask You to come and take possession of my soul. I cannot receive Holy Communion as often as I desire, but Lord, are You not all Powerful? Remain in me as in a tabernacle and never separate Yourself from Your little victim.

I want to console You, O my God, for all the ingratitude of the wicked, and I beg You to take away my freedom to displease You. Since through weakness I will sometimes fall, may Your divine glance cleanse my soul immediately, consuming all my imperfections, as a fire that transforms everything into itself.

I thank You, O my God, for all the graces You have granted me, especially the grace of making me pass through the crucible of suffering! It is with joy that I shall contemplate You on the last day carrying the sceptre of Your cross. Since You deigned to give me a share in this very precious cross, I hope in Heaven to resemble You and to see shining in my glorified body, the Sacred Stigmata of Your Passion.

After my exile on earth, I hope to enjoy You, my God, in the Fatherland, but I do not want to store up merits for Heaven. I want to work even in Heaven, until the end of time, for Your Love alone, with the one purpose of pleasing You, consoling Your Sacred Heart, and saving souls who will love You eternally.

In the evening of this life, I shall appear before You with empty hands. I do not ask You, Lord, to count my works, for I have given my merits away to my brothers and sisters. I wish to be clothed in Your own Mercy and to receive from Your Love, the eternal possession of Yourself.

Offering 2

16

I want no other throne, no other crown but You, My Beloved.

Time is nothing for You, and a single day is as a thousand years. You can then, in one instant prepare me to appear before You.

In order that I may live in an act of perfect love, I offer myself as a victim of holocaust of Your merciful Love, asking You to consume me incessantly, allowing the infinite Tenderness enclosed within You to overflow into my soul, so that I may become a martyr of Your Love, O my God!

May this martyrdom, after having prepared me to appear before You, finally cause me to die. Then may my soul take its flight without any delay, into the eternal embrace of Your merciful Love.

I want, O my Beloved, at each beat of my heart, to renew this offering to You an infinite number of times, until, the shadows having disappeared, I may be able to tell You of my love, in an eternal face to Face!

Offering 3*

*   *   *

All God's perfections appear to be resplendent with Love; even His Justice seems to me to be clothed in Love. What a sweet joy it is to think that God is Just, that He takes into account our weakness, that He is perfectly aware of our fragile nature. What should I fear then? Must not the infinitely Just God, who deigns to pardon the faults of the prodigal son with so much kindness, be just also towards me, for I am with Him always?

Victims of Love are souls who offer themselves to God's merciful Love in order to turn away the punishments reserved to sinners, drawing this punishment on themselves.

*

O my God, will Your Justice alone find souls willing to immolate themselves as victims? Does not Your merciful Love need them too? Your Love is unknown and rejected! Those hearts upon whom You would lavish It turn to creatures, seeking happiness from them with their miserable affection; they do this instead of throwing themselves into Your arms and accepting Your infinite Love. O my God, must Your Love, which is disdained, remain hidden in Your Heart? It seems to me that if You were to find souls offering themselves as victims of holocaust to Your Love, You would consume them rapidly; it seems to me, too, that You would be happy not to hold back Your infinite Tenderness. If Your Justice loves to release itself, this Justice which extends only over the earth, how much more does Your merciful Love desire to set souls on fire, since Your Mercy reaches to the Heavens. O my Jesus, let me be this happy victim. Consume Your holocaust with the Fire of Your Divine Love!

It seems to me that Love penetrates and surrounds me, that at each moment this merciful Love renews me, purifying my soul and leaving no trace of sin within it: therefore I need have no fear of purgatory. I know that the Fire of Love is more sanctifying than is the fire of purgatory. I know that You, cannot desire useless sufferings for us, and that You would not inspire the desires I feel unless You wanted to grant them.

"Take My Sacred Heart and offer It to your God. By It, you can pay all your debts. You now know why I attracted you to My house.

"I want you to fulfill My plan by being docile and surrendering to My Love, which seeks only to possess and consume."

*

"My Heart is a fiery Furnace to which you chosen souls must come to enkindle yours. It belongs to you with all the Graces It contains, that you may distribute them to the world, to the many souls who do not know where to seek them, and to so many others who despise them."

*

"The greatest reward I can give you or any soul, is to make you a victim of My Love and Mercy, rendering you like Myself, for I am the Divine Victim for sinners."

*

"If you give Me souls, I will give you My Heart. Which one of us will be giving the greater gift?"

*

"Since through you, I Will to pour out the treasures of My Mercy to other souls, do you think that I would not begin by giving them first to you?"

*

"You possess My Heart for all I ask you to do."

*

"For all that you give Me, I give you My Heart."

*

"Tell Me what you have to offer Me for the souls I have confided to you. Put it all in the Wound of My Sacred Heart, so that your offering may acquire an infinite value."

19

"Love transforms your ordinary actions and gives them an infinite value, but It does even more: My Heart Loves you chosen souls so tenderly, that I wish to use your miseries, your weaknesses, and even your faults. Your very abjectness clothes you with a humility that you would not have, if you saw yourself without any defects."

*

"Never forget that you are the victim of My Heart."

*

"I know your wretchedness. I will make reparation for you; you will make reparation for souls."

*

"Love Me and never cease telling Me of your love."

*

"Each time you acknowledge your unworthiness of My gifts, and confide fully in My Mercy, you acquit yourself of the debts you owe Me for these benefits."

*

"Love Me on behalf of each one of My creatures, of each heart that exists."

*

"A holy desire is a continuous prayer."

*

"There is a degree of love, which only those attain who have suffered much and suffered well, and this is mainly the suffering of the soul. If you really love God, the greatest suffering that you can endure is that of not being able to love Him as much as you desire. The pain of love is sweet and attractive; the more it prevails, the more it is sought; the souls who suffer it, desire to hear God spoken of, whom they love, thus seeking to be cured by a renewal of the wound."

"Whenever you desire to obtain anything from Me, offer Me My Heart, which I have so often given you as a bond of our mutual friendship, in union with the Love which made Me become man for the salvation of mankind. I give you this special mark of friendship, that this treasure shall be presented to whomever you pray for, as a rich man would present a coffer to his friend to supply all that is needed."

*

"In order to labor for the salvation of your neighbor, make the saving Sign of the Cross upon your heart; utter My Name once, and then say all that My grace shall inspire you!"

*

"I visited Saint Catherine when she was in prison, and I encouraged her by these words: 'Be firm My daughter, for I am with you.' For what purpose was this visit recorded? I visited John, My favorite apostle, and said to him: 'Come to Me, My beloved.' What purpose does it serve that it should be known? What purpose does it serve that these and many other sayings and conversations are known, unless it be to enkindle the zeal of you souls who shall read or hear about them, and to manifest to all mortals the greatness of My Love? In this manner you shall desire to obtain the same favors as those My Saints received.

"These sayings and conversations will produce devotion in your heart, when you consider the effusion of My grace and the excess of My Mercy, and you shall endeavor to change your present life for one which is more perfect."

*

"God delays answering your prayers and defers the fulfillment of your desires, in order to dispose you to receive and to oblige Himself to give much more than you ask or desire."

*

"Repeat these words after Me and ponder them carefully in your heart:

My dearest Lord Jesus, King of my soul, my Father, my Spouse, my God, I surrender myself from this moment forth into Your most Holy Hands. From henceforth I shall have no jurisdiction over myself, but shall be governed by You.

Whatever You ask of me, I shall give; whatever You permit to befall me, I shall gladly submit to it. Whether joy or sorrow, honor or dishonor, comfort or pain be my lot, I shall be equally happy, for all are gifts from You and I shall praise You and love You for all.

My God, the only reason for my existence is to give You honor. Under the guidance of Your Holy Virgin Mother Mary, I give myself to You forever and irrevocably to be Your slave. All I have, all I am, all I ever hope to be, all, dearest Jesus, is Yours. Do whatever You will with me, only give me the grace to love You and to serve You faithfully forever."

*

"Do you love Me? See, I give you My Heart, I entrust to you My most priceless Treasure. Guard It well."

*

"Every wound made in your heart is one more avenue by which I may enter into it."

"Don't lose a single minute. Time is short for saving so many souls. You know it is not merely by praying that souls are saved, but through the actions of even the most ordinary lives lived for God. Offer Me everything, absolutely everything, united to My Life on earth. What wealth! Give it to poor sinners: most of them are just ignorant. Since you have received so much, you must make every effort to help them. You will comfort this Heart of Mine so full of Tenderness, and you will satisfy justice. Offer Me all the crosses of the world. There are so many crosses and few think of offering them to Me in expiation for sins. You who know should help, so that nothing may be lost. Give Me hearts. Give Me souls. I am thirsty. Always give Me souls."

*

"You may be very sure that to do your duty is one way of loving Me. In this way you can love Me all day. You don't notice this, but I do, for you told me so in your morning offering.

"Are you so busy that you have not even a moment to glance at Me or think of Me? It would enrich Me, for My children don't think about Me very often.

"Forget that you are you. Be your Christ. Be the One who loves you at all times. Try to imitate Me."

*

"Charity not only covers sin, but like a burning sun, consumes the slightest imperfections, and overwhelms the soul with Merit."

*

"Those who leave all things for Me find all things in Me."

23

"My Love is an Ocean of Waters, sweeping before It and into It all that comes in Its path.

"My Love is a raging Fire, consuming all with which It comes into contact.

"My Love is an Eagle, soaring into the sky and swooping down surely and swiftly to catch Its prey, and carry it to Its Nest.

"Let this Ocean cleanse you. Let this glowing Fire consume you. Let this Eagle swoop down and bear you to Its Nest on the mountain top."

My Jesus, I am Yours. You may do whatever You please with me. Drown me in Your Divine Ocean of Love, consume me in Your flaming Furnace of Love, and carry Your prey to Your Eagle Nest.

*

"If you will not look with the eyes of your soul on the Mercies which I have bestowed on you, open at least the eyes of your body, and behold Me before you enclosed in the Blessed Eucharist. Know assuredly that the rigor of My Justice is limited within the bonds of Mercy which I exercise towards mankind in giving you this Holy Sacrament.

*

"When the Saints, whom you have invoked, pray for you, their prayers shine before Me as a monument of Mercy which I have promised mankind, which obliges Me to have pity on you."

*

"My Merits never come to an end. They only multiply as you take them, for My Merits are Myself. Your soul in a state of grace is My temple, since Grace is your Jesus."

Love of God

O my God, most worthy Object of my love, my supreme and infinite Good, I love You and will love You forever and ever. I embrace You with all the affections of my heart, for You are my sweetest Good. O most Gentle, most Beloved Lord, You are the Life of my soul. You are the Joy of my heart, my Peace, my God and my Love. I love You with all my soul and with all my strength; I do not love You as I should love You, nor even as I desire to love You. Would that I could love You a thousand times more; would that I could love You with an infinite Love: Your Love!

Pierce my heart with the arrow of Your Love, and wound it as the Wound of Your Heart. Grant that I may love You, for without Your aid I cannot love You. I desire to gather all created hearts, and contain them all in my heart, with all their love and desires. How I would love You then! I desire that You would give me, but for one hour, the glowing love of the Seraphim, that I might be inflamed with the ardor of that impetuous love, and enkindle it in every heart of all mankind!

How great is my grief that You are not loved! I mourn that You are neglected and despised, and that You are so cruelly offended and outraged! I console You for all the injuries and insults which are heaped on You; if I were able, I would most gladly make reparation to You for all the outrages and wrongs done to Your honor. Yes, for Your Love I would gladly suffer to my dying hour, all the pangs of holy desire which the heart of mankind has suffered or shall suffer to the end of the world, if so I might offer You a more worthy shelter within my soul, and make amends to You for all the contempt and ignominy which You sustain at the hands of ungrateful mortals. Amen.

*

Aspirations of a Loving Soul

O God of my heart, I love You with all my heart, and I desire to love You a thousand times more. Would that I could praise and love You beyond every other creature; would that I could give You thanks and console You, and practice all virtues in greatest perfection. Gladly would I do so, according to the pleasure of Your Divine Heart.

O my Sweet Love, I desire to bring before You, all mortals in whom You have desired to take Your delight. I would gladly go barefoot throughout the world, and bring to You in my arms all those in whose hearts You deign and delight to dwell, that I might satisfy the yearnings of Your infinite and Divine Love. If it were possible, I would willingly divide my heart into as many fragments as there are souls on earth, that I might communicate to all of them, a holy resolve to serve and obey You, to the joy and content of Your Divine Heart.

O God, worthy of an infinite love, I have nothing which can be worthy of Your dignity. If I had all that You have, I would gladly and thankfully resign all to You. Amen.

Holocaust

Eternal Father, God of glorious Majesty, Ruler of Heaven and earth, I, Your most unworthy creature, offer You, upon the most sacred Altar of the Sweetest Heart of Jesus, myself with all that I am, all I have, all I can do, together with every good gift which You have ever bestowed on me.

I offer You all the treasures and the wealth of this world, all kingdoms, royalties, honors, and dignities, with this intention: that were they all mine, I would distribute them to Your poor, or employ them in other pious uses, so that for love of You, I might abide with joy in my present state of poverty.

I offer to You, O Eternal Father, on the Altar of the Sacred Heart of Jesus, the virtues, merits, devotions, and holiness of all the just; the crosses, the afflictions, the poverty and needs of all the poor, the afflicted and the sick; the pangs, the torments, the wounds, the shedding of blood, and the death of all martyrs; the penance and vigils of all confessors; the love and purity of all virgins. I offer them all to You with this intention: that were they all mine, I would practice all virtues and suffer all afflictions with a most pure intention for Your glory.

I offer You all the fullness of grace and glory, transcending all human thought, with which You have so super-abundantly enriched Your Saints in Heaven, especially the most Glorious Virgin Mary, Mother of Your Only-Begotten Son.

Above all these, I offer You the Virtues and Merits which Your Son Jesus manifested on earth, and all the gifts of Grace, drawn from the infinite treasure of the most Holy Trinity, which You have bestowed on His most Sacred Humanity. On behalf of all in Heaven and earth, and through the most Sacred and Blessed Heart of Your Son, I desire to sing unto You praises and thanksgivings, and thus give back to You, Your own gifts.

Eternal Father, I offer You the priceless ineffable abundance of Riches and Perfections which You contain within Yourself, and which One Divine Person communicates to Another in sweetest, most transcending, and unimaginable manner. For all that, I give You thanks with all my heart and strength; I congratulate You that You contain within Yourself and for Yourself, such inexhaustible treasures and delights, and perpetually communicate them to Your elect. O my King, Live forever; enjoy evermore that Bliss which is Yourself, and bestow on us, wretched exiles in this valley of tears, some crumbs from Your heavenly Table. Amen.

Holocaust 2*

*   *   *

O most Loving Jesus, from the depth of my little heart, I beseech You with all my might, that You would work in me all my works, whether of body or of soul, to cleanse them all in Your Sweetest Heart, and to offer them, in union with Your own most perfect works, to God the Father as an eternal thanksgiving. Amen.

*

"The desire to love is love itself."

My Intention

O Lord, my God, for Your sake I resolve to perform all my actions, purely for Your glory, and for the salvation of the whole world; with such intention and in such manner as You desire, in union with that Love with which Your Son Jesus came down from Heaven, and wrought the whole work of our salvation, especially during His Passion. I completely disclaim all merit, all reward and grace which I might obtain by these actions, so that I may offer to You, my God, a pure sacrifice of praise, and give You a proof of my love.

*

A Covenant with God

O Almighty God, I sanctify, dedicate, and consecrate to You every beat of my heart. I desire to make this compact with You, that its every beat shall say to You: Holy, Holy, Holy Lord, God of Hosts. I beseech You to impute this meaning to them, so that they may be before Your Divine Majesty, an unceasing echo of that heavenly canticle, which the Seraphim sing without ceasing unto You. Amen.

*

A More Extended Covenant with God

O Lord God, my Creator, all my desires are before You. Since the necessities of this life prevent the constant application of my mind to Your praise, I make with You this covenant, desiring that it may remain in force all my life.

Whenever I look up towards Heaven, I desire to

29

rejoice with You in Your infinite Perfections: to rejoice that You are supremely Strong, Wise, Loving, and Just.

As often as I open or close my eyes, I desire to approve all the holy actions which Your Only-Begotten Son, and all the Saints in Heaven and the just on earth, have ever done, or shall ever hereafter do for Your glory, and I desire to be a partaker in them all.

As often as I draw my breath, I offer the Life, Passion and Blood of our Lord Jesus Christ, and the merits and sufferings of all the Saints, to Your eternal glory, for the welfare and peace of the whole world, and in satisfaction for the sins of all mankind.

Whenever I sigh, I intend to detest every sin, my own as well as those sins which have ever been committed from the beginning of the world against the honor of Your name. Would that the slight and worthless offering of my blood might be accepted in satisfaction for them!

As often as I move my hand or my foot, so often do I unite myself with entire resignation to Your most Holy Will. I desire that You would dispose of me in time and in eternity, according to Your good pleasure.

Lest this covenant should be in any way made void, I seal it with Your five Sacred Wounds, desiring that it may have its full force with You, even though in anyone of these actions, it may not actually be present to my mind.

An Act of Most Perfect Charity

My God, I love You, I love You, I love You. Were it possible, I would love You with an infinite love, and I desire even at the cost of my life a million times, to make all creatures love You with such a love.

O my God, I desire even with the sacrifice of my life, to be able to prevent not only all mortal sins, but also all venial sins and deliberate imperfections. I desire to cause all creatures to do good, the greatest good possible, all for Your Love, for Your Pure Love, if it were possible, because You would receive greater glory.

O my God, if to augment the glory that we, Your poor little creatures, can give You, it were necessary that I should give up every kind of enjoyment and happiness, that in regard to my personal enjoyment, I should become blind, deaf, and dumb, but that You through this sacrifice of mine, should have greater glory forever, O my God, I would desire it with my whole heart throughout eternity, if You would accept this little sacrifice.

God of my heart, You know that I love You, and that I desire nothing else but to love You and not offend You even involuntarily, if it were possible. O God of all Love, if it were necessary, in order to give You greater glory in eternity, that I should be deprived of all glory, provided Your grace, which is also Yourself, remained with me, I would accept it willingly that I might see You more glorified.

Act of Perfect Charity 1

My God, You who are so great and infinite, permit Your little creatures to love You. What condescension!

My God, my most bountiful God, the thought that in hell there are creatures who will never love You, fills me with sorrow.

Why can I not at the cost of my life, which I would give a million times for this end, change all the grains of sands, all the drops of water, all flowers, fruits, seeds, leaves, plants, animals, stars, objects, even change all the atoms of the universe, into so many hearts that would love You, my Jesus, with pure love until the end of the world and throughout eternity.

My God, You know that my heart is little, but I give it all to You; I reserve nothing to myself, it all is given to the Love of my God. If You would teach me an "Act of more Ardent Charity," I would make it instantly in order to give You greater glory.

My God, teach me and assist me to love You more and more. Teach me and assist me, my Jesus, to live only of love. Grant that I may live only of love, so that I may be able to die of love.

O Divine Fire of Love, I desire that all my life might be but one sigh of love for You, of most intense love for You, the only and supreme Good of my soul, whom I wish to love, whom I wish to serve, whom I wish to glorify with all my strength, sustained by Your divine grace, during my whole life.

Act of Perfect Charity 2*

Compact of Desires

My Jesus, I desire that every beat of my heart, whether by day or night, when I think of it, as well as when I do not think of it, would renew the "Act of most Perfect Charity" which You have taught me.

My God of Love, I desire to make an infinite number of acts of perfect charity, of adoration, thanksgiving, confidence, resignation, and of union through pure love with Your Divine Will. I desire to make billions of acts of faith, hope, perfect contrition, and of all the other virtues.

I desire to say billions of Holy Rosaries, for each soul living and for those who will live. I desire to say billions of ejaculations of piety for all souls, with every beat of my heart.

I desire to be able to give all souls Holy Baptism, Holy Confirmation, Holy Absolution, and Holy Communion. I desire to unite in the Sacrament of Matrimony, all those persons who should be living in these holy bonds of the Holy, Catholic, Apostolic, and Roman Church.

I desire to say and hear Holy Mass billions of times and to receive Your Precious Body and Blood at each Mass. I desire to make billions of Spiritual Communions. I desire to receive, as often as is necessary, Your Sacrament of Holy Absolution. I desire to consecrate many priestly souls, who will live in holiness while instructing and providing Your Holy Sacraments to all mortals.

I desire to give Holy Oils to all the dying, and to assist them in their agony. I desire to console all the afflicted, comfort and serve all the sick, draw back from desperation all those tempted to despair, practice, and cause all to practice, the works of mercy, spiritual as well as corporal.

I desire to teach all to know, love, thank, and serve You. I desire to teach all, not only virtue, but the perfection of virtue. I desire to be united with You in the distribution of Your grace in all Your Holy Sacraments, in all the prayers, good works, and sufferings of Your Mystical Body.

O unsurpassed Charity, I desire to remember all You have taught me in Your Holy Church by means of instruction, good books, prayers, and sufferings. I desire to be truly thankful for all Your blessings.

I desire, with every beat of my heart, to renew all the acts of virtue that You, my Jesus, Holy Mary, the Angels and Saints have ever made.

For Your greater honor and glory, I desire that I and my brothers and sisters have the same Love and desires of Your Sacred Heart, and renew them with every beat of our hearts.

O incomprehensible Beauty, I desire that all the atoms of my heart be changed into so many hearts, that would be placed before all the tabernacles of the world, loving You with pure love, such as would be rendered by the highest Seraphim, or rather, such as You, my dearest Jesus, would render Yourself.

Compact of Desires 2*

My God of Love, great are Your Sacraments and admirable Your mysteries. I contemplate them with sweet affection. Your greatness overwhelms me, and the greatness of Your Love overpowers me even while these mysteries inflame my heart. In the ardor of my soul I cannot rest satisfied, and I find no repose. My desires surpass all that I can accomplish and my obligations are greater than my desires. I am dissatisfied with myself, because I do not exert myself as much as I desire, because I do not desire to accomplish as much as I should, and because I find myself continually falling short and vanquished by the greatness of the returns which are due to You.

"O soul, your obligations surpass those of many, but they are to increase and advance continually. Never will your inflamed love equal its Object, since our God is Eternal and Infinite and without measure in His Perfection. You will always be happily vanquished by God's greatness, for no one can comprehend Him. Only the Almighty comprehends Himself and Loves Himself in the measure in which He deserves to be loved. Eternally shall you find in the all Merciful, all Powerful God, more to desire and more to love, since that is required by His Greatness and our blessedness as His creatures."

*

"Tell Me that you want to possess Me and to be possessed by Me, to love Me and to be Loved by Me. Tell Me all about your desires for Me and I will make it increase. Even if you do not desire Me, tell Me so and I will give you the desire; I will make your desires increase to the point where you will desire to leave the earth to meet Me."

35

"I am the Infinite God! When you unite the love and desire of your soul to My infinite Love and Desire, yours likewise becomes infinite."

*

How did Saint Aloysius rise to such a height of sanctity; in what time, and by what works?
"He rose to sanctity on the wings of great desires."

*

Lord Jesus, Your grace has prompted me to make many offerings to You, nevertheless I know that I offer You and desire to do more than I can possibly accomplish, yet on account of my own frailty I will forget what I have promised You.

"I accept your good desires for the act. My goodness is such, that when you have the desire to perform a good action, I count it as done, and recompense it as if it were accomplished, even if human frailty prevents its accomplishment. Your good will suffices and satisfies Me perfectly. What will it matter if you do forget? I will not allow what you have once given Me, and what you desire, to escape from My Hands, but I will always preserve it as a proof of your love for Me."

*

"Where is your lamp?"
Behold, Lord, I give You my heart for a lamp.
"I will fill your lamp abundantly with oil, that is, grace from My Heart."
Thank You, my dearest Jesus, but where is the wick to light it?
"Your pure intention of doing everything for Me alone will be a wick, and the light from your heart will be most pleasing to Me."
I desire that my life be consumed like a lighted candle before You, my Beloved, my Savior.

†

PREPARATION FOR HOLY MASS
AND HOLY COMMUNION

*　　*　　*　　*　　*　　*　　*

O most Sweet and Loving Jesus, I, the most unworthy of all Your creatures, propose now to receive the most Holy Sacrament of Your Body and Blood, as the most effectual remedy for all my miseries of body and soul. With confidence and faith I shall, by receiving You in Holy Communion, not only obtain the supply of all my needs, but also most perfectly please Your supreme Majesty and all the inhabitants of Heaven. O Supreme and Ineffable Majesty, before Your Face the heavens are not clean and its strong pillars tremble. How shall I, a creature of the earth, a sink of corruption and misery, dare to receive You into my heart, since You are the Fountain and Source of all Purity! How shall I presume to receive You into a heart surrounded with briars and thorns?

O most compassionate Love of my soul, I blush exceedingly; I am confounded before You. I fear lest I should outrage You by receiving You into an abode so foul, so unworthy of Your Majesty. You have said that the healthy do not need a physician. You invited the blind, the lame, the poor, and the needy, to Your Supper; as one of them, yes, as the poorest and most wretched of them all, I will draw near to the most Sacred Feast of Your Body and Blood, not in presumption, but with lowly confidence.

For love of You, I am heartily sorry for all my sins and my negligences, which have offended and grieved You and have polluted my soul with such defilement. Would that I could cause the whole sea to pour its mighty waters through my head and my heart, so that I who am filled with sin, might be cleansed, since You, my Last End, have chosen me for Your habitation. Would that my heart could be purified in fiercest fire, so that it might offer You an abode, not, alas, worthy of You, but at least not so unworthy.

Why, O my soul, am I so uneasy? Even if a thousand years were given me, I could not prepare myself to receive my Jesus in a proper manner; I have nothing whatever which could in any way avail towards so august and solemn a preparation, as is worthy of His adorable Majesty.

O most Loving Jesus, I humbly cast myself in the dust before You. I beseech You to prepare me, so that I may partake of this heavenly Banquet for Your glory, and for the profit of souls in the world.

I offer and abandon to You, all that I am and all I have, desiring that You would prepare within me, all that is most pleasing to Your Divine Goodness.

I offer and abandon to You, O Sweet Love of my soul, my whole heart, imploring You to wash it in the Water which flowed from Your most Holy Side, and adorn it for Your indwelling with the Precious Blood of Your most Sacred Heart, and the fragrant incense of Your Divine Love. Amen.

*

Ardent Desire for Holy Communion

O Jesus, my Spouse, I ardently desire You. The moment draws near, the rapturous moment in which I shall receive You, my God, into my soul. I come to You, I run to meet You with the utmost devotion and reverence of which I, as a little child, am capable. Stretch forth Your most Sacred Hands to embrace my soul, Your pierced Hands which were stretched forth amid the anguish of Your Passion, to embrace all sinners. O my crucified Jesus, I stretch forth not only my hands, but my heart and my soul, to embrace You and to lead You into the innermost and secret recess of my heart.

Would that I had within me as great a devotion, love, and purity, as You have ever been adored with by the heart of any mortal. Would that I were filled with all virtues, with all holy desires, with perfect devotion. Would that I had the purity of all Your Angels, the charity of all Your apostles, the holiness of all confessors, the chastity and cleanness of heart of all virgins, and the holy fire of love of all the martyrs. Would that I could receive You now with all that devotion, reverence, and love which Your most Blessed Mother received You in Your Incarnation, and in Your adorable Eucharist! Would that I had Your own Sacred and Divine Heart, that I might receive You as Your ineffable Majesty deserves!

I offer You, O Sweetest Jesus, to be my fitting preparation. To make amends for all my unworthiness, negligences, my lack of preparation, devotion, and affections, I offer You the love which the Saints and Holy Mary had when they received You in this Holy Sacrament.

I offer You, O most Holy Jesus, Your own meritorious Heart, and all the ineffable Virtues and Graces which the most Blessed Trinity bestowed without measure upon It, that all my vileness and all my unworthiness may be covered, and that a proper and most peaceful abode may be prepared for You in my soul. Amen.

"When you approach to receive Me in Holy Communion, receive Me with these intentions of feeling all the glowing desire and love with which the heart of any mortal has ever been inflamed. I will accept this love and preparation, not as it is in you, but what you desire your love and preparation to be."

*   *   *

O most Chaste Virgin Mary, by Your unspotted Purity, You prepared for the Son of God a dwelling of delight in Your Virginal Womb, pray that all my negligences may be expiated.

O most Humble Virgin Mary, by Your most profound Humility, You merited to be raised high above all the choirs of Angels and Saints, pray that all my negligences may be expiated.

O most Amiable Virgin Mary, by Your ineffable Love, You were united so closely and so inseparably to God, pray that I may obtain an abundance of all merits. Amen.

*

Jesus, Mary, I love You! Save souls!

*

Prayer to the Saints for Aid in Preparation for Holy Communion

All you Saints of God, I salute and venerate you with the most profound affection of my heart. I thank and bless the infinite Goodness and condescension of the ever Adorable Trinity, for all the grace which has ever flowed forth from that unfathomable and overflowing abyss for your salvation. I implore each one of you to offer prayers to the Trinity for my preparation for Holy Communion, in satisfaction for all my negligence and unworthiness. Offer all that fervent zeal and preparation you had when you stood before God on the day of your entrance into Heaven, to receive your everlasting reward.

*

Prayer to Jesus for Aid in Preparation for Holy Communion

O most Loving Lord Jesus Christ, I beseech You, by all the Love of Your Sacred Heart, to please offer for me all that Perfection with which You stood before God the Father, when You ascended on High to enter into Your Glory. I beg You through Your sinless and unspotted manhood, to render my soul pure and free from every sin, and to prepare my soul to receive You. Through Your glorious Divinity, endow and adorn it with every virtue. I beg You through the virtue of that Love, which has forever united Your Divinity to Your Immaculate Humanity, to furnish my soul in a proper manner, with Your best gifts. Amen.

*

Jesus, Mary, I love You! Save souls!

Invitation to Jesus

O Jesus, surpassingly sweet, You have said that Your delight is to be with the children of mortals. My soul desires You, my heart yearns for You. I invite You to come into my heart with all that devotion and love which any loving soul has ever invited You to itself. Come, then, O most Beloved Spouse of my soul. Come to a little child, come for a while into the poor and wretched hovel of my little heart. O Physician, come and heal my stricken soul. O Friend, You are a thousand times better than other friends, and You can enrich my poverty.

Come, O bright Sun, and scatter the thick darkness which hovers upon my heart. O sweetest Manna, satisfy my soul's exceeding hunger. O Jesus, incomparable in Your loveliness, Beloved of my heart, come and eat with me in the chamber of my heart. Although I have made nothing ready which will be worthy of You, yet will You find within me, a food such as You desire when a soul tends to You alone, for my affections are wholly Yours, and I desire to follow Your Holy Will.

O my only Love, I ardently desire Your coming. I await Your coming with yearning love. O fairest of the sons of mortals, O Spring of inexhaustible sweetness, sweeter than all the sweetest delights, come to me, and disdain not Your poor, little, and needy servant. Good Jesus, O Spouse of my soul, come into my heart with that Love with which You entered into the Virgin Mary's Womb.

*

"All night long I waited for you in My Eucharist, to give Myself to you in the morning. Why should this astonish you? You believe in My presence in the tabernacle, don't you? You believe in My immense Love? When you wake up during the night, think of Me who already long for the dawn to bring you to Myself."

*

"Love gives Itself as Food to Its own and this Food gives mortals their life and sustains them. Love humbles Itself before Its own and in doing so, raises mankind to the highest dignity. Love surrenders Itself in totality; It gives in profusion and without reserve. With enthusiasm, with vehemence It is sacrificed, It is immolated, It is given for those It Loves. The Holy Eucharist is Love to the extreme of folly."

*

"When I rose to Heaven, I remained in the midst of My Apostles hidden in the Eucharist, in the Heart of My Mother Mary. Could I have deserted My poor children completely? Seek Me always in the Eucharist. I am there for you, for everyone."

*

"If you are hungry to receive Me, I too, hunger to be received by you. I come to you with joy."

*

"Those who approach the Sacrament of Holy Eucharist for love of My glory, receive the Food of My Divine Body and the delicious nectar of the Divinity; they are adorned with the incomparable splendors of My Divine Virtues."

*

"Pray with Me: O Eternal Father of Mercies, accept the Blood of Your Son, accept His Wounds and His Heart for souls. Consider His Head which is crowned with thorns. Let not His Blood be once more shed in vain. See His thirst to save souls for You. Do not allow them to be lost. Save souls, that they may eternally glorify You."

*

My Lord, give me the strength to go to receive You in Holy Communion; if I cannot receive You, we shall both be the losers, since You find Your delight with Your weak creatures.

*

O Jesus, Beloved of my soul and Light of my eyes, I am not worthy to ask You what I desire from my inmost soul. You, O Lord, are my Life and my Hope. I beseech You, if such be Your pleasure, to make me a participant in the ineffable Sacrament of Your Body and Blood. You, my Love, have resolved to institute the most Holy Eucharist as a pledge of Your glory and I desire in receiving You in my heart, to share the effects of this admirable Sacrament. Well do I know that no creature can ever merit such an exquisite blessing, which You have set above all the works of Your magnificence. In order to induce You to confer it upon me, I have nothing else to offer except Your own Self and all Your infinite Merits.

If, my Jesus, by perpetuating these Merits through the same humanity which You received from Your Mother Mary, create for me a certain right, let this right consist, not so much in giving Yourself to me in this Holy Sacrament, as in making me Yours by this new possession by which I shall have Your sweetest companionship. This prospect enkindles my heart with most ardent love. May I never be separated from You, who are the infinite Good and Love of my soul.

Divine Victim of Calvary

My Jesus, Divine Victim of Calvary, Victim of Love perpetually immolated on our altar in the sight of Your Heavenly Father, I approach the sacred altar to hear Holy Mass and to receive Your Precious Body and Blood. My Jesus, this Church is Holy and Sanctified by Your Holy Presence; grant that I may not approach It without taking off the shoes of useless thoughts, of distractions, of all that might in the least withdraw me from You. O Jesus, grant that I may have the fervor of a Seraph in this Holy Sacrifice.

O Jesus, as You really immolate Yourself during Holy Mass, although in an unbloody manner, grant me also the grace never to refuse to immolate myself with You and for You. Jesus, Sweet Jesus, the Sacramental Species are the veil which You draw over Your Divine Sacrifice, to cover it from the eyes of Your creatures. The silence is like a mysterious shadow under which You hide Yourself, yet, now, You are no less present in a true Sacrifice, the renewal of the Sacrifice of Calvary; I believe it, with all my heart. Jesus increase my faith.

My God, God of Love, You in Your thirst for the salvation of souls, seek victims who will immolate themselves in union with You. My Jesus, the spirit is willing but the flesh is weak. How many fly from the thought of suffering! Have You not redeemed these souls with Your most Precious Blood? Give me a little zeal for the salvation of souls. You can do it, O Jesus, my only Love, the sovereign Good of my soul. You sacrificed Yourself for my sake. Grant that I may follow Your holy example.

O Jesus, I implore of You yet one more grace, which I am sure of obtaining from the inexhaustible Goodness of Your most Sweet Heart: the grace to begin truly to know You, in order that I may begin truly to love You; to love You with a strong love, that is nourished by continual sacrifices, ever more painful, more interior, and if possible, known to You alone. Give me as many sacrifices as You please; grant that I may be generous in giving You all You require of me.

*

Act of Humility

My God, my sovereign Love, my All, I am only nothingness, with nothing of good, no virtue, no fidelity, no correspondence with Your grace, no gratitude. Out of the abyss of my misery I invoke the abyss of Your Mercy, that I may have the grace to be able to know You and make You known, to love You and make You loved, to serve You and make You served as perfectly as possible, by a poor creature for Your greater glory.

"Everytime you make this 'Act of Humility' with sincere sentiments of humility, you wound My Heart with a golden arrow. From this wound your soul has made, a torrent of graces flows over your soul and over Holy Church."

*

"Charity covers a multitude of sins; pure love not only covers sins, it destroys them. Sins covered may be uncovered; sins destroyed are no more."

†

46

My most tender, most sweet and most lovable Spouse Jesus, Lily of the Valley, Brightness of Eternal Light, Mirror without a spot, You, the God of infinite Sanctity are with me. O my God, God of my heart, Heart of my God, how annihilated I feel before You who are my All, yet I trust in Your tender Goodness.

Precisely because I am nothing I trust the more, for You have come to seek me in the abyss of my misery. O Jesus, Source of Love, give me a true love for You. O Jesus, Source of Humility, grant me a real and profound humility. O Jesus, be to me a Jesus, defend me from my enemy, hide me in Your Sacred Heart, and teach me to become what You desire of me.

*

You see, my Jesus, that I desire to love You; You see that I desire to be faithful to You, and You see that I desire to please You in all things. O Jesus, out of this nothing, create one of the prodigies of Your Omnipotence. The sanctification of this poor soul will be a trophy of Your Mercy and Love.

*

O Jesus, the souls whom You Love have need of You, be to them a Jesus; they have need of counsel, be to them a Master; they have need of light, be to them a Light; they have need of support, be to them a Brother; above all, O Jesus, be to them a Jesus.

*

My Jesus, my only Love, my God, my All, I come

to You, O Divine Prisoner of Love, enshrined in our tabernacles for us, Your poor creatures. I come to You, to bear You the weight of my miseries, the multitude of my needs, all my desires and those of friends dear to me.

O Lord Jesus, You are here in the tabernacle as long ago You were at the well awaiting the Samaritan woman. My Jesus, You say to me: "Give Me to drink." What, O Jesus, would You have of me?

Tell me, my dearest Jesus, will you have my weakness, will You have my infirmity, will You have my desires? Yes, Jesus, I give You all, and beg of You in charity, Your Mercy. I have so great a need of Your Mercy.

My Jesus, since You are thirsty, I also thirst; You are thirsting for my sanctification, and I thirst to give You pleasure.

Listen, My Jesus, I will remain at Your Feet as long as You deign to hold me here. When duty shall call me away, I will leave as a pledge of my love for You, my poor heart, which I beg You to hide with Yourself in Your tabernacle, so that I may nevermore leave You. O Jesus, my Beloved, give me Your Benediction.

*

My Jesus, only Love of my heart, I wish to suffer what I suffer and all You will have me suffer for Your Pure Love; I will suffer, not for the merits I may acquire, nor for the rewards You have promised me, but only to please You, to bless You, to praise You, in sorrow as well as in joy.

My Jesus

My Sweet and dearly loved Jesus, were You not my Savior, I should not dare to come to You, but You are both my Savior and the Spouse of my soul, and Your Heart loves me with the most tender and burning Love, as no other heart can love. Would that I could correspond with Your Love for me; would that I had for You, who are my only Love, all the ardor of the Seraphim, the purity of the Angels and Virgins, the holiness of the Blessed who possess You and glorify You in Heaven.

Were I able to offer You all this, it would still be too little to honor Your Goodness and Mercy. That is why I offer You my poor heart such as it is, with all its miseries, its weaknesses, and good desires. Deign to purify my heart in the Blood of Your Heart, to transform and inflame it with an ardent and pure love. Thus the poor creature that I am, who can do no good but is capable of every evil, will love and glorify You as do the Seraphim, who in Heaven are consumed with adoring love.

I ask of You, O Gentle Jesus, to give my heart the Sanctity of Your Sacred Heart, to plunge it in Your Divine Heart, that in It I may love, serve, and glorify You; may I lose myself in You for all eternity! I beg this same grace for all those whom I love. May they render You for me, the glory and honor of which my sins have deprived You.

*

Jesus, Mary, I love You! Save souls!

My Jesus, God of infinite Charity, Goodness inexhaustible, I, a miserable creature worth nothing, in order to honor Your ineffable Mercy, offer myself, give, consecrate, and abandon myself forever to the Love of Your most loving and Tender Heart. My dearest Jesus, as it is impossible that fire should not burn and consume a little blade of straw cast into it, so let Your burning Furnace of Charity consume this poor little heart of mine, which wishes to be all Yours. Jesus, be to me a Jesus; Jesus, be to me a Jesus; Jesus, be to me a Jesus.

*

My Sweetest Jesus, God infinitely Merciful, most Tender Father of souls, especially of the weakest, the most miserable, the most infirmed, whom You bear with singular tenderness in Your Divine Arms. I come to beg of You through the Love and Merits of Your Sacred Heart, the grace to confide more and more in Your merciful Goodness, the grace to repose securely, for time and eternity, in Your Divine and loving Arms.

*

I go to You, O Jesus, in confidence. I will not lose trust, but I will place myself in Holy Mary's care, asking Her to remove all that is imperfect and supply for my deficiencies. Thus my prayer will please You, no matter how feeble it is. Even if I should become as dry as a stick, I would still go on loving You, my God, and praying until You can no longer resist me. My dearest Jesus, illumine my soul, so that I can have no doubt about what You desire me to do. I am ready to fulfill Your Divine Will. Bless my intentions, and give me the grace to carry them out with perfection.

†

THE HOLY EXERCISE OF THE WAY OF THE CROSS

*   *   *   *   *   *   *

First Station: Jesus is Condemned to Death

"I Pontius Pilate, presiding over lower Galilee and governing Jerusalem in fealty to the Roman Empire, condemn to death, Jesus of the Nazarean people, a Galilean by birth. He is seditious and opposed to our law, our senate, and our great emperor Tiberius Caesar. I decree that Jesus shall die on the cross and that He shall be fastened to it with nails as is customary with criminals. Every day, He has gathered many men, poor and rich; He has continued to cause confusion throughout Judea, proclaiming Himself the Son of God and King of Israel.

"Near the top of the cross shall be placed the inscription: 'Jesus of Nazareth, King of the Jews.'"

*

"Meditate on the martyrdom of My supremely tender and loving Heart at finding Barabbas preferred to Me, at seeing Myself so scorned, and on hearing the cries of the crowd urging My death. I, the Son of God, who hold the universe in the palm of My hand, willed that I should appear as the last and most contemptible to all mortals. Far from flying from such humiliations, I willingly endured them to expiate mankind's pride and draw souls to follow in My footsteps."

*

O Jesus, my only God, Love of my heart, You are condemned to death for me. With Your divine assistance, I will not dread humiliations and fly from mortifications; I will love You more and more and never again offend You.

Second Station: Jesus Receives His Cross

"O cross, beloved of My Soul, come to Me that I may be received in your arms, and that attached to you, I may be accepted by the Eternal Father as I offer this Sacrifice for the redemption of the human race. In order to die upon you, I have descended from Heaven and assumed mortal and passible flesh; you are to be the sceptre with which I shall triumph over all My enemies, the key with which I shall open the gates of Heaven, the sanctuary in which the guilty children of Adam shall find Mercy, and the treasury for the enrichment of their poverty. Upon you I desire to exalt and recommend dishonor and reproach among mortals, in order that My friends may embrace them with joy, seek them with anxious desires, and follow Me on the path which I through you shall open up before them."

*

"While the loss of the soul of Judas was filling My Heart with sadness, the executioners, devoid of every feeling of humanity, placed a cross of thick and heavy timbers upon My lacerated shoulders. I was to consummate on the cross the mystery of mankind's redemption. In order that I might carry the cross, the executioners loosened only the bonds holding My hands, since they wished to drag Me along by the ropes that bound My Body."

*

O Jesus, You run to the cross as to a nuptial feast. I have such a dread of every suffering; only to behold it from afar terrifies me, and I try to escape it, because I am wanting in love. My Jesus, give me a love of the cross. Cheerfully do I desire to follow You on the way to Calvary.

Third Station: Jesus Falls the First Time

"In order to torment Me even more, the executioners looped ropes around My throat. Some jerked Me forward in order to accelerate My passage, while others pulled from behind in order to retard it. This jerking and the weight of the cross caused Me to sway to and fro and to fall to the ground. When I fell on the rough stones, great wounds were opened, especially on My knees, and they were widened at each repeated fall. The cross which fell on Me, crushed Me with its weight."

*

"By this, My first fall under the cross, I obtained for sinners rooted in evil, the grace of conversion.

"See how roughly the inhuman soldiers raised Me to My feet. One seized an arm, another My garments which clung to My open wounds, a third grasped hold of Me by the neck, and another by the hair. Some showered blows on Me with their clenched fists and others brutally kicked My prostrate Body."

*

"Tell Me that it doesn't bother you to go along beside Me. What you do cheerfully for Me pleases Me more. I do not want to impose on My friends; I am joyful when you express your ever new happiness to be with Me."

*

My King, You lie stretched under the cross. How clearly I behold the result of my sins! Grant that I may weep over those sins of mine, since they are the cause of such great pain to You, and grant that I may nevermore return to them.

Fourth Station: Jesus Meets His Mother Mary

"Consider the martyrdom of two Hearts. Who does Holy Mary Love more than Her Son? Far from being able to help Me, She knows that the sight of Her anguish increases Mine. Whom do I Love more than My Mother? Not only can I offer Her no comfort, but I know that the terrible plight in which She sees Me, pierces Her Heart with sorrow as My own. I suffer death in My Body, My Mother suffers death in Her Heart. Her eyes are fixed on Mine, and Mine dulled and blinded with Blood are fixed on Hers. No word was spoken, but what a world of thoughts Our two Hearts exchanged in one heart-rending glance."

*

"Never leave your Immaculate Mother. She won't leave you either. Since suffering increases love, just imagine the tenderness She feels for you. Nothing could ever diminish Her Love for you, not even your ingratitude. Love Her, thank Her! Speak to Her about your Love, and this will draw you nearer to Me. Ask My Mother to teach you to live for Me. Put all your trust in Her. She will help you on your uphill climb; it is strenuous work climbing the mountain of perfection. Just when you think you are going up, you find that you are slipping back. Who will purify you? Who will put light into your mind? Light can only come from those who possess it: the Saints and Holy Mary, the Queen of all Saints!"

*

O Jesus, grant that I also, while bearing the cross after You, may meet Your most tender Mother and receive from Her a word of comfort, so that I may follow You faithfully until death.

Fifth Station: The Cyrenean Aids Jesus

"Fearing that I might die before crucifixion, those wicked men inspired by hatred, not compassion, looked for someone to help Me carry the cross, and for that purpose, offering a small reward, seized on a man of that neighborhood, called Simon.

"Contemplate Me on the way to Calvary loaded with My heavy cross; watch Simon carrying it behind Me and consider: though he was a man of good will, he carried My cross only because he was paid. When he began to tire, he allowed the weight to bear more and more on Me, and that is how I fell twice.

"When you, O soul, love truly, you neither measure what you do nor weigh what you suffer; never looking for a reward, but seeking only what you believe to be for My greater glory. You are not mercenary; you only want Me to be consoled; you desire only My rest and My glory."

*

"You are My Cyrenean whom, in My infinite Love, I have chosen to give the burden of My Love, of My Mercy. It will be your mission to console the infinite Love of God, which seeks solace from Its little creature. The secret of sanctity, known only to few, resides in this: to be what God wills; to do what God wills; to will what God wills."

*

My Jesus, I come to You because You have called me. What a sublime mission You offer me to fulfill. O Jesus, O Love, O Sanctity, teach me Yourself to do that which You have willed for me.

55

Sixth Station: Veronica Wipes the Face of Jesus

"While I was carrying My heavy cross, Veronica courageously walked into the procession and wiped My Face. I left My image on the cloth as a reward for a kind human action. What comforted Me on that terrible way of the cross, was not only the gesture of Veronica and the softness of her veil, it was that I could reward her. It is My joy to give. My grace is inexhaustible. I wait for opportunities to be able to make them known to you, for occasions on which you offer Me a heart ready to receive them. I wait and watch, I stand at your door and knock."

*

"Religious soul, you wipe My Face as Veronica did, every time you mortify yourself; the veil with which you wipe My Face is your soul on which I leave My divine features portrayed. The more pure and spotless your soul is, the more are you capable of receiving My divine aid. If you would come near to Me to wipe My Face, you must pass by My enemies, who are yours also, and from whom you will have much to suffer. The consolation which a single one of My divine looks will impart, will repay you with interest."

*

O Good Jesus, I will use the very finest linen, the whitest and most delicate; I will prepare this linen for You by my fidelity in three things: purity of intention, charity toward my neighbor, and the most ardent love possible toward You. O Jesus, Celestial Beauty, give me a perpetual remembrance of You. Thank You for rewarding Veronica by leaving Your image on the cloth. Thank You for leaving Your image on our souls.

Seventh Station: Jesus Falls the Second Time

"My Face, bruised and torn, was covered with Blood and dirt. My eyes were blinded with the dust of the road. I was treated as the vilest and most contemptible of all creatures! I should have died there because My exhaustion had reached its utmost limits, but all had not been accomplished. My Love gave Me strength to rise again. I fell a second time during My journey to Calvary to merit for souls the grace to rise from their falls and to teach them the means of doing so. I encourage weak souls blinded by sadness and anxiety, so that rising again they might make a new start in the way of virtue."

*

"The infernal enemy conquers religious souls more easily by discouragement than by any other temptation. It is of supreme importance to know how to triumph over him. The enemy is overcome by unlimited confidence in your Jesus; the more frequent the falls, the more should confidence increase in the Divine Mercy."

*

"What gives Me the most pain is to see the indifference, the hatred mankind has for Me. They fly from Me as they would fly from a robber or an assassin, from Me, who ask only to replenish souls with My graces, but I cannot do it because they do not desire them."

*

My Jesus, You use our continual miseries to feed the fire of Your Divine Mercy. Help me to rise from my falls; look with pity on Your child who lets not a moment pass without giving You something for Your fire of Mercy.

Eighth Station: Jesus Consoles the Pious Women

"Daughters of Jerusalem, I approve of your compassion for Me as good and just, but much more do I desire you to weep over your sins for which I suffer. By this weeping you shall acquire for yourselves and your children the price of My Blood for your redemption.

"Come, it is I who Love you, it is I who pour out all My Blood for you. I pity your weakness, I desire to open My arms and clasp you in Love's embrace! Come, My chosen one, come. I am infinite Mercy; do not fear that I shall punish you. I shall not repulse you, but I shall open My Heart to you and Love you with even greater tenderness. I shall wash away your sins in the Blood of My Wounds. All Heaven will rejoice and wonder at your regained beauty, and My Heart will find rest in yours."

*

"My Heart desires to console those who suffer, to compassionate the miseries of My poor creatures, and ever to show them Mercy. You can purchase relief and Mercy by presenting for payment your very miseries. My most Merciful Heart will accept them provided they are offered with humility, confidence, and love."

*

"Have no fear, where I am, there is My cross. Carry it with reverence and affection for the salvation of many souls that are in peril."

*

O my Good Jesus, I will console Your Heart so desirous of consuming our miseries; console my heart, by giving me Your holy peace.

Ninth Station: Jesus Falls the Third Time

"Wearily I dragged Myself forward, for My Body was broken by many torments and bathed in sweat and Blood. I suffered, but there were few to compassionate Me besides My Mother Mary. The crowd followed Me, the soldiers pitiless as ravenous wolves surrounded Me. We had nearly reached Calvary. I dragged Myself along with the utmost difficulty. So great was My exhaustion and so heavy the cross that I fell for the third time. I willed to bear the torture of this third fall, so that it would help souls to repent in the supreme hour of death."

*

"See Me once again on the ground, exhausted. Did I stop there? Death would have been sweet. I had suffered far beyond what was necessary to redeem the human race! These additional sufferings were nevertheless necessary for so many souls who, through lukewarmness and conceit, run the risk of losing the gifts that have been bestowed on them and of losing themselves."

*

"In one instant I can bring souls who have fallen, who live in sin, to Holiness, to Myself, as I did for Saul on the way to Damascus, for Magdalen, for Dismas the thief, who asked for My Mercy on the cross, and even for you. It only requires that you look on Me as a Merciful, Forgiving Savior."

*

O dear Jesus, O most Sweet Jesus, when I shall experience some pain which like a thorn shall pierce my heart, I will rejoice to be able to suffer a little for You. O Jesus, give me the grace to suffer willingly for Your greater glory.

Tenth Station: Jesus is Stripped of His Garments

"Look at the officiousness with which these hardened sinners surround Me; some seize hold of the cross and lay it on the ground. Others tear My garments from Me, reopening all My wounds.

"Think of My shame in seeing Myself exposed to the gaze of the mob; what physical agony, what confusion for My Soul. The tunic woven by My Mother, with which She had so lovingly clothed Me in My Infancy, and which had grown with My stature, these cruel men despoil Me of it and draw lots whose it shall be. Think of the affliction of My Mother as She witnessed this terrible scene. She ardently desired to take possession of that tunic, impregnated with My Blood!"

*

"Calvary, in Religion, is holy perfection: it is a mountain because souls ascend it with pain. While you ascend the mountain of holy perfection, Love strips you of all self-will, that you may no longer will but what God wills; Love strips you of every desire which has not God for its end; Love strips you of every desire for natural satisfaction. All this makes you, O soul, suffer much, but you suffer with joy because you are the prey of Love. If you did not love, you would suffer all the more, you would be more weighed down, but because you love, Love renders your trials sweet."

*

O Jesus, You are Sweetness, and You have the power to sweeten the most bitter bitterness. I will drink the chalice of detachments after You have blest it, and I shall find it, with Your grace, more sweet than every other sweetness.

Eleventh Station: Jesus is Nailed to the Cross

"The executioners violently seize and extend My arms so that My Hands may reach the holes they have prepared in the wood. Hear the first sound of the hammer that fixes My right Hand. Listen again: they fasten My left Hand. I remain silent, not a murmur escapes My lips. Every shock causes My thorn-crowned Head to come into violent contact with the cross. Having nailed My Hands, they pull pitilessly at My Feet; My wounds burst open anew, the nerves are severed, the bones are dislocated. They pierce My Feet and My Blood is poured forth upon the ground."

*

"If the hands of a robber were nailed, even though he wished to rob again, could he do so? I let My Hands be nailed as if to render Myself unable to punish poor sinners. I Love these poor sinners so tenderly! I wish they could see how much I Love them! I suffered so much pain in My Head from the crown of thorns, and also from the Blood which trickled into My eyes, that I was scarcely able to open them, yet from time to time I opened My eyes to look with tenderness upon My executioners."

*

O Jesus, You did not withdraw Your Hands and Your Feet when the executioners came to nail You to the cross. Give me the strength never to draw back from the loving operations of Your grace, which nails me to the cross, that is, to Your Love, with the hammer of Your Divine Will, and the nails of the trials that You present to me. Grant me the grace to second these operations as much as I can by my faithful correspondence.

Twelfth Station: Jesus Dies on the Cross

"Father, forgive them for they know not what they do. I am their Life, but they have not known Me. On My shoulders they have heaped the fury of their iniquities, but I beseech You, My Father, heap upon mankind the full measure of Your Mercy.

"Today you shall be with Me in Paradise. Your faith in your Savior's Mercy has wiped out all your offenses and it will lead you to eternal blessedness.

"Woman, behold Your son! O Mother Mine, these are My brethren; keep them, Love them!
Son behold your Mother. You souls for whom I die are no longer alone; you have a Mother to whom you can have recourse in every necessity.

"My God, My God, why have You forsaken Me? After My death, mankind will inherit Eternal Life.

"I thirst! O My Father, I thirst indeed for Your glory, and behold now the hour is at hand! I thirst for souls, and to appease this thirst, I will give the last drop of My Blood.

"All is consummated! Now is accomplished that great mystery of Love in which God delivers up His own Son to death. I came into this world to do Your Will. O My Father, it is accomplished!

"Into Your Hands, O Lord, I commend My Spirit. To You I give back My Soul. Thus shall souls that do My Will, have the right to say in all truth: 'All is consummated. Receive, O Eternal Father, my soul.'"

Thirteenth Station: Jesus is Removed from the Cross

"Contemplate these pierced Hands and Feet, this Body covered with wounds, this Head pierced by thorns, fouled with dirt, bathed in sweat and Blood. Gaze on My Wounds and desire to comfort Me, the Victim of sin."

*

"Longinus, a soldier, thrust his lance into My side, which pierced My Heart, and from the Wound flowed Blood and Water.

"The men placed the ladders against the Holy Cross; rising they detached the crown, laying bare the wounds it had caused. They gave the crown of thorns to My Mother with great reverence, amid abundant tears. The nails were removed, handing them first to My Mother for veneration and afterward showing their own reverence. Joseph of Arimathea, Nicodemus, John the Apostle, and Mary Magdalen tearfully placed My Body into the arms of My sorrowful Mother Mary."

*

"When you receive with faith and love any occasion of suffering, it is as if you received Me in your arms when I was taken down from the cross. The two arms with which you receive Me, are resignation and love for My Divine Will."

*

O infinite Charity, You suffered so much for me. Behold I do not esteem suffering at its real value. Enlighten me so that I may know its true worth. Grant me the grace to suffer through love all that Your Love reserves for me, and move my heart to love that which nature so much abhors.

Fourteenth Station: Jesus is Laid in the Sepulchre

"Death separated My Body and My Soul, but My Divinity did not withdraw from either one."

*

"Joseph of Arimathea and Nicodemus brought spices, aromatic ointments, and linens which were used to prepare My Body for burial. My anointed Body was placed on a bier which was carried by John the Apostle, Joseph of Arimathea, Nicodemus, and Longinus. The men were followed by My Virgin Mother Mary, Mary Magdalen, and by the other men and women who gathered at the sight of the crucifixion. All of them proceeded in silence toward a nearby garden where Joseph had hewn into the rock a new grave, in which no one had yet been buried. My Body was reverently placed in the sepulchre. My Mother adored My Body, and the faithful in imitation of Her also adored It. Then they closed the sepulchre with a very heavy stone and departed."

*

"Religious soul, your heart is the sepulchre from which I wish to arise. I come to beg of you, in alms, a place in your heart, where I may shelter My Love, not dead in a cold sepulchre, but all inflamed with a fire of love. You shall be to Me, My solace, and I shall be to you, your All."

*

O Jesus, I, a poor little nothing, have no existence except by Your Mercy. I come to give You with all my heart that which Your Love asks of me. Jesus, close the door of this new sepulchre of my heart which You have chosen. Seal it, so that no one may enter there. May my heart beat only and ever with love for You.

†

At the cross Her station keeping,
Stood the mournful Mother weeping,
Close to Jesus to the last.

Through Her Heart, His sorrow sharing
All His bitter anguish bearing,
Now at length the sword had passed.

O how sad and sore distressed
Was that Mother, highly blest
Of the Sole-Begotten One!

Christ above in torment hangs;
She beneath, beholds the pangs
Of Her dying Glorious Son.

Is there one who would not weep,
'Whelmed in miseries so deep,
Christ's dear Mother to behold?

Can the human heart refrain
From partaking in Her pain,
In that Mother's pain untold?

Bruised, derided, cursed, defiled,
She beheld Her Tender Child,
All with bloody scourges rent.

For the sins of His own nation,
Saw Him hang in desolation,
Till His Spirit forth He sent.

Holy Mother, Fount of Love,
Touch my spirit from above,
Make my heart with Yours accord.

Make me feel as You have felt,
Make my soul to glow and melt
With the Love of Christ my Lord.

Holy Mother, pierce me through,
In my heart each Wound renew
Of my Savior Crucified.

Let me share with You His pain,
Who for all my sins was slain,
Who for me in torment died.

Let me mingle tears with Thee,
Mourning Him who mourned for me,
All the days that I may live.

By the cross with You to stay,
There with You to weep and pray,
Is all I ask of You to give.

Virgin of all virgins blest!
Listen to my fond request:
Let me share Your grief divine.

Let me to my latest breath,
In my body bear the death
Of that dying Son of Thine.

Wounded with His every Wound,
Steep my soul till it has swooned
In His very Blood away.

Be to me, O Virgin, nigh,
Lest in flames I burn and die,
In His awful judgment day.

Christ, when You shall call me hence,
Be Your Mother my defense,
Be Your Cross my victory.

While my body here decays,
May my soul Your Goodness praise,
Safe in Heaven eternally. Amen.

*   *   *   *   *   *   *

My Jesus, my most Pure Jesus, Immaculate Lamb, Divine Pelican, in this Sacrament of Mercy You have created a saving bath out of Your Precious Blood, in which we may cleanse and purify our souls from every stain. You are a most Pure Lily and love to be surrounded by lilies. Grant that I may approach this Divine Sacrament with the dispositions Your Heart desires to find in me, so that I may participate in the treasures of grace enclosed in this Mine of Love. What You desire most is to find in my soul a great depth of humility; fill it with Your Divine Mercy. Infuse in my heart a lively faith, a firm hope, an ardent charity, and an unlimited confidence, so that I may share in all the treasures of grace reserved for me in this Divine Sacrament.

*

"Everything contributes to the cleansing of your soul. Your imperfections are in My Divine Hands like so many precious stones, because I change them into acts of humility, which I inspire you to make. If you lend yourself to My design of Love, your imperfections are transformed in an instant. If those who build houses could transform the debris and all that obstructs their work into materials of construction, how fortunate they would consider themselves! O faithful soul, you transform your debris: your faults, even the gravest and most shameful sins, with the aid of My Divine Grace, into stones which are used to build the edifice of your perfection."

*

"My Heart is comforted when I forgive. I have no

67

greater desire, no greater joy, than when I can pardon a soul. When you return to Me after a fall, the comfort you give Me is your gain, for I regard you with very great Love. Have no fear whatever. As you are nothing but wretchedness, I wish to make use of you."

*

"Always remember that I Love you because you are little, not because you are good."

*

"I make the most beautiful masterpieces with the most miserable subjects, provided you souls let Me. When you souls repent of your faults and deplore them, do you think I am so hard as not to receive you? If so, you know not My Heart. My most loving Heart has such a thirst for the salvation of souls, that when they return to Me, I cannot contain My joy; I run to meet them. The greatest injury the demon can cause a soul, after having made it fall into sin, is to incite that soul to distrust. As long as a soul has confidence, its return is easy, but if the demon succeeds in closing the heart with distrust, oh how I have to struggle to reconquer it."

*

"As fire is fed with combustibles, and increases accordingly as they are supplied, so My Mercy is nourished with the miseries It consumes, and the more It receives, the more It increases. My Heart rejoices when mortals believe in My Love! If mankind only knew how I Love them and how My Heart rejoices when they believe in My Love! They believe in It too little!"

*

"Place no limits on your confidence in Me, then I will place no limits on My graces for you."

†

THANKSGIVING AFTER HOLY CONFESSION

*   *   *   *   *   *   *

My most loving, most Benign Jesus, You have deigned to cleanse, purify, and enrich with grace, my soul redeemed with Your Precious Blood. Be pleased to confirm my good resolutions, so that I may never again give You the least displeasure.

My Jesus, create in me a solitude, so that I may love You and enjoy the immense grace You have granted me. O Jesus, be the Strength of my weakness, the Repairer of my frailties, and above all, O Jesus, be to me a Jesus!

*

"You cannot conceive the pleasure I take in fulfilling My mission as Savior. When your sins have been pardoned, they become for your soul fountains of grace, because they are perpetual sources of humility."

*

"Tell Me of your sorrow for your shortcomings, not because they have sullied you, but because they have pained Me; you had the sad courage to hurt your God who gave His Life for you. You disregarded Me; you resisted My Will, and did what you pleased; My eyes followed you with distress. Come and place your sins quickly within My Heart; then strengthen your determination to strive for the opposite virtue, but with great calmness. In that manner your every fault will help you to advance in virtue."

*

"Do you think that I, the Lamb of God, can roar as a lion? I do not reproach sinners, however loaded with sins, provided they come to Me with contrite and humble hearts. It is the demon who taunts them after their fall."

*

"Feel grief for your falls, tearless grief, and your renewed resolution will lead you to humble love and a sense of your nothingness. I will swoop down as an eagle, and carry you away to the 'enclosed garden'. When you speak to Me of the past, I will place My Hand over your mouth and you will hear Me speak of My Tenderness and Mercy. You will thirst for a new life. Humbly now, fully aware of your dependence on Me, surrender your faculties to Me, one by one. You and I will walk together, patiently striving day by day."

*

"Don't you know that because of My Compassion, a single act of perfect love atones for a whole lifetime of sin? Don't you know that one humble and tender look from you pierces My Heart with Love? Don't you know that I am sensitive to every cry of your heart?"

*

"Your defects are very advantageous to you. Each day I heap upon your soul such an abundance of grace, that to preserve your human frailty from the assaults of vanity, I conceal graces from your own eyes, under the cloud of slight failings."

*

"You would like to have Me promise that I would never permit you to fall, but always to remain faithful, always perfect. No, I do not wish to deceive you. You will commit faults; you will be guilty of infidelities and imperfections; these will help you to advance, for they will cause you to make many acts of humility."

†

*　　*　　*　　*　　*　　*　　*

In the name of the Father...

O all Holy God, in Your presence the Angels and Saints are not worthy to stand. Forgive all the sins committed this day. Receive in expiation of these sins the thorn-crowned Head of Your Son. Accept His Blood which flows so copiously from His wounds. Purify minds that are sullied; enlighten their minds, and may this Blood be their strength and their Life.

O Holy and Eternal Father, receive the sufferings and merits of all who, united to the Sufferings and Merits of Jesus, offer themselves to You, that You may extend Your pardon to all mankind. O God of Mercy and Love, be the Strength of the feeble and the Light of the blind. May all souls love You!

*

My Jesus, by Your most Loving Heart, I implore You to inflame with zeal for Your Love and glory, all the priests of the world, all missionaries, and those whose office it is to preach Your Word. On fire with holy zeal, may they snatch souls from the devil and lead them into the shelter of Your Heart, where forever they may glorify You.

*

O Jesus, I deplore so many hours and so many seconds passed without loving You! I beg Your pardon. With Your grace I will love You ardently. I offer You to the Eternal Father to supply for my weakness, my insufficiency, and my misery.

*

Jesus, Mary, I love You! Save souls!

71

My Jesus, I, Your servant, come to You in my extreme poverty of all good, rich only in miseries, defects, faults, and infidelities, which I cast with confidence into Your Loving Heart, that You may consume them in the Fire of Your Pure Love.

O Jesus, why are You the sweet Spouse of our souls, if not to sustain our weakness? Why are You our most tender Father, if not to give us our daily Bread? Why are You our most gentle Physician, if not to bind up our wounds, to heal our bruises, to cure our infirmities? We come to You, O Jesus, with our miseries; we come to implore Your Mercy, to beg Your help, to obtain the gift of Your Holy Love.

O Jesus, make of us, Your humble servants, seraphs of love, that are consumed night and day for Your greater glory. Since You have told us that we are the trophies of Your Mercy, make us also the masterpieces of Your Love.

*

My Jesus, You are the Resurrection and the Life! Will You let those souls for whom You have died on the cross, hasten to perdition? Be the Resurrection and the Life to the many hearts that have been buried in the darkness of sin!

I thank You, my Jesus, from this moment for the victory You have gained over the infernal enemy, who held so many souls slaves of sin, because You have assured me that I should obtain everything when I pray with confidence.

*

Even if I should be cast into hell, You, O Lord, will deliver me.   (Prayer of Confidence)

72

"If you only knew what joy it gives Me to sanctify your soul! Everybody should become holy in order to procure Me this pleasure."

*

"If you only knew how I suffer when I must dispense Justice! My Heart needs to be comforted; It wishes to dispense Mercy, not Justice!"

*

"Only those go to hell who want to go there. How foolish is your fear of being damned!"

*

"Offer Me your shortcomings of today."
O Lord, my memory is poor, I cannot recall them!
"I too have forgotten them."

*

"Tell Me that you love Me, for love shall be your penance! Go in peace, for your sins do not exist any more."

*

"I grant you pardon of all your sins, that you may truly amend your life. I enjoin you each day to perform some action by which you may gain this indulgence. I will accept the least thing which you do with this intention, even if it be only to lift a pebble or a straw from the ground, to utter a single word, to show kindness to anyone, to pray for the faithful departed, for sinners or the just. All who wish to share with you in this satisfaction which I have imposed on you, will also receive a similar indulgence and remission of their sin."

*

"My Heart is comforted when I forgive. I have no greater desire, no greater joy, than when I can pardon a soul. When you return to Me after a fall, the comfort you give Me is your gain, for I regard you with very great Love. Have no fear whatever. As you are nothing but wretchedness, I wish to make use of you."

*

"Every evening before you fall asleep, say with much respect and confidence: 'O Jesus, You knew my misery before You looked on me, yet You did not turn away from my wretchedness. Because of my misery, Your Love for me is more sweet and tender. I beg pardon for having corresponded so little to Your Love. I beg You to forgive me, and to purify my actions in Your Divine Blood. I am deeply grieved at having offended You, because You are infinitely Holy. I repent with heartfelt sorrow and I promise to do all in my power to avoid these faults and sins in the future.'

"During the night you will rest in My Heart! My Heart will listen to the beats of your heart, which will be so many acts of love and desire. Thus even while you are sleeping, you will bring back to Me souls that so offend Me."

*

"Before going to rest as you must, place on the powers of your soul the obligation of rendering Me all night the worship of your love. Let all the tenderest love, thanksgiving, and desire of your heart remain in the presence of the only Object of your love, even while your senses slumber. Say to Me: 'Lord, I am going to sleep, but my soul will keep You company. The body alone will rest tonight, but all the powers of my soul will still belong to You, and my heart will keep for You its tenderest, and most constant love.' After which, in all tranquility and joy, take your rest."

†

"Just think, I am perfectly happy with My Father in Heaven, yet I must be with My children, for My Love for them is beyond all their power to imagine."

*

"The Seraphim love Me ardently, the Saints love Me and their love is pure and perfect, yet I come to earth to seek love, because on earth souls can freely give Me their love. I have good souls even in the world, and in them I take My delight. These souls are the oases in which I repose in the midst of the desert."

*

"Ask Me for all you have lost through neglecting to harmonize with My grace. Ask humbly, with confidence, and My Compassionate Heart will give it to you because with Love nothing is impossible, and My Love is victorious. I will help you pick up those dropped stitches of your life. You will have the light that you have missed. Don't ever give way to the distress that could keep you away from Me. Be sure that My Goodness is infinitely greater than the sinfulness of My children."

*

Lord, at times I feel so close to You, and at other times I feel dry and deserted.

"Sometimes I leave you to your littleness, so that you can take stock of all that you lack and send Me those secret cries for help with sincere and humble tenderness. I am always in you, for of yourself you are only nothingness. I am Life and you live by Me alone."

"Remember that nothing happens without My permission, so be very serene. There is nothing like serenity for convincing people of the existence of good."

*

My dearest Jesus, how can we console You, since we are so full of miseries?

"I make little account of all your miseries, if you souls come to Me with confidence and love. I make up for all your frailty."

*

"Many souls forsake Me and are lost. What wounds Me most is that they are souls whom I have chosen specially and overwhelmed with My gifts. In return, they show Me only coldness and ingratitude. Few souls correspond with My Love!"

*

"Pray for religious souls who live in a state of tepidity: O Jesus, You have granted to religious souls the special grace of serving You in a more perfect state. Do not permit them to abuse so great a treasure, by passing their lives in tepidity and negligence. Revive in their hearts the Fire of Your Love, so that repairing the past and sanctifying the future, they may enjoy You in Heaven for all eternity."

*

"I want you to speak to Me of all your concerns; consult Me at every turn; ask favors of Me. I live in you to be your Life; I abide in you to be your Strength. Yes, I repeat, remember that I delight in being One with you. Remember that I am in your soul; there I see you, hear you, and Love you; in your soul I look for a return from you."

*

"I am all Love. My Heart is an abyss of Love. It was Love that made mankind and all things, that they might be at their service. It was Love that moved the Father to give His Son for mankind's salvation which, through their own fault they had lost. It was Love that caused a Virgin, who was little more than a child, to renounce the charms of life in the Temple and consent to become the Mother of God, thereby accepting all the suffering involved in the Divine Maternity. It was Love that caused Me to be born in the inclemency of winter, poor and destitute of everything. It was Love that hid Me thirty years in complete obscurity and humble work. It was Love that made Me choose solitude and silence; to live unknown and voluntarily to submit to the commands of My Mother and adopted father.

"Love saw how, in the course of ages, many souls would follow My example and delight in conforming their lives to Mine. It was Love that made Me embrace all the miseries of human nature, for the Love of My Heart saw far ahead. I knew how many imperiled souls would be helped by the acts and sacrifices of others and so would recover spiritual life.

"It was Love that made Me suffer the most ignominious contempt and horrible tortures, and shed all My Blood; Love made Me die on the cross to save mankind.

"Love saw, how in the future, many souls would unite themselves to My torments and dye their sufferings and actions, even the most ordinary, with My Blood in order to win many souls to Me."

"It is because I Love you that I have simplified your life: I have given you no other responsibility than to be faithful to your daily duty.

"It is because I Love you that I have given you poor health, in order that from the beginning of your natural life you might feel your dependence on Me, and receive strength every day from Me.

"It is because I Love you that I want you to be poor, altogether poor, so that I can be your Wealth.

"It is because I Love you that I gave you the gift of Holy Faith and brought you into My Holy Church.

"It is because I Love you that I put fervent souls in your path who have prayed much for you.

"It is because I Love you that I have confided you since your birth to the Blessed Virgin Mary.

"It is because I Love you that I have given you a desire for penance and the strength to do penance.

"It is because I Love you that I have given you the Vows which bind you to Me in Holy Religion.

"It is because I Love you that I died for you on the Cross.

"My Love prevents you from understanding My Passion. If you understood how much I suffered, you would be crushed.

"What will you give Me?"

The Martyrdom of Love

"The martyrdom of Love consists in surrendering yourself to Love as wood to the fire, or gold in the crucible. Fire consumes wood and reduces it to ashes; fire purifies gold and makes it resplendent. When you surrender to Love, you can no longer interrupt the work of Love unless by infidelity you deprive yourself of Its action. As fire consumes wood entirely, so Love continues to work until your soul has arrived at the degree of perfection which God requires of it. It suffices to surrender wholly to Love, then Love will do the rest. When wood is dry, it is immediately consumed; when wood is green, the fire must first consume its humidity, and this takes time; wood is more rapidly consumed as it is drier. So it is with souls: those who are still full of themselves find great difficulty in yielding to the action of Love, but souls dead to themselves are quickly consumed.

"Provided I find good will in your soul, I am never weary of looking on your miseries. My Love is fed by consuming miseries; the soul that brings Me the most, if the heart is contrite and humble, is the one that pleases Me most, because it gives Me an opportunity of exercising more fully My office as Savior. You should never be afraid of Me, because I am all Merciful. The greatest pleasure of the Heart of your Jesus is to lead to His Father numerous sinners; they are My glory and My jewels. I Love poor sinners so much! The greatest pleasure you can give Me is to believe in My Love. The more you believe in It, the greater is My pleasure; if you wish that My pleasure should be immense, then place no limits to your faith in My Love.

"The martyrdom of Love requires that you let your soul be consumed by Love. Love is ingenious enough to know how to take everything away from you, without appearing to take away anything. Let Love act, and It will despoil you. It will commence by the exterior, as the fire first consumes the bark; then It will penetrate into the interior. Give to Love all that It asks, and never say: 'It is enough'. The more you give, the more Love will demand, but always with the greatest sweetness. Love will augment in you the desire of giving.

"Very few souls are surrendered wholly to Love, because it is painful. Certain souls commence well, but turn back; they are afraid of sacrifice; I compare them to those persons who will not pluck a rose for fear they will be scratched. True love does not act so; wherever it sees a sacrifice, it darts upon it as its prey; it enfolds and embraces it; the more hidden the sacrifice, the more interior and known to God alone, the more willingly it is performed. Courage then! Tell Me that you give Me your will forever, because you have no other desire than that of Love; then remain firm, and know that when you commence generously, you will always be well received by My Heart. You may repair for lost time by greater fidelity in the present and especially by using the Treasures of My most Sacred Heart.

"You cannot imagine the pleasure I experience in remaining with My creatures! I am always in search of hearts that love Me, and I find only a small number, upon whom I lavish the plenitude of My graces."

The Martyrdom of Love 2*

"Give Me souls."

My Jesus, how can a little child like me give You souls?

"By sacrifices! I ask no great thing of you, only a word withheld, a look repressed, a pleasant thought banished, and all that restrains and mortifies nature."

*

"Annihilation means death. A thought comes which pleases you; banish it, forget it, and it is the death of that thought. Sacrifice a desire, and it is the death of that desire. When you will to do something and renounce it, it is the death of that will. Every act of death is an act of life, because the moment you die to nature, you live to Me. Strengthen your free will by performing acts of virtue, so that you can reject, with your free will, that which is sinful, during temptation."

*

"Only love is required in all your actions. Suffer because you love, work because you love, and abandon yourself to Love. These little things united to My infinite Merits acquire great value. When I let you feel anguish of spirit and great loneliness, suffer in love. I want to make use of you as a tired man uses a stick to lean upon. I want to possess you, to envelop you, to consume you entirely, but all in great sweetness, so that enduring a martyrdom of love, you will thirst to suffer still more."

*

"My infinite Love puts into your hand a net in which you shall catch souls for Me. I fashion the net which I give you, out of your acts of fidelity."

81

"I will immolate you with the sword of Love, and I will enchain you with the bonds of Love.

"I shall be the one Love of your heart, the sweet torture of your soul, and the welcome martyrdom of your body.

"You will be the victim of My Mercy and the consolation to My Love. You shall be the victim of My Sacred Heart through a bitter dislike for all that is not Me; the victim of My Soul by all the anguish of which yours is capable; the victim of My Body, by the denial of all that could satisfy yours."

*

"One faithful soul can repair and obtain Mercy for many ungrateful ones.

"Why are you afraid? I know well what you are, but I say again: I do not mind your helplessness.

"If you concern yourself with My glory, I will look after you. I will establish My peace in you so that nothing will be able to trouble you; I will set up in your soul the reign of My Love, and no one shall take your joy from you. Tell Me what you have to offer Me for the souls I have confided to you. Put it all in the Wound of My Sacred Heart, so that your offering may acquire an infinite value."

*

"Say to Me: O Father, Merciful and Good, look on Your child; make me so entirely Your own, that I may lose myself in Your Heart. May my one desire be to accomplish Your Holy Will."

*

"See My Wounds! Who has suffered for love of you as I have? Contemplate Me in this state of ignominy. Will not My Wounds give you strength to conquer and resist temptation? My grace will help you to do whatever I ask of you.

"Offer My Father the sufferings of My Passion: O Heavenly Father, look upon the Wounds of Your Son and accept them, that souls may accept Your grace. May the nails which pierced the Hands and Feet of Jesus, pierce those hardened hearts; may His Blood lead them to repentance.

O Heavenly Father, may the weight of the cross on the shoulders of Jesus, Your Divine Son, obtain for souls the grace to unload themselves of their sins in the Sacrament of Penance. I offer You the crown of thorns. By the agony the crown of thorns caused Jesus, grant true contrition to souls for all their sins.

O Eternal Father, O God of Mercy and Love, I offer You the abandonment of Your Son on the cross, His thirst and all His pain, that sinners may recover peace and consolation in sorrow for their sins.

O God of all Compassion, in the name of Jesus who persevered in prayer for the men who were crucifying Him, I implore You to grant to souls, love of God and perseverance in prayer.

Just as the torments of Your Beloved Son ended gloriously in Eternal Bliss, may the sufferings of penitent souls be crowned by the everlasting reward of Your glory."

"Peace has come to the world! The cross, formerly an instrument of torture on which criminals were made to die, is changed into the Light and Peace of the world and the object of most profound veneration. Sinners will draw pardon and life from My Sacred Wounds. My Blood will wash away their filth and foulness. Pure souls will come to My Wounds to slake their thirst and kindle flames of love in their hearts. In My Wounds souls will find a refuge, and forever make a home. The world has found a Redeemer, and chosen souls, the Model they must copy."

*

"Religious soul, if you contemplate Me, you love Me. Look upon Me not with a passing glance, but regard Me as very near to you. You will see that all My Wounds bear the sign of Love. As objects of gold and silver have a seal to distinguish them, so all My Wounds have the stamp of Love. If you regard them superficially, they will seem to have been made only by the executioners, but the executioners would have been powerless had not Love permitted it. You cannot, like Me, put yourself into the hands of executioners, but if you observe your Rule faithfully, if you observe the Commandments, it is as if you were in their hands, because the Rule and the Commandments scourge you, crown you with thorns, and nail you to the cross."

*

"Do not go seeking the love of creatures. Were they to give themselves to you entirely, you would not be satisfied. You need a Heart that loves you, that understands you. It is the Heart of God you must have. Speak to Me as you would to an earthly friend to whom you tell everything."

†

* * * * * * *

"For all that you give Me, I give you My Heart."

*

Lord, what shall I do?

"I want you to rest in My Heart as a child, to love Me as a spouse, and to console Me as a victim. I want you to love Me and to be faithful to Me. Remember, no one else can make you happy. I will reveal to you the riches of My Heart. Love Me without measure."

*

"Do you love Me?"

Lord, you know very well that I love You, but poor as I am, I can only offer You Your own Love, and that of my Mother, the Blessed Virgin.

*

"Leave yourself entirely in My Hands. I will use you as I desire. I will take you when I need you, for you are Mine. What of your littleness and weakness? It does not matter. I ask you to love and console Me. I want you to know how dearly My Heart loves you, and how great are the riches It contains. You must be like soft wax, that I may mold you to My desire. I want you to offer Me all, even the smallest things, so as to comfort My suffering Heart, especially those sufferings which I have to endure from souls consecrated in Religion. I want you to rest in My Heart without any fear. Gaze on It; cannot Its flame burn up all your imperfections? Remain in My Heart and be busy only in pleasing Me. I am your Father, your Spouse, and your God."

"Come, enter in, lose yourself in My Heart."

*

"What is there to fear, if you are in My Hands? Never doubt the Goodness of My Heart, nor the Love I bear you. All I ask of you is that you should always be ready to console My Heart, when I call on you. The comfort given Me by one faithful soul compensates for the coldness and indifference of so many others. You will sometimes feel in your heart the anguish that is in Mine, and that is how you will comfort Me in My sorrow. Fear nothing, I am with you."

*

My Jesus, why do You Love me so much?

"Your misery attracts Me. What would you do without Me? Do not forget that the more humble in spirit you become, the nearer I shall be to you. Let Me do as I please with you."

*

"Have I asked you to merit the graces I give you? What I ask is that you should accept them. I will show you the School of Love in which this lesson can be learned. Leave Me free to do as I like in you."

*

Jesus!

"Why do you call Me?"

Lord, I cannot live without You.

"I love to hear you calling Me, I thirst for your love. If you are resolved to be faithful, I will pour into your heart the flood of My Mercy, and you will know what Love I have for you."

"Always remember that I Love you because you are little, not because you are good."

*

"All I ask of souls is their love, but many give Me only ingratitude; I should like to fill their souls with grace, but they pierce My Heart. I call them and they turn away from Me. If you accept, I will give you charge of souls, and by your sacrifices and love, you will win them for Me."

*

"Where are you coming from?"

I have been closing the windows, Lord.

"Where are you going?"

I am going to finish doing so, my Jesus.

"That is not the answer I desire! Say: 'I come from Love and I go to Love.' Regardless of your occupation, you are ever in My Heart, for It is an abyss of Love. I am always with you."

*

"You must not grieve excessively over your falls. I could make you a saint instantly. I ask you never to oppose My Will. Do what I ask you. Let Me act! Humble yourself! I will seek you out of your nothingness, and unite you to Myself."

*

"Love Me; never cease telling Me of your love!"

*

"Do you love Me?"

My Jesus, I love You.

"I also Love you."

"Say: 'My Jesus, I love You' often, to make up for the forgetfulness of so many. Many souls think that love consists in saying: 'My God, I love You.' No, love is sweet, and acts because it loves, and all that it does is done out of love. I want you to love Me in that way, in work, in rest, in prayer and consolation, as in distress and humiliation, constantly giving Me proofs of your love by acts; that is love. If souls really understood this, they would advance in perfection rapidly. How greatly they would console My Heart!"

*

"Are you happy in suffering?"

Yes, because it is for You that I suffer, Lord.

"Will you carry the burden of other souls?"

Yes, provided they love You, Lord.

"You shall suffer because you are the victim of My Love, but your suffering must always be in love, joy, and peace.

"As you are prepared to suffer, let us suffer together. Never mind your littleness, for I am your support."

*

"Courage! I can give you no better gift than suffering. It is the same road that I trod. I allow tribulations for two reasons. First, to convince you that when you are alone you are not capable of anything, that the graces I give you spring only from My Goodness, and the great Love I bear you; secondly, because I want to use your sufferings for the salvation of many souls."

"You will suffer to gain souls, because you are the chosen victim of My Heart, but you will not be harmed, for I will not allow it."

*

"My Heart is only wounded by My chosen souls."

*

"The sins committed are so many and so grave, that the wrath of My Father would overflow were it not for the reparation and love of My consecrated souls. Many souls are lost!"

Lord, is the number of sinners, then, so great?

"Yes, but one faithful soul can repair and obtain Mercy for many ungrateful sinners."

*

"The Love I bear for souls is so great that I can no longer contain the flames of burning Charity that consumes Me; in spite of your unworthiness and helplessness, I mean to make use of you to accomplish My plans."

*

"Tell Me what you have to offer Me for the souls I have confided to you. Put it all in the Wound of My Heart, so that your offering may acquire an infinite value."

*

"I want you to be so forgetful of yourself and so abandoned to My Will, that I shall be able to warn you of your slightest imperfections, for I will allow none in you. You must never lose sight, on the one hand, of your nothingness, and on the other, of My Mercy. Never forget that it is through your nothingness that My treasures will be poured forth to other souls."

*

"Do not forget that it is your nothingness and littleness that act as magnets to attract Me to you."

*

"If you concern yourself with My glory, I will look after you. I will establish My peace in you so that nothing will be able to trouble you, I will set up in your soul the reign of My Love, and your joy none shall take from you."

*

Lord, what is meant by "saving souls"?

"There are some Christian souls, and even very pious ones, that are held back from perfection by some attachment, but when victim souls offer Me their actions united to My infinite Merits, they obtain grace for other souls to free themselves and make a new start. Many other souls live in indifference and even in sin, but when helped by victim souls, recover grace, and will eventually be saved. Others again, and these are very numerous, are obstinate in wrongdoing and blinded by error. They would be damned if some faithful souls did not make supplication for them. Thus grace is obtained to touch their hearts, but their weakness is so great, that they run the risk of a relapse into their sinful life. These I take away into the next world without any delay, and that is how I save them."

Jesus, how can I save many souls?

"Unite all you do to My Actions, whether you work or whether you rest. Unite your breathing to the pulsation of My Heart. You will be able to save many souls that way."

Lord, teach me how to humble myself and how to surrender myself in a way that pleases You.

"You can humble yourself by adoring the Divine Will, which in spite of your worthlessness, uses you to make known God's Mercy. You can humble yourself by thanking Me for having placed you in Religious Life, though you have done nothing to merit it. Never complain about being humbled."

I beg You, O Jesus, to have compassion on me, for no one is more in need of it than I.

"If through you, I will to pour out the treasures of My Mercy to other souls, do you think that I would not begin by giving them first to you?"

*

"I will give you a lesson of very great importance: the devil is like a mad dog, but he is chained, that is to say, his liberty is curtailed. The devil can, therefore, only seize and devour his prey if one ventures too near him, and that is why his usual tactics are to make himself appear as a lamb. The soul does not realize this, and draws nearer and nearer, only to discover his malice when in his clutches. When he seems far away, do not relax your vigilance, child; his footsteps are padded and silent, so that he may take you unnoticed."

*

"You are an abyss of miseries, but I am an abyss of Mercy and Goodness."

*

"Do not fear pain, it is a treasure both for you and for souls."

"My child, why are you afraid? I know well what you are, but I say again: 'I do not mind your helplessness.'

"My Heart is comforted when I forgive. I have no greater desire or joy, than when I can pardon a soul. When you return to Me after a fall, the comfort you give Me is your gain, for I regard you with very great Love. Have no fear whatever. As you are nothing but wretchedness, I wish to make use of you. I will supply for all your deficiencies. Let Me do it. Let Me act in you."

*

"The greater your helplessness, the more My power will sustain you. I will make you rich with My gifts. If you are faithful to Me, I will take up My abode in you and I will take refuge there. I shall rest in you, and you will have Life in Me. Come to My Heart and there find all you need. Have confidence and love."

*

Feast of the Sacred Heart of Jesus

"Today is the Feast of My Love. Those souls that I Love so much, delight My Heart, coming as they do to seek strength and remedy in My Heart, which so ardently desires to enrich them; that is what glorifies and consoles Me most."

*

"Take My Sacred Heart and offer It to your God. With My Heart you can pay all your debts. You know now why I attracted you to My House. I want you to fulfill My plans by being docile and surrendering yourself to My Love, which seeks only to possess and consume."

*

"Your Daily Schedule!"

"When you awake, enter at once into My Heart, and when you are in It, offer My Father all your actions united to the pulsations of My Heart. Unite all your actions to Mine, so that it will no longer be you, but I, who act in you.

"During Holy Mass, present souls that I want to save to My Father, so that He may pour over them the Blood of the Victim, that is about to be immolated.

"After you have received Holy Communion, offer the Divine Wealth you then possess, to pay the debt of souls.

"During your prayer, place yourself beside Me in Gethsemane, share My anguish, and offer yourself to My Father as a victim, ready to endure all that your soul is able to bear.

"When you eat or drink, think that you are giving Me that alleviation, and do the same whenever you take pleasure in anything whatever.

"Do not be separated from Me even for one instant.

"Make the Stations of the Cross every day.

"Look solely to My Will in all you do and accomplish It with the greatest submission.

"Humble yourself profoundly, but always join confidence and love to your humility.

"Today you are going to console Me. Enter into My Heart and offer yourself to My Father with the Merits of your Spouse. Beg Him to forgive the many souls that are ungrateful. Tell Him that even in your littleness you are prepared to repair for the sins mankind commits against Him. Tell Him what a miserable little victim you are, but that you are veiled in My Blood.

"You should spend the day imploring forgiveness and repairing for sin. I want you to unite your soul to the zeal that consumes My Heart.

"Repeat these words every day:
My dear Jesus, by Your most Loving Heart, I implore You to inflame with zeal for Your Love and glory all the priests of the world, all missionaries, and those whose office it is to preach Your Word; on fire with holy zeal, they may snatch souls from the devil and lead them into the shelter of Your Heart, where forever they may glorify You.

"Do everything out of love, and do not lose sight of what I suffered for souls.

"During the night you will rest in My Heart! My heart will listen to the beats of yours, which will be so many acts of love and desire. Thus even while you are sleeping, you will bring back to Me souls that so offend Me.

"Offer My Father the Divine Victim and the Blood of My Heart for souls.

"You possess My Heart for all I ask you to do."

Your Daily Schedule 2*

94

"Whatever you do for love of Me, however small in itself, will give Me much pleasure, and will be of great benefit for yourself and for souls. Give Me your heart, that I may there take My rest. Now say once more that you love Me for those who offend Me."

*

"Shall I tell you what I want? I want to envelop, consume, and annihilate you, so that I may reign alone in you."

*

"The greatest reward I can give you or any soul, is to make you a victim of My Love and Mercy, rendering you like Myself, for I am the Divine Victim for sinners."

*

"Do not stop uniting your actions to Mine and offering My Precious Blood to My Father."

*

"Never forget that you are the victim of My Heart."

*

"Look at My Heart. It is all Love and Tenderness, but there are those who do not realize this."

*

"If religious souls only knew how great My Love for them is and how they wound Me by their coldness and tepidity! These souls do not know the dangers they run by neglecting their faults. They begin by a small infidelity and end by relaxation. Today, they grant themselves a slight indulgence; tomorrow, they are deaf to an inspiration of grace, and little by little without realizing it, they allow their love to become cold."

*

"I want you to burn with love of Me. You will find happiness nowhere but in My Heart. I want you to love Me. I hunger for love, but I also want you to burn with desire to see Me loved. This must be the one food of your soul."

*

"I have so many souls who forsake Me and are lost! What wounds Me most is that they are souls whom I have chosen specially and overwhelmed with My gifts. In return, these souls show Me only coldness and ingratitude. How few souls correspond with My Love!"

*

"My Heart is your Refuge."

*

Jesus, how can we console You, since we are so full of miseries and weakness?

"I make little account of all your miseries, if you souls come to Me with confidence and love. I will make up for all your frailty."

*

"Ask forgiveness for the whole world, especially for those that know Me and yet sin; offer yourself in reparation!"

*

"Now I am satisfied, for you have made your vows. Now I hold you a prisoner in My Heart. From all eternity I have been yours; now, you are Mine forever. You will work for Me, and I will work for you. Your interests will be Mine, and Mine yours. I have been faithful to you."

*

"Every time you renew your vows, I tighten the bonds that unite you to Me."

*

"Behold the Heart that gives life to souls. The Fire of this Love is stronger than the indifference and ingratitude of mortals.

"Behold the Heart that bestows on the souls I have chosen, a vehement desire to consume themselves, and, if necessary, to die to prove to Me their love.

"Sinners tear Me to pieces and fill My Heart with sorrow. Will not you, My chosen little victim, repair all this ingratitude?"

*

"My Will is that you should enter into My Heart today; There you will find strength to suffer. Do not reflect on your helplessness; My Heart is powerful enough to sustain you. It is yours; take from It all you need. Be consumed in It! Offer this Heart and this Blood to the Eternal Father. Live only a life of love, reparation, and suffering."

*

"The better you know who you are, the better you will know WHO I AM."

*

"I do not look at the act itself, I look at the intention. The smallest act, if done out of love, acquires such merit, that it gives Me immense consolation. I want only love. I ask for nothing else."

*

"Take My cross. Ask Mercy for sinners, Light for the blind, Love for hearts that are indifferent. Comfort Me, love Me, and surrender yourself to Me. One act of abandonment glorifies Me more than many sacrifices."

*

"Many souls are willing to entertain Me when I visit them with consolation. Many receive Me with joy in Holy Communion, but few welcome Me when I visit them with My cross. When a soul is stretched on the cross and is surrendered to My Will, that soul glorifies Me, consoles Me, and is very close to Me."

*

"What would become of the world if reparation were not made for offenses committed? There are too few victims, too few."

Lord, how can I make reparation when my own infidelities are so great? I am full of miseries.

"It does not matter! The Sun of Love purifies you and makes your sufferings worthy to be used in reparation for the sins of mankind."

*

"In spite of your miseries, you souls can love Me to folly. You must realize that I am speaking only of faults of frailty and inadvertence, not of willed sin or voluntary infidelity."

*

"Love transforms your most ordinary actions and gives them an infinite value, but it does even more: My Heart Loves you chosen souls so tenderly, that I wish to use your miseries, your weaknesses, and often even your faults.

"You souls who see yourselves overwhelmed with miseries, attribute nothing to yourselves, and your very abjectness clothes you with a humility that you would not have, if you saw yourselves without any defects."

*

"My Heart is not only an abyss of Love, It is also an abyss of Mercy. Since I know that even My closest friends are not exempt from human frailties, I will that each of their actions, however insignificant, be clothed through Me with immense value for the help of those in need and for the salvation of sinners.

"All souls cannot preach nor evangelize distant uncivilized peoples, but all, yes, all can make My Heart known and loved. All can help one another to increase the number of the saved by preventing the loss of many souls, and that through My Love and Mercy.

"I will tell you, My chosen souls, that My Love for you goes further still; not only shall I make use of your daily life and of your least actions, but I will make use of your very wretchedness, your frailties, even of your falls, for the salvation of souls.

"Love transforms everything; Mercy pardons all."

*

"Love will despoil you of 'self' and allow you to think only of My glory and of souls."

*

"The one desire of My Heart is to imprison you in It, to possess you in My Love, and to make of your frailty and littleness a channel of My Mercy for many souls who will be saved by your means. I will reveal to you the burning secrets of My Heart, and they will be for the good of many souls. It is not for your merits that I use you, but that souls may see how I make use of weak and despicable instruments."

Union with God

"You souls who constantly unite your lives with Mine glorify Me and do a great work for souls. Thus, even when you are engaged in work of no value in itself, if you bathe it in My Blood or unite it to the work I did during My mortal Life, it will greatly profit souls, more perhaps, than if you had preached to the whole world and that, whether you study, speak, or write, whether you sew, sweep, or rest, provided first that the act is sanctioned by obedience or duty and not done from mere caprice; secondly, that it is done in intimate union with Me, with great purity of intention, and covered with My Blood. I so much want you souls to understand this! It is not the action in itself that is of value; it is the intention with which it is done. When I swept and labored in the workshop of Nazareth, I gave as much Glory to My Father as when I preached.

"There are many souls who in the eyes of the world fill important posts, and they give My Heart great glory. I have many hidden souls who in their humble labors are very useful workers in My vineyeard, for they are moved by love, and they know how to cover their deeds with supernatural gold by bathing them in My Blood. My Love goes so far that souls can draw great treasure out of mere nothing. As soon as you awake, unite yourselves to Me and offer Me your whole day with a burning desire, so that My Heart may use it for the profit of souls. With love you should perform your duties, hour by hour and moment by moment. How great is the treasure you souls amass in one day!"

"If you give Me souls, I will give you My Sacred Heart. Which one of us will be giving the greater gift?"

*

"Virgin souls are the dwellings of Love, where the Immaculate Lamb takes His rest. Among these souls some are even admired by the Angels and Saints. On them, the Heavenly Spouse fixes His most pure gaze and imbues them with sweet fragrance from His Heart."

*

"Do not think of what you are. I will give you the necessary strength for anything I may ask of you. Remember that I permit your miseries and falls, so that in spite of the graces I bestow on you, you may never lose sight of your nothingness."

*

"I need victims to repair the bitterness inflicted on My Heart and to relieve My sorrow. Many sins are committed! Many souls are lost!"

*

Jesus, how is it that when one prays for a soul, month after month, there seems to be no result? How is it that You who desire the conversion of sinners, leave their hearts untouched, so that many sacrifices are lost?

"When you pray with an intense desire for the conversion of a sinner, your prayer generally obtains the sinner's conversion, though sometimes only at the last moment, and the offense given to My Heart is repaired. Prayer is never lost, for on the one hand, it consoles Me for the pain sin has occasioned, and on the other, its efficacy and power are applied, if not to that sinner, then to

101

others souls better disposed to profit by it.

"There are souls who during life and for all eternity, are called to give Me not only the glory they owe Me themselves, but also that which other souls who are lost should have given Me. In this way My glory is not impaired, and a just soul is able to make reparation for many others.

"Let this be your constant prayer:
Eternal Father, out of Love for mankind You gave Your Beloved Son up to death. By His Blood, His Merits, and His Heart, have pity on all souls, and forgive all the sins that are committed. Receive the humble reparation offered You by Your chosen souls. Unite it to the Merits of Your Divine Son, so that all they do may be very effective. O Eternal Father, have pity on souls, and remember that the time has not yet come for strict justice, but for Mercy."

*

"Say with Me:
O God, infinitely Holy, I adore You. Humbly I kneel in Your presence; I beg You in the name of Your Divine Son, to pardon the many sinners who offend You. I offer You my life; I desire to make reparation for so much ingratitude."

*

"Say with Me:
My Father, God Holy and Merciful, accept my desire to console You. Would that I could repair for all the sins of mankind. Since this is impossible, I offer You the Merits of Jesus Christ, the Redeemer of the human race, in order to satisfy Your Justice."

*

My Jesus, do You remember our faults and sins after we have been sorry for them and have obtained Your forgiveness?

"I forget all the sins of any soul who comes to My Feet and implores My forgiveness."

*

"I pursue sinners as justice pursues criminals. Justice seeks them in order to punish them; I, in order to forgive."

*

What time is it?

"It is Love's hour!"

*

"Let us now ask pardon for souls; let us repair the offenses committed against the Divine Majesty. Say with Me: O God most Holy and Just, Father of all Clemency and of infinite Goodness, You created mankind out of Love, and through Love have made them heirs to eternal Blessings. If they have sinned against You through frailty, and if they deserve chastisement, accept the Merits of Your Son, who offers Himself to You as a Victim of expiation. By those Divine Merits, forgive sinful mortals, and deign to reinstate them as heirs of Heaven. O Eternal Father, have Pity and Mercy for souls!"

*

"Let us repair for this multitude of sins!
O God, infinitely Holy, Father infinitely Merciful, I adore You. I desire to expiate the insults heaped upon You by sinners all over the world, at every moment of the day and night. Would that I could at least repair for those being committed at this hour. O my Father, I offer You all the acts of

103

adoration and reparation made by souls who love You. Above all, I offer You Your Divine Son, immolated on the altars in every corner of the world, at every moment of this hour. O Father, You are infinitely Good and Compassionate, accept His Pure Blood in reparation for all the outrages committed by mankind, wipe out their sins and have Mercy on them."

Dear Jesus, I feel so unworthy to do this, as I also am a great sinner.

"If your unworthiness and your sins are great, come and immerse them in the torrent of My Heart's Blood and you will be purified. Then accept generously all the sufferings My Will sends you, and offer them up to My Heavenly Father. Your heart should burn with desire to console an outraged God, and repair for so many sins through My Merits."

*

"Do you know a heart more loving than Mine, and any that meets with less response to Its Love? Is there a heart to be found that consumes itself with greater willingness to forgive? In payment for so much Love, I receive only great outrages. Poor souls! Let us go and ask pardon, and repair for their sins:

O my Father, have pity on souls. Do not chastise them as they deserve, but have Mercy on them according to the entreaties of Your Son. I desire to make reparation for their sins, and render You the glory which is due to You, O God, infinitely Holy! Cast Your eyes on Your Son. He is the Victim who will expiate all these sins."

"Renew your vows; it gives Me glory when you tighten the bonds that unite Me to you, and I fill your soul with so much grace, that not only is it as pure as on the day of your first vows, but each time, it gains a new degree of merit which makes it more pleasing in My sight. Thus all souls united to Me by these close and sacred bonds, clothe themselves in new merit and draw nearer to My Heart which delights in them, each time they renew their vows."

*

The Sacrament of Penance

"I will reveal to you the secret thoughts that filled My Heart, while I was washing the feet of My disciples.

"The Twelve were gathered together. John the Beloved was there, as well as Judas who was so soon to deliver Me to My enemies. I gathered them together, because the moment had come for My Church to be manifested to all souls in the world, and for all the sheep to have but One Shepherd. It was My intention, also, to show souls that I never refuse grace even to those who are guilty of grave sin, nor do I separate them from the good souls whom I Love with predilection. I keep them all in My Heart, that they may receive the help required by their state of soul.

"How great was My sorrow to see in the person of My unhappy disciple, Judas, the throng of those souls, who, though gathered at My Feet and washed in My Blood, would yet hasten to their eternal perdition! I want you to understand that it is not the fact of being in sin that should keep them from Me. They must never think that there is no remedy for them, nor that they have forfeited forever the Love that once was theirs. No, poor souls, the God who has shed all His Blood for you, has no such feelings!

"Come to Me and fear not, for I Love you. I will wash you in My Blood and you shall become whiter than snow. All your offenses will be washed from you, nor shall anything or anyone be able to tear from My Heart Its Love for you. Let your soul be seized by an ardent desire to see all souls, especially sinners, come and purify themselves in the waters of repentance. Let them give themselves up to thoughts of confidence, not fear, for I am a God of Pity, ever ready to receive them into My Heart.

"I washed the feet of My Apostles before the Last Supper, to teach souls how pure they must be to receive Me in Holy Communion. I also wished to remind souls who would have the misfortune to sin, that they can always recover their innocence through the Sacrament of Penance.

"I washed the feet of My Apostles so that those who have consecrated themselves to apostolic work may follow My example, and treat sinners and all other souls that are entrusted to their care with humility and gentleness. I girded Myself with a white linen cloth to remind them that apostles need to be girded with abnegation and mortification, if they hope to exert any real influence on souls. I wished to teach them mutual charity, which is ever ready to excuse the faults of others, but never to reveal them."

Sacrament of Penance 2*

The Blessed Sacrament

"The hour of Redemption was at hand. My Heart could no longer restrain Its Love for mankind, nor bear the thought of leaving them orphans.

"To prove My tender Love for them and, in order to remain always with them till time ceased to be, I resolved to become their Food, their Support, their Life, their All. I desire to make known to all souls the loving sentiments with which My Heart overflowed at My Last Supper, when I instituted the Sacrament of the Holy Eucharist.

"I saw the multitudes in future ages who would receive My Body and Blood, and all the good It would effect; how many hearts I saw that from Its contact would bud forth virginity; how many others that It would awaken to deeds of charity and zeal! How many martyrs of love did I see!

"How many souls who had been enfeebled by sin and the violence of passion, would come back to their allegiance and recover their spiritual energy by partaking of this Bread of the Strong!

"Who can describe the overwhelming emotions that filled My Soul? Joy, Love, Tenderness, but, alas, bitter sorrow also filled My Soul.

"Who made you? Has anyone shown you more love than I? Who has forgiven you as often as I, and who will do so again?

"I want to tell you chosen souls of the sorrows

which filled My Sacred Heart at the Last Supper. It was bliss for Me to think of all those to whom I should be both Companion and Heavenly Food, of all who would surround Me to the end of time with adoration, reparation, and love, yet, this in no way diminished My grief at the many souls who would leave Me deserted in My tabernacle and who would not even believe in My Real Presence.

"Into how many hearts defiled by sin I would have to enter, and how often this profanation of My Body and Blood would serve for their ultimate condemnation!

"Sacrileges and outrages, and all the nameless abominations to be committed against Me, passed before My eyes; the long, lonely hours of the day and night in which I would remain alone on the altars, and the multitudes who would not heed the appeals of My Sacred Heart.

"It is Love for souls that keeps Me a Prisoner in the Blessed Sacrament. I stay in the Eucharist that all may come and find the comfort they need in the tenderest of hearts, the best of fathers, the most faithful of friends, who will never abandon them.

"The Holy Eucharist is the invention of Love, yet how few souls correspond to that Love which spends and consumes Itself for them!

"I live in the midst of sinners that I may be their Life, their Physician, and the Remedy of the diseases bred by a corrupt nature.

The Blessed Sacrament 2

"In return for living with mortals, they forsake Me, insult and despise Me! O poor pitiable sinners, do not turn away from Me. Day and night I am watching for you in the tabernacle. I will not reproach you. I will not cast your sins in your face; I will wash the sins from your soul in My Blood and in My Wounds. You need not be afraid to come to Me. If you only knew how dearly I Love you!

"Dear souls, why this coldness and indifference on your part? Don't I know your concerns and the requirements of your position in life make continual calls upon you? Do not allow yourselves to be involved in useless and incessant cares, but spare a few moments to visit and receive Me, for I am your Prisoner of Love.

"If you were weak or ill in body surely you would find time to see a doctor who would cure you. Come then to One who is able to give both strength and health to your soul, and bestow your alms of love on the Divine Prisoner who watches for you, calls for you, and desires to see you with Him.

"My best-loved and specially favored souls, My priests and My consecrated souls, I want to tell you this: your infidelities wound Me deeply, but your love consoles and delights My Heart to such a degree that I, so to speak, forget the sins of many others on your account.

"I am going to reveal to you the greatest mystery of My Love, of Love for My consecrated and chosen souls.

"When I was about to institute the Holy Eucharist I saw the privileged multitude of souls who would be nourished by My Body and Blood. Some would find in It the remedy for their short-comings, others a consuming fire for their imperfections. I likewise saw you, consecrated souls, gathered around Me as in a garden, each causing Me to rejoice with flowers and their scent. As a vivifying sun, My Sacred Body gave you spiritual life, and warmed your cold hearts. To some souls I went for comfort, to others for refuge, to others again for rest. Would that all you cherished souls knew how easily you can console Me, harbor Me, or give rest to Me, your God.

"It is your infinitely Loving God, who after freeing you from the slavery of sin, has given you the incomparable grace of your religious vocation and has mysteriously attracted you into the enclosed garden of His delights. I am your God and your Savior; I have also made Myself your Spouse.

"I feed you with My Immaculate Flesh, and quench your thirst with My Blood. If you are sick, I will be your Physician; come to Me, I will cure you. If you are cold, come to Me, I will warm you. In Me you will find rest and happiness. Do not wander away from Me, for I am Life. When I ask you to comfort Me, do not sadden Me by a refusal. Alas, what sorrow it is to see so many who have been endowed with My choicest graces, become a cause of pain to My Sacred Heart! Am I not always the same? Have I changed? My Love is unalterable, and will endure to the end of time with the same tenderness and predilection.

The Blessed Sacrament 4

"That you are unworthy I well know, but not because of that do I turn away from you. On the contrary, with anxious solicitude I look for your coming, that I may not only ease your troubles, but also grant you many favors.

"I ask for your love; do not refuse it. It is so easy to love Love Itself.

"If I should ask you for things that cost, know that at the same time I will give you all the grace and strength you need to conquer yourself.

"All sinners were present to Me when I instituted the Blessed Sacrament, and My Heart glowed with desire to become the Food for just such souls. Since I have taken up My abode among mortals, it is not merely to live among the perfect, but to uphold the weak, and sustain the lowly. I will make them grow and become strong. Their good resolutions will be My solace and I will rest in their wretchedness. Are there not some among these chosen souls who will inflict sorrow on Me? Will they all persevere? Such is the cry of grief that comes from My Heart. I want souls to hear it.

"I will tell you of the pain endured by My Sacred Heart, when being constrained by the Fire that consumed It, I devised the marvel of Love: the Holy Eucharist. While I looked at those many souls that would feed on this Heavenly Bread, I could also see the indifference of so many other consecrated souls and priests, who would neglect Me in this Sacrament. There were those who would grow cold, gradually yield to routine, and,

The Blessed Sacrament 5

worse than routine, to weariness and little by little to tepidity.

"Still I wait all night and watch in the tabernacle for souls who are cold, fervently hoping that they will come and receive Me, that they will converse with Me with all the trust of a bride, telling Me their sorrows, temptations, sufferings, asking advice, and begging for the graces needed for themselves and for others. Yes, I yearn for your coming, that I might rest in you and share your anxieties. I have prepared new graces for you. Ask Me for advice and strength.

"Come, I say to you souls, let us discuss all your tribulations with perfect freedom. Be concerned about sinners. Offer yourselves to make reparation. Promise Me that at least today you will not leave Me alone, then see if My Heart is not asking something more of you to comfort It. This is what I hope to obtain from many souls, especially from My chosen souls.

"The Blessed Sacrament is the Invention of Love. It is Life and Fortitude for souls, a Remedy for every fault, and Viaticum for the last passage from time to eternity. In the Blessed Sacrament sinners recover spiritual life for their souls; tepid souls, true warmth; fervent souls, tranquillity and the satisfaction of every desire; saintly souls, wings to fly towards perfection; pure souls, sweet honey and rarest sustenance.

"Adieu, do not forget Me. Desire Me as I desire you; love Me as I Love you; seek Me as I seek you. You see that I never forsake you."

The Blessed Sacrament 6*

Holy Thursday

"Today is My great day, the day of Love: Love's Feastday. Today is the day on which I give Myself to you souls, that I may be for you just what you wish: if you will look on Me as your Father, I shall be a Father to you; if you desire Me as your Beloved, I shall be your Beloved; if you need strength, I will be your Strength, and, if you desire to console Me, I will let you console Me. All I want is to give Myself to you and to fill you with the graces I have prepared for you. I cannot withhold them any longer. What shall I be for you?"

My Jesus, I am nothing, be to me my All!

"It is on account of your nothingness and utter misery that you must let Me kindle your heart's fire, consume and destroy your miseries. Yes, I did indeed say that Love gives Itself to Its own, and it is true. Come, draw near to My Heart and enter in; taste and see what Its overwhelming emotions are.

"Love gives Itself as Food to Its own. This Food gives you your spiritual life and sustains you.

"Love humbles Itself before Its own, and in so doing, raises mankind to the highest dignity.

"Love surrenders Itself in totality; It gives in profusion and without reserve. With enthusiasm, with vehemence It is immolated for the souls It Loves. The Holy Eucharist is Love to the extreme of folly."

"Come, enter into My Sacred Heart and spend the day therein. You are in Me and that is why you do not see Me, but I see you, and that suffices.

"Never be afraid of suffering or of sacrifice; such are God's ways. If you want to come out victoriously from the assaults of the devil, pay great attention to two things: first, humble yourself, for you are nothing and deserve nothing. Everything comes to you as a grace from God. Second, when you feel lonely and given up to temptation, when your soul is cold and you have no courage to go on, do not give up prayer. Pray humbly and confidently, and go at once to seek guidance from the person God has given you for that purpose. Believe Me, if you do this, you will make no mistakes."

*

"Peace has come to the world! The cross, formerly an instrument of torture on which criminals were made to die, is changed into the light and peace of the world and becomes the object of the most profound veneration.

"Sinners will draw pardon and spiritual life from My Sacred Wounds. My Blood will wash away and efface all their filth and foulness.

"Pure souls will come to My Wounds, There to quench their thirst and kindle flames of love in their hearts. There they will find a Refuge and forever make a home. All souls have found their Redeemer, and chosen souls have found the Model they must copy."

"The Father Loves Me; the Son Loves Me; the Holy Spirit Loves Me. We are One in Sanctity, in Wisdom, in Power, and in Love. The Father and the Spirit are One with the Son, and by Him communicate Themselves wholly to souls, for the Son, uniting in His Divine Person the two natures, Divine and Human, has made Himself the bond between God and mankind. Mankind, whose human nature is divinized by grace, becomes one with God, each time when, in a state of grace they receive Holy Communion. Souls are identified with God and are lost in Him. Thus does God reside in souls that are in a state of grace. Thus do the Three Divine Persons take up Their abode in them, making these souls Their habitation of delight.

"Every soul can be instrumental in the sublime work of the salvation of souls. Nothing great is required, the smallest acts suffice: a step taken, a straw picked up, a glance restrained, a service rendered, a cordial smile — all these offered to Love are in reality of great profit to souls and draw down grace on them. No need to remind you of the results of prayer, of sacrifice, of any act offered to expiate the sins of mankind, to obtain for them the grace of purification, that they too may become fitting sanctuaries for the indwelling of the Blessed Trinity.

"When souls devote their lives to work either directly or indirectly for the salvation of other souls, and reach such a degree of detachment from self that, without neglecting their own

115

perfection, they leave to others the merit of their actions, prayers, and sufferings, they draw down abundant graces on all souls, and they themselves reach a high degree of sanctity, far higher than they would have attained had they sought only their own advancement."

*   *   *

"Souls that eat My Flesh possess God, the Author of Life and of Life Eternal. That is how they become My Heaven. Nothing can compare with their beauty. The Angels are in admiration and, as God is with them, they fall down in adoration. O souls, if you only knew your dignity!

"Your soul is My Heaven; every time you receive Me in Holy Communion, My grace augments both your dignity and your beauty."

*

"My Heart is a fiery Furnace to which you chosen souls must come to enkindle yours. It belongs to you with all the graces It contains, that you may distribute them to the world, to the many souls who do not know where to seek them, and to so many others who despise them."

*

"Console Me! Love Me! Glorify Me through My Heart; make reparation and satisfy Divine Justice by It. Offer Me to God the Father as a Victim of Love for souls and, in a special way, for those vowed and consecrated to Me.

"Live with Me and I will live with you. Hide in Me and I will live in your heart."

*

"Ask Mercy for sinners, Light for the blind, Love for hearts that are indifferent."

116

My Lord Jesus, I give You my heart, my life, my liberty . . . all!

"I desire nothing else. What does all the rest matter? Your sins? I can wipe them out. Your miseries? I consume them. Your weakness? I will be your support. Let us remain united."

Jesus told me my failings.

"What are you, after all? You are a mere pinch of dust that one blows away with a breath.

"You know that I always forgive you. If I tell you your faults, it is because of My Love for you, that your 'self' may disappear and I may live in you. I will change the flame in your heart and kindle it anew to give you new vigor for the work of your own destruction.

"You know that it is the property of fire to destroy and to enkindle. In the same way My Heart's property is to Pardon, Love, and Purify. Never think that I shall cease to Love you because of your miseries. No, My Heart Loves you and will never forsake you."

*

"Do not fear. My one desire is to forgive. Do not think that I have chosen you because of your virtues; I know well that you have nothing but misery and weakness, but as I am a purifying Fire, I will wrap you in the flame of My Heart, and destroy you by transforming you into Myself! My one desire is for souls to bring Me their miseries! Come, and let Love consume you.

117

"I have chosen you and I will provide your every want. I require nothing of you beyond what is already yours. Give Me an empty heart and I will make it beautiful. Give it to Me with all its miseries and I will consume them. What is hidden from you I will reveal, and all that you lack I take on Myself to supply. You know well, that had I been able to find anywhere a creature more miserable than you, I would assuredly have chosen her, in order to manifest the desires of My Heart through her to all souls in the world, but not finding one, I chose you.

"Think what would have become of you if I had left you, frail and miserable as you are, to the cold of winter, the heat of summer, to be the sport of wind and rain; assuredly you would have died. It is because I want you only to live in Me that I transplanted you into the garden of My Sacred Heart, tending you with My own Hands, that you may grow up under the beams of the Sun with Its vivifying and restoring Power, whose Strength is tempered in your regard, so that no injury may come to you. Leave yourself, such as you are, to My care, and let the sight of your nothingness never lessen your trust, but only confirm you in humility."

*

"Would that you souls understood that never are you more free than when you have given yourselves up to Me, and that never am I more inclined to grant your desires than when you are ready to do My Will in everything. Clasp tight those chains that sweetly bind you to Me. Go and renew the vows that bind you to My Feet, to My Hands, and introduce you into My Heart."

"My Appeal!"

"I am Love! My Heart can no longer contain Its devouring flames. I Love souls so dearly that I sacrificed My Life for them.

"It is this Love that keeps Me a Prisoner in the tabernacle. For nearly twenty centuries I have dwelt there, night and day, veiled under the Species of Bread and concealed in the small white Host, enduring through My Love, neglect, solitude, contempt, blasphemies, outrages, and sacrileges.

"For Love of souls, I instituted the Sacrament of Penance, that I might forgive them, not once or twice, but as often as they need to recover grace. There I wait for them; I desire to wash away their sins, not in water, but in My Blood.

"How often in the course of the ages I have in one way or another, made known My Love for mortals; I have shown them how ardently I desire their salvation! I have revealed My Heart to them. The devotion to My Sacred Heart is a powerful means of gaining souls, and so thereby extending My Kingdom.

"Now I want something more! I desire love in response to My Love, but this is not the only return I desire from souls; I want you to have confidence in My Mercy, I want you to expect all from My Clemency, and never to doubt My readiness to forgive.

"I am God, but a God of Love! I am a Father,

but a Father full of Compassion and never harsh.

"My Heart is infinitely Holy but also infinitely Wise, and knowing human frailty and infirmity, I stoop to poor sinners with infinite Mercy.

"I Love you after a first fall when you come to Me for pardon. I Love you still more when you beg pardon for your second sin, and should this happen again, I do not say a million times but a million million times, I still Love you and pardon you, and I will wash away in My Blood, your last as fully as your first sin.

"Never shall I weary of you repentant sinners, nor shall I ever cease hoping for your return. The greater your distress, the greater My welcome shall be. Does not a father love a sick child with special affection? Are not his cares and solicitude greater? The Tenderness and Compassion of My Heart is likewise more abundant for sinners than for the just.

"This is what I wish all to know. I will teach sinners that the Mercy of My Sacred Heart is inexhaustible. Let those souls that are calloused and indifferent know that My Heart is a Fire which will enkindle them, because I Love them. To devout and saintly souls I would be the Way, that making great strides in perfection, they may safely reach the harbor of Eternal Beatitude.

"Since you possess nothing but miseries, faults, and sin, these I desire. I beg you to give them to Me. Trust in My Heart: I forgive you, I Love you, I will sanctify you.

My Appeal 2

120

"You consecrated souls, priests and religious, My elect and chosen ones, I ask once more for all your love. I ask that you do not doubt My Love; I ask that you trust Me and never doubt My Mercy. It is so easy to trust completely in My Heart.

"I want to forgive. I want to reign over souls and pardon all nations. I want to rule souls, nations, the whole world. My peace must be extended over the entire universe. I am Wisdom and Beatitude! I am Love and Mercy! I am Peace; I shall reign! I will shower My Mercies on all souls in the world, to wipe out their ingratitude.

"To make reparation for their crimes, I choose victims who will obtain pardon, for there are in the world many whose desire is to please Me; there are also generous souls who will sacrifice everything they possess, that I may use them according to My Will and good pleasure.

"My Reign will be one of Peace and Love; I shall inaugurate it by compassion on all: such is the end I have in view and this is the great work of My Love.

"My appeal is addressed to all souls: to those consecrated in religion and to those living in the world, to the good and to sinners, to the learned and to the illiterate, to those in authority and to those who obey. To each of them I say: 'If you seek happiness, you will find it in Me. If you seek riches, I am infinite Wealth. If you desire peace, in Me alone is Peace to be found. I am Mercy and Love! I must be the Sovereign King.'

"Understand well, you My consecrated souls who form the court of the Immaculate Lamb, that the glory you give Me surpasses incomparably that of the Angelic Spirits, for they have never experienced the frailties of your human nature, and they have neither to struggle nor to conquer in order to remain pure. You thus acquire a relationship with My Holy Virgin Mother Mary, who being a mortal creature was nevertheless of spotless Purity. She was subject to all human miseries, yet, at every instant of Her Life was absolutely Immaculate. She has glorified Me more than all the Celestial Spirits, and God Himself, drawn by Her Purity, took flesh of Her and dwelt in His Creature.

"I want you to console Me, and I shall be your shield against anything that anybody may think or say of you. Are you not Mine? Since I am with you, what does it matter if the whole world is against you? I want you to burn with desire to save souls. I want you to place yourself in My Heart, and to make My glory your sole occupation.

"Make an oblation of yourself and repair for sins, in union with Me, the Divine Victim.

"See how My Heart is consumed with Love for souls! You, too, must burn with desire for their salvation. I want you to enter into My Heart and make reparation with Me. We must repair. I am the great Victim, and you are a very little one; since you are united to Me, My Father will listen to you.

"Love is reparation and reparation is love.

My Appeal 4

122

"In My Church I have chosen you as My elder children: you who are consecrated by the priesthood or by the vows of Holy Religion. You live nearest to Me; you share in My choicest graces, and to you I confide My secrets, My desires, and also My sufferings. I have committed to you the care of My little children, your brethren, and through your ministry you must directly or indirectly, guide them and transmit My teaching to them.

"If you, chosen souls, know Me truly, you will make Me known to others; if you love Me, you will make others love Me. How can you teach your brethren, if you hardly know Me yourselves? I ask you: 'Can there be much love in your heart, for One who is barely known? What intimate conversation can be exchanged with One who is avoided, or in whom you have little confidence?' This is precisely what I wish to recall to your minds. Nothing new, doubtless, but you have need to re-animate your faith and your love.

"I look for greater intimacy and confidence in the way you religious souls treat Me. Seek Me in your hearts, for you know that a soul in the state of grace is a tabernacle of the Holy Spirit. In your heart consider Me as I truly am, your God, but a God of Love. Let love triumph over fear; never forget that I Love you. You are convinced that it was because of this Love that you were chosen. When you are discouraged at the sight of your miseries and faults, you become sad at the thought that I have changed, and Love you less than before.

My Appeal 5

123

"How little you consecrated souls know Me! You have not understood My Heart! It is your very destitution and failings that inclines My Goodness toward you. When you acknowledge your helplessness and weakness, when you humble yourselves and have recourse to Me trustfully, then indeed you give Me more glory than you did before your fault. If you waver and doubt when you pray, either for yourself or for others, you do not glorify My Heart; you do glorify It, if you are sure that I shall give you what you ask, knowing that I refuse you nothing that is good for your soul.

"When the centurion came to beg Me to cure his servant, he said very humbly: 'I am not worthy that You should enter under my roof,' and faith and love prevailing, he added: 'Say but the word, and my servant shall be healed.' This man knew My Heart. He knew that I would not resist the prayer of one who trusted Me absolutely. He gave Me much glory, for to humility he joined confidence. Yes, this man knew My Heart, yet I had made no manifestations to him as I have to My chosen ones.

"Hope obtains innumerable graces for yourself and for others. I want this to be understood, so that My Heart's Goodness may be revealed to those poor souls who as yet do not know Me.

"I once again repeat what I have already said, and it is nothing new: 'As a flame needs to be fed, if it is not to be extinguished, so souls need constant fresh urging to make them advance, and new warmth to renew their fervor.'

My Appeal 6

"There are few among you religious souls that are consecrated to Me who possess an unshakable confidence in Me, because there are few who live in intimate union with Me.

"I want you to know that I Love you as you are. I know that through frailty you will fall more than once. I know that you will often break the promises you have made Me. Your will to do better glorifies Me; your humble avowals after your falls, your trust in the forgiveness I will grant, glorify My Heart so much, that I will give abundant graces to you.

"I want you to know how greatly I desire a renewal of your union and intimacy with Me. You must not be satisfied with merely conversing with Me in Church, where doubtless I am truly present, but remember that I abide in you, and delight in this union.

"Speak to Me of all your concerns, consult Me at every turn, ask favors of Me. I live in you to be your Life, I abide in you to be your Strength. Yes, I repeat, remember that I delight in being one with you. Remember that I am in your soul; there I see you, hear you, and Love you; in your soul I look for a return from you.

"Many are accustomed to daily meditation, but for how many souls it becomes a mere formality, instead of a loving interview! They say or assist at Holy Mass and receive Me in Holy Communion, but on leaving the Church become once more absorbed in their own interests, to such an extent, that they scarcely say a word to Me.

"I am in some souls as in a desert. They neither speak to Me nor ask anything of Me. When they are in need of comfort, they solicit it from creatures whom they must seek rather than from Me, their Creator, who abides and lives in them. Is this not want of union, want of interior spirit, in other words, want of love?

"Let Me once more tell you souls who are consecrated to Me, how I specially chose you, that you might live in union with Me, to comfort Me, and repair for the sins of those souls who offend Me.

"I want you souls to remember that it is your duty to study My Heart, in order to share in Its desires, insofar as it is in your power to realize Its desires.

"I call you souls to live a life of intimate union with Me.

"It is your privilege to know My desires and to share in My joys and sorrows.

"It is your privilege to labor for My interests, never sparing yourselves trouble or pain.

"It is your privilege, by prayer and penance, to make reparation for many, many souls.

"It is your privilege to become more and more closely united to Me and never to abandon Me, never to leave Me alone! Please understand and do not forget that it is your privilege to give Me companionship and consolation.

My Appeal 8

126

"I ask you religious souls to combine together in a 'league of love,' in My Heart, to implore for souls the knowledge of Truth, Light, and Pardon. When you see with deep sorrow the outrages I receive, you will offer yourselves to make reparation and to labor at My work.

"Let your trust be firm, for I shall not refuse your supplications, and all you ask for will be granted to you.

"You should apply yourselves to the study of My Heart and to the understanding of My desires, striving to live in union with Me, to converse with Me, and to consult Me.

"You should clothe your actions in My Merits, bathe yourselves in My Blood, and consecrate your lives to the saving of souls and the extension of My glory. You should rejoice at seeing yourselves clothed with the power of My Blood and of My Merits.

"If you rely on yourselves, you will do little or nothing, but if you labor with Me, in My Name, and for My glory, you will be powerful.

"Sometimes I leave you to yourself, so that you might see how little you can do without Me.

"You should revive your desire for reparation and beg confidently for the advent of the Divine King.

"Have no fear, hope in Me, and place your trust in Me.

"You should be burnt up with zeal and charity for sinners, praying for them with compassionate hearts, and treating them with all gentleness.

"Let all souls hear from you how great is My Kindness, My Love, and My Mercy.

"Armed with prayer, penance, and reliance on Me, never on yourself, go forward to your apostolic labors in the Power and Goodness of My Heart which is ever with you.

"My apostles were poor and ignorant men, but rich and wise in My Wealth and Wisdom. Their watchword was: 'In Your name, O Lord Jesus, we shall labor and be all-powerful.'

"I ask three things of you, My consecrated souls:

1. "Reparation: that is, a life of union with Me, for I make Divine Reparation. Work for Me, with Me, and in Me, in a spirit of reparation, in close union with My desires.

2. "Love: that is, intimacy with Me, for I am all Love. I humble Myself to ask My creatures not to leave Me alone, but to give Me their love.

3. "Confidence: that is, trust in Me, for I am Goodness and Mercy; in Me you live day and night. Have confidence in Me, for I know you and you know Me; I Love you and you love Me. Have confidence in Me, for I call you to live with Me in a special way, to know My Heart, and so to trust Me in everything."

*   My Appeal 10*

"Look at My Wounds and greet them with a kiss. Do you know where they came from? Love! Do you know what opened My Heart? Love! Who crowned Me with thorns? Love! Since I have Loved you so much as to refuse no suffering for your sake, cannot you suffer without refusing Me anything? Abandon yourself to Me."

*

"Don't you know that I and the cross are inseparable? If you meet Me, you meet the cross, and when you find the cross, it is I whom you have found. Whoever loves Me loves the cross, and whoever loves the cross loves Me. Only those who love the cross and embrace it willingly for love of Me, will possess Eternal Life. The path of virtue and of holiness is composed of abnegation and suffering. Whoever generously accepts the cross, walks in true Light, follows a straight and sure path, with no danger from steep inclines to slide down, for there are none.

"My cross is the door of true Life. Souls that know how to accept and love it, just as I have chosen it for them, will enter by the cross into the glory of Life Eternal.

"Do you now understand how precious the cross is? Do not shun it. Love it, for it comes from Me, and I shall never leave you without strength to bear it. I bore it for Love of you. Will you not bear it for love of Me?"

*

"Do not regard your littleness; look rather at the Power of My Heart sustaining you. I am your Strength; I will repair your abjectness. I will give you courage for anything I ask you to endure."

"I know your extreme wretchedness! I will make reparation for you; you will make reparation for souls."

*

"Unite your sorrow and your anguish to Mine, and offer them to My Eternal Father together with all the merits and sufferings of all the just souls. Offer Him the agonies of My crown of thorns to expiate the perverse thoughts of souls."

*

"Our work in Heaven will be to teach souls how to live united to Me, not as if I were far away, but in them, because by grace I dwell in them, and in Holy Communion My Sacred Humanity becomes, so to speak, Incarnate in them."

*

"My Heart is a Book into which you must look and meditate. It will teach you all virtues, especially zeal for My glory, and zeal for the salvation of souls.

"My Heart is the Sanctuary of the miserable, hence yours, for who is more miserable than you?

"My Heart is the Crucible in which the most defiled are purified and inflamed with love. Draw near this Furnace, cast your miseries and sins into It; have confidence and believe in Me!

"My Heart is a Fountain of Living Water. Throw yourself into Its depths and appease your thirst. I desire that all may find refreshment at this Source. I have found a hidden place for you in the depths of My Heart. You are so little that you could not attain to It alone. Use well the grace I have stored in My Heart for you."

†

130

JESUS SPEAKS TO ME
THROUGH SISTER BENIGNA CONSOLATA

*   *   *   *   *   *   *

"No longer go begging for the love of creatures; were they to give themselves entirely to you, you would not be satisfied. God alone can suffice, for you have need of a Heart which Loves you, which understands you; it is the Heart of God you need. Speak to Me as you would to an earthly friend, to whom you tell everything."

My Jesus, I want to be a Saint! Is it not pride and presumption for me to aspire to an end so elevated, I who am weakness itself?

"It would be indeed, if you depend on your own strength. If you will hope for all from Me, I will sustain you in your conflicts and will help you to surmount all the obstacles that could hinder the reign of pure love in your soul."

*

"Say to Me: My Jesus, You are the Resurrection and the Life! Will you let those souls for whom You have died on the cross, hasten to perdition? Be the Resurrection and the Life to the many hearts that have been buried in the darkness of sin. From now on I shall thank You for the victory You gained over the infernal enemy who held so many souls slaves of sin, since You have assured me that I should obtain all I ask of You with confidence."

*

"Pray to Me: O Jesus, You have granted to religious souls the special grace of serving You in a more perfect state. Do not permit them to

131

abuse so great a treasure by passing their lives in tepidity and negligence; revive in their hearts the flame of Your Love, so that repairing the past and sanctifying the future, they may enjoy You in Heaven for all eternity."

*

My Jesus, pardon me the liberty I take in speaking thus to You; You can do all things; grant then that souls may know You, love You, and serve You with all the respect and love You merit.

"I use creatures for this end, making them the instruments of My Mercy. I choose those souls destined to revive the Christian spirit; I form them, I overload them with My graces, and so prepare them for their mission. Such souls have existed in the past, they live at present, and I will raise up others in the future. You are one of these souls."

My Jesus, with humility I go to Your Feet, and with love I go to Your Sacred Heart.

*

"You shall say to your Spouse: O my Jesus, only Love of my heart, I wish to suffer what I suffer and all You will have me suffer, for Your pure Love; I will suffer, not because of the merits I may acquire, nor for the rewards You have promised me, but only to please You, to praise You, to bless You in sorrow, as well as in joy."

*

"Mortification is the channel through which My choicest graces pass. If the channel is small, few graces pass, but if it is great, many graces will pass."

"The most precious gift I can make to My friends is that of the cross. I send to the soul what costs it most, what it dreads most; this is the best means of making it advance. It is because I Love you that I give you the cross. I tell you this to comfort you. I assure you that you are far from displeasing Me when you are in this painful state, since it is I who permit it. I am beginning to nourish you in your youth with the substantial bread of sorrow, and during your whole life I shall satiate you abundantly with this Celestial Manna."

*

"I am going to ask a gift of you. Will you, in exchange for the infinite Love I have for you, give Me a special testimony of your affection? I desire that you should offer it to My Divine Heart to save sinners. By joining your works to prayer you will obtain more easily what you desire so ardently: the salvation of souls. I ask you therefore to make Me a generous sacrifice of that portion of merit, which still remains to you after the donation you have made in favor of the souls in purgatory, by an heroic act of charity. Nothing will remain to you of what you shall do or suffer; surrender all to Me, that I may dispose of it, according to My Will, in favor of the souls whose conversion you seek. This generous offering will attract to you the choicest benedictions of God, and make you participate in the benefits of Redemption, since you sacrifice all that you are, all that you have, and all that you do, for those poor souls who, thanks to you, will obtain Mercy and Pardon from My Heart.

"You must therefore have a loving and constant generosity which does not recoil even before the greatest sacrifices. Be avid not to let one pass without offering it to Me; the more you shall vanquish your repugnances, the more grace you shall receive. Let this promise encourage you not to tremble in the face of trial; accept it, bear it sweetly through love. In exchange, you shall obtain from Me all you hope for, and all you can desire."

*

"You shall make your purgatory in the flames of My Pure Love."

*

"Courage, My spouse. I, your God, am always near, although you do not see or hear Me.

"Sentiment, while giving certitude, diminishes faith; I take away sensible consolation from the soul that I wish to exercise perfectly in this virtue. You should believe without understanding and without wishing to understand; you should believe without wishing to see. In this way reason is subjected and your soul glorifies Me. Do you wish to give Me pleasure? Do not scrutinize My designs in your regard; let Me treat you as I please. I can do in one instant, by a single act of My Will, a thing which would require many years of labor."

*

"I want you to lend Me your mind, your life, and your faculties, which are My gifts because you have received them from Me, so that you may become wholly the instrument of My Mercy. The desire of seeing My Adorable Heart ever more known and loved should move you to receive this mission I give you with docility. Accept it, then, through the love you have for My Sacred Heart."

"I beg the love of My creatures, who refuse it to Me and squander it upon things which pass away. They do not even think of giving it to Me. If you knew how painful it is to Love so much and not to be loved! I do not grow weary, I am always seeking love and few give it to Me. Some not only do not love Me, but they hate Me. Do you know what hinders Me from striking sinners? It is the prayers of the just; they disarm My Divine Justice."

*

"You cannot imagine the pleasure I experience in remaining with My creatures! I am always in search of hearts that love Me, and I find only a small number. I lavish upon them the plenitude of My graces; I have so great a Love for the souls who are faithful to Me and let Me do what I please with them, that I am as ready to gratify them as if it were a law to Me."

*

"Do you know the shortest way to arrive at Heaven? It is that of confidence in My Merits and fidelity to grace."

*

"My beloved, seek for Me victims who are willing to immolate themselves for the glory of My Heart. My Heart is full of Mercy, not only for you, but for all."

*

"My child, when you shall have tasted the life of the cloister, you will not desire to return to the world at any cost. There you will find humiliation, recollection, and all that is needful for you. In the monastery, you shall win souls to Me. I desire ardently that you should be all Mine.

"The monastery will be the pulpit in which you shall make Me known. I, having no need of strength, shall lean upon your weakness. I use the ignorant to confound the intelligent."

My Jesus, one would say that You cannot live without me. What is it that attracts You to my soul? Have You not the Angels? Do You not find Your Happiness in Yourself?

"It is true that I have the Angels, but it is also true that I have a human Heart, and that I Love mankind. I tell you of My Love so that you may write it, My little 'secretary of Love'. Then I will cause it to be read, that souls may believe in My excessive Love."

*

"My child, the farther you advance in the way of mortification, the nearer you will draw to God; it is only the first step that costs. Look upon your Jesus on the cross, and you will see your program of mortification. Spiritual consolations will be your recompense; the more you mortify the flesh, the more capable will you be of comprehending the things of God. I will dwell in you according to the capacity I find there."

*

My Jesus, I am sleepy.

"I have compassion on you. Even if you passed all the time of the Holy Hour in struggling against sleep, it would be an agreeable offering, because it is the sacrifice which pleases Me."

*

"Sacrifice means love and love means sacrifice."

*

136

"The whole secret of sanctity lies in these two words: distrust and trust. Distrust always in yourself, but not stopping there, rise immediately to trust in God; since I am Good to all, I am especially Good to those who trust in Me. Do you know what souls profit most by My Goodness? Those who trust the most! Trusting souls are the robbers of My graces. The pleasure I take in trusting souls is inexpressible.

"As fire is fed with combustibles, and increases accordingly as they are supplied, so My Mercy is nourished with the miseries It consumes, and the more It receives the more It increases. If souls only knew how I Love them and how My Heart rejoices when they believe in My Love! They believe in It too little!

"Souls do not know the wrong they do to Me in doubting in My Divine Goodness! Sins may be enormous and numerous, but if souls return to Me, I am always ready to pardon all, to forget all. You are the apostle of the Mercy of God; I have chosen you, so that you may become the channel of the Divine Mercy.

"I make the most beautiful masterpieces with the most miserable subjects, provided souls let Me. When souls repent of their sins and faults and deplore them, do you think I am so hard as not to receive them? If so, you do not know My Heart. My most Loving Heart has such a thirst for the salvation of souls, that when they return to Me, I cannot contain My joy; I run to meet them. The greatest injury the demon can cause a soul after having made it fall into sin, is to incite that soul to distrust. As long as a soul has confidence, its return is easy, but if the demon succeeds in closing the heart with distrust, O how I have to struggle to reconquer it!

"It is certain that a hundred sins offend me more than one, but if this single sin is distrust of Me, it wounds My Heart more than the one hundred others. Distrust wounds My Heart to Its innermost core. I Love mankind so much.

"Mankind has no idea of the Goodness of God, of His Mercy and Love for His creatures. They measure God by creatures, but God has no limits; His Goodness is without bounds. Souls are able to use God and will not do it, because they do not know Him. I am an infinite Treasure which My Father has placed at the disposal of all. The souls who reject Me will comprehend their misfortune only in eternity. I Love mankind. I Love them tenderly as My dear brethren. Although there is an infinite distance between them and Me, I make no account of it."

*

"Little things are little things, but fidelity in little things is a great thing."

*

"The thirst I experience of saving the greatest possible number of souls, impels Me to seek generous souls with whom I can associate in My work. You will be the victim of My Justice and the consolation of My Love. You will be consumed by Love. I will immolate you with the sword of Love; I will enchain you with the bonds of Love; I will consume you in the fire of My Love."

*

138

Decalogue of Mercy

1. "I am the God of all Mercy.

2. "I always desire to be Merciful.

3. "To exercise Justice is for Me to go against the current; it does violence to Me.

4. "The door of My Mercy is never closed; it is always ajar; however lightly it is touched, it opens; even a little child can open it, or an old man who has lost his strength.

5. "The door of My Justice, on the contrary, is shut and locked. I open it only to those who compel Me to do so, but I never open it spontaneously.

6. "Once your soul or any soul has crossed the threshold of the door of My Mercy, you fall into the power of Love, which employs every means possible to hinder you from escaping, and to attract you to love your new Home.

7. "When you become the happy prisoner of Love, Love sets you at liberty, but only within the precincts of Love, because if you should leave this enclosure, you would meet death. Love does not prevent your departure, but will avert it.

8. "The more evil the state to which the soul is reduced by the sins of the past, by disorders and passions, that Love is even more pleased to have so much to accomplish in that soul.

9. "You souls who are the most miserable, the most weak, the most infirmed, are the best clients of Love, the most desired by the Divine Mercy.

10. "You souls thus become, as it were, the most favored of God. You will exalt and praise God for His Mercy. You will send up to God the reflections of living Light, His own Light, which you have received from Him during your mortal life; you will thank Him for the many acts of Kindness, by which He conducts you to Heaven. You souls will shine like precious gems, and will form the crown of the Divine Mercy."

*   *   *

Desire for Heaven

O Blessed Jerusalem, O most sweet Country which awaits me, O beautiful Paradise, Blessed Abode of my Sweet Jesus! I already seem to breathe the ineffable delights which my Jesus is preparing for me. Why have I not the wings of a dove to fly away and be at rest in my Beloved? Why can I not be immersed in that delicious sea of infinite Delights that You are, O God of my heart? Jesus, Jesus, Jesus, can You bear to see this little soul languish with the desire it has of being with You? Take me quickly, O my Jesus, in order that soon I may love You perfectly. If to obtain this grace sooner I must suffer much in a little time, must love You more ardently, be humbled more profoundly, and suffer more patiently, O Jesus, do all this in me!

*

"I call you: 'The heart of My Heart.' "

"You cannot conceive the pleasure I take in fulfilling My mission as Savior. When sins have been pardoned, they become for the soul fountains of graces because they are perpetual sources of humility. Everything contributes to the advancement of your soul; even your imperfections are in My Divine Hands like so many precious stones, because I change them into acts of humility, which I inspire your soul to make. If those who build houses could transform the debris and all that obstructs their work, into materials of construction, how fortunate they would consider themselves! O faithful soul, you transform your debris: your faults, even the gravest and most shameful sins, with the aid of My grace, into stones which are used to build the edifice of your perfection."

*

I had placed a statuette of the Infant Jesus near the sheet of paper on which I was writing; a slight movement I made caused the statuette to fall. I raised it immediately and gave a kiss to the Little Jesus saying to Him: "If You had not fallen, You would not have had that kiss."

"When you have committed an involuntary fault, you do not offend Me, but the act of humility and love you make deliberately after your fall, is the kiss you give Me, which I would not have received had you not committed that imperfection."

*

"The shortest, safest, and easiest way to arrive at perfection is love. Love tends directly to its end, which is God; it is safe, because it lies between two walls which prevents one from falling — trust

141

in God and distrust of oneself. It is the easiest way, because when one loves, everything is easy. I am with these souls and I make them take the short cut, which is humiliation.

"When you humble yourself without being troubled, when you recognize your faults, deplore them, repent and beg My pardon, resolving, with the aid of My grace, nevermore to commit them, I raise you up from the ground, take you in My arms, kiss you, caress you, and show you with joy to My Eternal Father and the Holy Spirit as My Benjamin."

My Jesus, You already foresee that I will relapse and fall again.

"Do you think that My Mercy is exhausted as easily as a provision of wine, of bread, or corn?

"Lose not even a moment of time in thinking of yourself, either of body or of soul. You have a Spouse who cares for you; think only of loving Me as perfectly as you are able.

"Do you think that I, the Lamb of God, can roar as a lion? I do not reproach sinners, however loaded with sins they may be. I am always ready to receive them, if they come to Me with a contrite and humble heart. It is the demon who taunts them after having done the evil. If you knew the Compassion My Heart feels for two classes of souls: for those poor sinners who are more deeply immersed in sin than a fish in water, and for those souls who are afflicted with distrust of My Goodness and with discouragement."

"My infinite Love puts into your hand a net in which you shall catch souls for Me. I fashion the net I give you out of your acts of fidelity."

*

"To say Jesus and to say Love is the same thing; to say Jesus and to say Mercy is the same thing; to say Jesus and to say Compassion is the same thing; to say Jesus and to say Tenderness is the same thing. I am the Oil to heal your wounds; I am the Balsam to cure your bruises; I am the Milk that nourishes you; I am the Fountain of Water that quenches your thirst."

*

"Would that souls could comprehend the value of patience! If a martyr going to the rack, could see the Holy Angels that were supporting it, with what respect would he or she not regard it!

"It is Love that supports and sustains those souls who suffer, for It gives them strength to go on working and suffering. One should not fly from the smallest suffering."

*

"When nothing stays in its nothingness, God looks upon it with complacency and makes it something great. When nothing remains in its nothingness, God sanctifies it. When nothing remains in its nothingness, God descends from Heaven to take possession of it and carries it to Paradise."

*

"I have made for you a law for all, and I desire that you have it always before you. These words are the law: Charity covers a multitude of sins; pure love not only covers them, it destroys them. Sins covered may be uncovered; sins destroyed are no more."

"I cannot make you a saint unless you give Me the key of your will, but if you give it to Me, I can make you, not only a saint, but a great saint.

"In a moment I can repair all the past of your soul, if you do not limit My Goodness by your distrust, if you do not circumscribe My Mercy by your narrowness, nor measure My Love by your own. If My Love were proportioned to your fidelity, I should Love you intermittently, since for a while you are faithful to Me and then become less faithful. I am Immutable.

"Just as the sun is constantly shining and does not in the least diminish its light nor the heat of its rays, whether a person is covered with mud or clothed in beautiful robes, so My Love for you remains constant."

*

"Why can I introduce so few souls into My Sacred Heart? Why do I find so few despoiled of all things? In My Heart is everything. I am Food and Drink; I am Repose and Strength."

*

"Generally speaking, no one comes to death but through disease, which little by little consumes life; so also to attain to the interior death, continual mortification is necessary. A soul that is abandoned to Love, is borne by Love to the interior death; a soul who labors with Love, who assists Love, arrives very quickly at this interior death. When a soul has reached this state, I reign in the heart. Since self-love no longer reigns there, My Love reigns, and My Love will have all."

"If you only knew the hunger I have to be loved by souls! I Love souls and I am not loved according to My desire. Souls in the world do not believe in My desires; even those who do, have a very uncertain belief.

"Little spouse of My Heart, I give you My intimate confidence. I wish to speak to all hearts, but they will not listen to Me; hence when I find a heart that receives My graces, I inundate it. I am an exiled King; if one person alone seeks to exile Me, it cannot be done, but many souls can truly do so. Those who commit mortal sin drive Me away, then I go to knock at the door of My spouses.

"There are souls who open to Me, true, but only after solicitation; others open to Me, but only after bargaining; while others, on the contrary, open wide the door and invite Me to enter. The first are those who forsake evil only through fear of punishment for sin; the second open to Me, but they wish that I should gratify them with spiritual pleasures and caresses; the third open the door and receive Me with My cross, My thorns, and My Love, desiring only to please Me.

"I am, as it were, oppressed with My graces, because they are turned back upon Me; souls do not want them. When I find a soul that gives Me liberty to bestow favors upon it, My Heart is relieved, so to say.

"When I tell you that I suffer and that I am oppressed, I do not mean it absolutely; I speak after a human fashion so that I may be understood. I can no longer suffer, though I suffer in My Mystical Body: the Holy Church, for since My Resurrection, I am Immortal, Impassible, and Glorious."

*

"Consider how a farmer fills his granary. Is it by sitting under a shady tree and watching the harvest, or rather is it not by wearisome labors under the heat of the sun? Little sacrifices have great value in My sight."

*

"A martyr whose head is cut off with one stroke suffers less than another who dies of many small wounds. You do understand Me? Is it not so?

"Continual fidelity to grace, continual prayer of so many souls who give up all, habitual renunciation of self, and ever with a smile, these sacrifices have no less value in My eyes than the martyrdom of blood. This is martyrdom of the heart that the creature does not see, but which Love sees and which Love will also crown. Would that you could know how much you souls please Me who immolate yourselves thus in silence!"

*

"There is too little devotion to the Holy Spirit. Souls have too little recourse to Him, yet He completes the great work of sanctification of souls. He forms in the soul My features. My image is seen in all souls, because all are created in the image and likeness of God.

"It pleases My Eternal Father to see My image increase ever more beautifully in the faithful soul, and it also pleases Me and the Holy Spirit who forms it."

146

"Do not think of Paradise without thinking of Calvary, and think not of Calvary without thinking of Paradise. If My elect are in Paradise, it is because I went up to Calvary. I conduct the souls of My chosen ones to Calvary before conducting them to Paradise, some with more suffering, some with less. If it were necessary that I should return to suffer for one soul alone, so great is My Love for My creatures that I would return to suffer, but it is no longer necessary since My Merits are infinite."

*

My Jesus, how could You permit this state of aridity to last so long a time?

"It was for your good. I wish to prepare you to receive new graces; I have taken away consolations, so as to give you an opportunity to practice perfect charity. One Ave Maria said without sensible fervor, but with a pure will in time of aridity, has much more value in My sight than an entire Rosary recited in the midst of consolations."

*

"Religious soul, be the apostle of My Love. Cry aloud so that all souls in the world may hear, that I hunger, I thirst, I die to be received by My creatures.

"I am in the Sacrament of My Love for My creatures, and they make so little account of it. At least you should make as many spiritual Communions as possible to supply for the many Sacramental Communions which are not made. One every quarter of an hour is not enough. Make them shorter, but more numerous."

147

"When you make the Sign of the Cross, do it always with the interior spirit. The cross should be the distinctive sign of all your actions; this sign honors the most Blessed Trinity."

*

"From all eternity I have fixed the design of perfection to which I call a soul, and afterward when in time I create it and it commences to have the use of reason, from that moment it should cooperate with My grace. If the soul does not cooperate, it stops the work of grace.

"Represent to yourself the Holy Spirit who is about to form a mosaic and has the pieces already prepared. The design is before Him; He asks for the pieces that suit His purpose; at one time He will ask for two pieces of the same color, another time not, but the one who is handing Him the pieces should give them according to His request.

"A soul is the masterpiece of the Holy Spirit, and the Holy Spirit labors over it; He calls to the soul for an act of obedience, then for an act of charity, then for two of humility in succession, and the soul should give at once without keeping Him waiting. The soul that does not cooperate, binds, as it were, the Hands of the Holy Spirit."

*

"My beloved, say to yourself: 'It is because I want to be a saint, I will tell such a fault. Why should I repress such words? It is because I want to be a saint. Why should I receive with a beautiful smile those things that are annoying? It is because I wish to be a saint'. Let these words: 'I wish to be a saint,' be your watchword. Become a saint only to please Me."

"If a seed could speak, it would beg to be cast into the earth and covered with earth that it might germinate; so a soul enlightened to know the value of the spirit of mortification, of contempt of self and loss in God, would desire only these things. Loss in God is, indeed, pleasing to the soul, but one must adopt the means to attain it. The soul that clings ever so little to self, will never attain perfectly to that sublime state."

*

"In one instant a soul can have a thought of love that will last for all eternity."

*

"The little prayer: 'I trust in You,' ravishes My Heart, because faith, love, and humility are comprised in this short prayer."

*

"The Furnace of Love is that Divine Furnace in which I purify, perfect, and form My Saints. Just as to bend iron it must be placed in the fire, and when heated is molded to any form the designer wishes, so in the fire of My Divine Love, must souls be molded to all forms of sanctity. There is an austere sanctity and souls honor Me by their austerity; there is a sanctity more sweet, more accessible, and other souls honor Me by their sweetness."

My Jesus, which sanctity pleases You the most?

"It always pleases Me most where there is most love. I Love the heart which beats only for Me more than a body exhausted by fasts, but in which there still resides a little selflove. I prefer less austerity and more charity, than more austerity and less charity."

149

"Am I not sufficient for you? Where can you find a heart that loves you more?"

*

"My Sacred Heart is an abyss of Mercy. Give Me your miseries and I will pay you; I will draw you from your troubles and it will give Me pleasure. I desire to be your Rag-collector, that is, one who buys rags, who even pays for those you offer Me. You must sell your miseries to Me by an act of profound humility, not spiteful, but fervent and affectionate. Give Me those things which you know not what to do with, and I will fashion of them something useful for souls. Allow My Love to act. Call Me what you please, either the Rag-collector of Love or the Rag-collector of Mercy. Both titles please Me.

"Love and Mercy are, as it were, the breath of My most Meek Heart. I draw into Myself the miseries of My poor weak creatures to consume them in the fire of My Divine Charity; then I breathe forth from My most Loving Heart, that Fire which devours the soul and is capable of inflaming many hearts."

*

"Fire gives warmth; a soul full of the Love of God also gives warmth and inflames other souls without knowing it. That soul is like a magnet, which attracts unknowingly."

*

"Those who are lost in God are well kept."

*

"Say: Whoever wishes to find me should look in the Sacred Heart of my Jesus. There I am lost and buried in the abyss of Mercy and Love."

*

150

A Decalogue of Confidence

1. I have a God of Love who is all mine.

2. My God of Love is also my Father.

3. My God of Love wishes that I be His forever.

4. My God of Love came down from Heaven to earth on purpose to seek me.

5. My God of Love asks me for my heart.

6. My God of Love wishes to be my Brother, my Friend, and my Consoler.

7. My God of Love carries His Tenderness so far as to wish to be my Physician, my Medicine, and more than all, my Spouse.

8. My God of Love wishes to be despoiled of His gifts. A tree, stripped of its fruit does not complain, but rather produces more fruit. The tree must wait another year, but my God of Love produces grace and virtue at once.

9. My God of Love seeks only imperfections to destroy, miseries to consume, weak wills to fortify, and good resolutions to strengthen.

10. My God of Love goes in search of sinners whom the world despises, and abandons. If after having converted them through His Charity and His Mercy, He meets with the correspondence He seeks, He makes them masterpieces of holiness.

"What should your soul do in a state of aridity?

1. "Humiliate yourself.

2. "Confide in the immense Goodness of Jesus.

3. "Watch over yourself with greater fidelity.

4. "Call your Savior by most sweet Names.

5. "Prepare for Jesus beautiful surprises on His arrival.

6. "When Jesus returns to comfort your soul, embrace Him closely, so closely that He can nevermore depart."

*　　　　*　　　　*

"What should your soul do in a state of Spiritual Consolation?

1. "Humiliate yourself.

2. "Be supremely grateful to God, and find all your delight in Jesus alone.

3. "Provide and store away a good stock of virtue for the time of aridity.

4. "Be always ready for the privation of sensible favors, and to persevere in the faithful service of God, even in the midst of aridity and disgust."

*　　　　*　　　　*

O Jesus, Lover of souls, You died to redeem them. Do not let them be lost at whatever cost!

*

"What did I do when I was in the womb of My Mother Mary? I had come to save all souls, and I did the Will of My Father even in My Mother's womb. There are many souls who would like to do great things for My glory, who would wish to go through the world converting souls, but who are nailed fast to a bed of illness, and are, besides, a burden to others. These souls would do more by a simple act of resignation to My Will than if they were to run over the whole world to save sinners. Such persons should not waste their energies in useless desires for action. They are anxious to do great things for Me, but meanwhile they fail in resignation to My Holy Will and their desires are without any merit. On the contrary, if they are perfectly resigned, their desires to do good to souls are in conformity with My Will, and they will reap the merit of those desires. Just as many branches are a burden to a tree, so desires contrary to My Will are a burden to souls."

*

"Every religious soul is My sanctuary because the Religious Profession is a Consecration, but this is not enough; Love must renew this consecration every day, every hour, every minute, and every second."

*

"You are Martha because you have received Jesus into your heart, but take care not to leave Him alone. Martha received Him but after a while left Him; true, it was to prepare food for Him, but nevertheless she left Him. Mary Magdalen on the contrary, enjoyed His presence. What end did it serve to prepare food for Him? His food is to do His Father's Will. Be attentive, even amid a multitude of things, not to forsake the vocation to which you are called. You forsake your vocation when you cease to listen to Jesus."

*

"There are souls who have so many vocal prayers to say, that resolved to say them all, they will not listen to Me until they have finished. I do not disapprove of vocal prayer, but it is better to listen to Me.

"Consider: I wish to raise up your Lazaruses, your sinful brethren of whom there are so many: conduct Me to their sepulchres. Where are their sepulchres? Behold, some are buried in the vice of gluttony; well, this is their sepulchre; by practicing mortification of the taste you will conduct Me to their sepulchres; others are immersed in other vices; they are dead; you, by living an angelic life will lead Me to their sepulchres. Be attentive: I gave the command and made the dead arise, yet he was bound, and I ordered those around to loose his bonds. You should pursue the practice of mortification to complete the work of the resurrection of sinners and obtain for them deliverance from their evil habits."

*

"If you would please Me, trust in Me; if you would please Me more, trust Me still more; if you would please Me immensely, trust in Me immensely. Your trust will never equal the desire of My Heart. An act of confidence pleases Me so much because it honors my dearest attributes, which are Goodness and Mercy."

*

"Always more, always better, always with love, always with Holy Mary."

A Decalogue of Love

1. "Give yourself to Love.   I am Love. I give Myself to you if you give yourself to Me without reserve, without falling away, and without absorption in other things.

2. "Abandon yourself to Love.   I take loving care of your soul abandoned to Me entirely.

3. "Follow Love.   I guide, hold by the hand, and if necessary carry your soul, if it is wholly surrendered to Me.

4. "Never go aside from Love.   I enclose within Myself your soul that is once surrendered to Me, and permit it not to leave except by your free will; nothing else can withdraw you from My power.

5. "Believe in Love.   I rejoice when you believe in Me, in all My operations, even the most painful.

6. "Support Love.   I love to be supported, favored, and assisted; I make wonderful progress in your soul that aids Me.

7. Give Love to others!   I love to be given to others. I increase in your soul in the same measure with which you give Me to other souls.

8. "Let yourself be inflamed by Love.   I burn everything that is ready to burn; the drier it is, the more quickly and easily it will burn.

9. "Let yourself be used by Love.   I rejoice in disposing not only of your soul, but of all your activities in favor of whomever I please.

10. "Let yourself be consumed by Love.   I consume completely whatever is given to Me, if you offer no resistance."

* * * * *

"I am raising an army and I call souls to combat for Love. The most generous are those who serve in the front line."

*

"It is not the faults of frailty that arrest the work of Love in a soul, it is the self-love and the seeking of self-interest."

*

My Jesus, You can do all things. Will You not take away my troubles?

"No! In taking away your troubles, I would deprive you of many graces. When I permit temptation, it is not through cruelty, but to give your soul an opportunity of merit. My Love has a thousand inventions for enriching souls."

*

"I have chosen you because you are wretched and miserable, in order that you may attribute nothing to yourself and know that all good comes from God."

*

"Learn for your own benefit and teach this to others: to obtain solid virtue, you will find it in the Heart of Jesus. Whoever wishes to be saved, must take refuge in My Blessed Ark, from where one can look out upon the tempest without being shaken by its fury."

†

"Tell Me that you languish for love of Me."

My Jesus, how can I, a poor sinner, presume to say that I languish for love of You?

"Whenever you willingly offer yourself to suffer anything in order to please Me, you truly glorify Me, and, glorifying Me, you tell Me that you are languishing for love of Me; provided that you continue to be patient, and that you never turn your eyes away from Me."

*

My Lord Jesus, why don't You deliver me from the ill-regulated habits and defects which I have implored You so many times?

"It is said of Me, when I was in My Childhood, that I advanced in Wisdom, in age, and in Grace with God and man. You will also advance from hour to hour, changing your faults into virtues. I will deliver you from all the infirmities of nature, so that after this life, you may possess the Blessedness which I have prepared for mankind, whom I have exalted above the Angels."

*

"Behold, I promise to preserve inviolate the gifts which I have bestowed on you; if, however, I suspend their effects for a time, by way of dispensation, I oblige Myself, by the Omnipotence, Wisdom, and Love of the Trinity, in which I live and reign True God through all ages, to recompense you afterwards threefold."

*

O Bountiful Lord, how can You give graces so full of consolation to one who is so unworthy?

"My Love compels Me."

*

My Jesus, permit me to leave this valley of tears.

"Consider how agreeable your concert of praise is, not only to My ears, but even to My most Loving Heart. Do not urgently desire to be separated from your body in which I pour forth so freely the gifts of My grace, for the more unworthy you are to whom I condescend, the more I merit to be glorified for it by all creatures."

*

"As you desire in all your actions the glory of God, and not your own, the fervor of your zeal increases a hundredfold the gifts which you offer your Spouse, not only by the pious works which you actually accomplish, but even by those which you desire to do yourself or to see done by others, although it is not in your power to perform them. I will supply before My Heavenly Father, your needs and your defects, and those of others for whom you are solicitous; I will regard all you desire to perform as if you had accomplished it. Know that the Angels and Saints rejoice in your advancement; they return thanks and praise to God for love of you."

*

"My Love will increase in you, as a fire which is enclosed burns with great force. The delight which I will find in you, and the love which you will have for Me, will be like a pentup ocean, which seems to increase by the impediments placed to its progress, until at last it breaks forth impetuously."

Sister Gertrude was confined to bed, and was unable to assist at Holy Mass at which she hoped to prepare herself to receive Holy Communion.

O Jesus, how shall I prepare myself to receive the Communion of Your adorable Body and Blood, since my intention at Holy Mass always seemed to be my best preparation?

"I will console you! I will make you hear the songs of joy with which Heaven resounds when I espouse a soul in Holy Communion.

"My Blood is your Redemption; meditate on those thirty-three years during which I labored for you in exile, and sought only to unite Myself with you. Let this serve for the first part of the Mass, in preparation for Holy Communion.

"I have showered you with the riches of My Spirit. Even as I endured so much bodily labor during the thirty-three years in which I sought you, so also My Soul feels an ineffable joy at the union and spiritual marriage which we have contracted. Let this be your consolation. Let this serve for the second part of the Mass, in preparation for Holy Communion.

"You are replenished with My Divinity, which has the power to make you taste the purest delights and the most ravishing sweetness inwardly, while exteriorly you are suffering the severest pain. This will serve for the third part of the Mass, in preparation for Holy Communion.

"You are sanctified by My Love; know that you

are nothing of yourself, and that all which renders you agreeable to Me comes from Me. Occupy yourself with these thoughts. Let this serve for the fourth part of the Mass, in preparation for Holy Communion.

"You have been united to Me in the sublimest manner; I want you to know that, as 'all Power has been given to Me in Heaven and on earth,' I cannot be hindered from exalting you, as a king exalts his queen to his throne, and consequently renders her an object of his love. Rejoice, then, in reflecting on these things, and do not complain when you are deprived of assisting at Holy Mass, in preparation for Holy Communion."

*　　*　　*

My soul, why delay any longer receiving Holy Communion? Even if I had a thousand years, I could not prepare as I should, having nothing which could serve to promote the right dispositions in me. I will meet my Jesus with confidence and humility. When Jesus beholds me from afar, He will fill me with all the grace which His Love desires that I should have to appear before Him."

*

"I grant you by My authority, a full remission of all your sins and negligences. Do you think that I possess less power than I have bestowed on My creatures? I have given to the material sun such virtue, that if a discolored garment is exposed to its rays, it will not only recover its former whiteness, but even become brighter than before. How much more can I, who am the Creator of the sun, by directing My looks upon sinners, remove all their stains, purifying them by the fire of My Love, from every spot?"

"What do you desire for N . . . , for whom you have prayed?"

Lord, I only ask that Your most peaceful Will may be perfectly accomplished in them.

"What do you desire that I should do for you?"

My Jesus, I have no other joy than to desire that Your Will may always be accomplished in me, and in all creatures; I am ready, for this end, to offer every member of my body to be exposed, one after the other to the acutest suffering.

"Since you have desired with such ardor to have the designs of My Will executed, I will reward you with this recompense: you shall appear as agreeable in My sight as if you had never violated My Will, even in the most trifling manner."

*

"Before work say: O Lord Jesus, in union with Your most perfect actions, I commend to You my work, to be directed according to Your Holy Will, for the salvation of all mankind."

"Before prayer say: O Lord Jesus, in union with the intention and Love You gave to God the Father, I offer You my prayers."

*

"When I behold any soul in agony, who has thought of Me with pleasure, or who has performed any works deserving of reward, I appear to that soul at the moment of death, with a countenance so full of Love and Mercy, that the soul repents from its inmost depths for having offended Me, and that soul is saved by this repentance."

161

O my Savior, why have I not a fire sufficiently strong to melt my heart, so that I might pour it forth entirely into You?

"Your desire is the fire which you will."

*

"Whenever you desire with all your heart to be delivered from the prison of the body, yet, at the same time, are perfectly willing to remain therein so long as it shall please Me, I unite the Merits of My Life to yours, which renders you perfect in the sight of the Eternal Father."

*

Lord Jesus, may I pray to You now?

"You may, My beloved one! I will always comply with your will in all things, as a servant would obey the commands of his master."

*

O God, full of Charity, I am assured that Your words are always true, but since You manifest such condescension toward me, although I am so unworthy of it, why is it that my prayers so often remain without effect?

"I always hear your prayers, but in My inscrutable Wisdom, I answer your prayers in a manner more useful for you, though human frailty prevents you from knowing this."

*

"I sometimes reveal to you My secrets in contemplation, and at other times I exclude you from them to preserve your humility. By receiving this grace you will know who you are in Me, and by being deprived of it, you will know who you are of yourself."

162

"I inclined your will to desire death, and consequently, you wanted to receive Extreme Unction. I have preserved in My Sacred Heart, for your eternal salvation, all that you have done in thought or act to prepare yourself for this Sacrament. If you were deprived of this Sacrament by sudden death, or if you receive It after having lost consciousness, which often happens to My elect, you would not suffer any loss thereby, because all the preparation for death which you have made for so many years is preserved in My Divinity, where, by My cooperation, it always remains for your eternal salvation.

"When anything is offered to Me for the faithful departed, I immediately use it for them according to My inclination to show Mercy and Pardon, either for the remission of their sins, for their consolation, or for the increase of their eternal happiness, according to the condition of those for whom the offering is made. When a similar offering is made for the living, I keep it for their benefit, because they can still increase their merit by their good works, by their good desires, and by their good will. They should endeavor to acquire by their labor, what they desire to obtain through the intercession of others."

*

"When you confide in the prayers of another, confident that through their intercession you will receive grace from God, I pour forth My benedictions on you, according to the measure of your desires and your faith, even when the person to whom you have recommended yourself, neglects to pray for you."

You, O God, are the Life of my soul! May all the desires of my heart be united to You by Your burning Love! You are the Beauty of all colors, the Sweetness of all taste, the Fragrance of all odors, the Harmony of all sounds, the Charm of all embraces! In You is all delight; from You flows forth a torrent of Love; to You all are drawn by Your powerful attractions, and by You all experience the influences of Love! You are the overflowing Abyss of the Divinity, a King greater than all kings, Supreme Emperor, Sovereign Prince, Peaceful Ruler, and Faithful Protector!

You are a Worker full of skill, a Master full of Clemency, a Counselor full of Wisdom, a Defender full of Kindness, a Friend most Faithful! You are the sweet Savor of all delights! You are the Springflower of unchanging beauty! O Loving Brother, Beautiful Youth, Joyful Companion, Liberal Host, Careful Administrator! I prefer You to every creature; for You I renounce all pleasure; for You I seek all adversity, and in all this I desire only Your honor and glory. My heart and lips testify that You are the Source and Stimulator of all Good. I unite, by the Merits of Your Love, the fervor of my devotions to the virtue of Your prayers, so that by the union of my will, my desires, and my love to Yours, I may be raised to the highest perfection.

*

O Sweet Jesus, I commend to Your Heart all that I have done in the hour that is past, to be purified, and offered to God the Father for His eternal praise. Whatever I shall do this next hour, I resolve to do for Your glory, for the salvation of all mankind, in union with Your Holy Passion.

O Holy Virgin Mary, I humbly and lovingly offer You, Your Son, whom You conceived in Your spotless womb, brought forth, nourished and pressed to Your Heart with tender embraces; in His Countenance You find joy and new delights, and He has this day given Himself to me in the ineffable condescension of His Divine Love: the Eucharist. I offer Him to You that You may fold Him in Your arms, kiss Him, Love and worship Him for me and with me, offer Him in deepest adoration to the Holy Trinity for my sins and the sins of all souls, so that the prerogative of Your great dignity may obtain for me what I dare not presume to hope for by myself.

*

All you Saints of God, especially my beloved patrons, behold Jesus your Lord and Spouse, whom you loved while you lived in the flesh, with all your heart and strength; in and through Him whom I have now received in the Holy Sacrament, I salute all of you and offer Him to you for an increase of your joy, glory, and blessedness, with all the Love and the faithfulness which He showed you in time, and now shows you in eternity. I beseech you Saints to adore Him for me, and to offer Him to the Holy Trinity with all your devotion on my behalf, on behalf of the souls of the whole Church, and in thanksgiving for all the benefits He has ever bestowed upon me. Whatever I am unable to obtain of myself, do You, my companions, obtain for me through your merits and intercessions.

*

"When you wish to honor any particular Saint and give Me thanks for all the graces I have bestowed on that Saint, I increase grace in your soul through the merits of that Saint. When you commit the end of your life to any of the Saints by special prayers, those prayers are borne up before the Judge, and I appoint those Saints to be your advocates and to provide whatever you need at that hour.

"If you say an 'Our Father' to all the Saints, with the intention, were it possible, of saying one for each of the Saints, your intention is accepted by them as though you had really done so.

"It is likewise most pleasing to the Saints to greet them in and through the Sacred Heart of Jesus, especially if you offer them My Divine Heart; because through It and from It they receive the greatest delights."

*

Lord, I offer You all the petitions of those persons who have been recommended to my prayers.

"You have enkindled as many flames in My Heart, as there are persons for whom you pray."

My Jesus, teach me how to enkindle this Fire of Your Divine Heart in every soul in the Church.

"My Fire of Love can be inkindled in souls: 1. Praise Me for all souls whom I have created in My image and likeness. 2. Thank Me for all the good which I have done for them, or which I may yet do for them. 3. Grieve for all the obstacles which souls put to My grace. 4. Pray for all souls, that each may be perfected in the state in which My Providence has placed it, for the good of the soul and for My honor and glory."

"If anyone desires health, wisdom, conveniences, rest, or any other advantages, My Goodness often makes Me believe it is I whom they seek in these things, that I may give them a greater reward; unless they deliberately turn their intention away from Me, such as, by desiring wisdom that they may satisfy their pride, or health that they may commit some sin. It is for this reason that I am accustomed to afflict those who are dearest to Me with corporal infirmities, with mental depression, and other trials, so that when they desire the goods which are opposed to these evils, the ardent Love of My Heart may reward them with greater profusion."

*

"By your moderation in speech, by your guard over your senses, by all your desires, by all your prayers, and by all the good dispositions with which you have prepared to receive My Adorable Body and Blood, these are to Me as the most delicious food and refreshment."

*

"Behold how, for your love, I have been fastened to this cross, naked, despised, torn, and wounded in My Body, and in all My members; still My Heart has such tender Charity for you, that were it necessary for your salvation, and were there no other means of saving you, I would even at this moment suffer for you alone, all that I have suffered for all souls in the whole world."

*

"My beloved, I am pleased with those souls who honor the image of My crucifixion very devoutly, when it is offered purely for My Love, when the cross is not desired for itself, but that it may serve to renew the memory of the Love and

167

fidelity with which I endured the bitterness of My Passion, and when there is an ardent desire to imitate the example of My Passion."

*

"My beloved, since I am the Sovereign Priest and true Pontiff to whom you can have recourse, I can renew in your soul, with greater efficacy, the grace of the seven Sacraments, by a single operation, than either priest or bishop could by conferring each separately. 1. I Baptize you in My Precious Blood. 2. I Confirm you in My victorious Strength. 3. I absolve you from all your sins by My Tenderness. 4. I feed you with Myself and I feed Myself on you. 5. I consecrate you in the perfection of My Holy Life. 6. I Espouse you in My faithful Love. 7. I purify you inwardly by so powerful an Anointing of the sweetness of My Spirit, so that all your senses and actions will breathe the most fervent piety, which pouring down on you like Holy Oil, will sanctify you more and more unto Life Eternal."

* * *

Holy Mary speaks to me through Sister Gertrude

"If you or any soul greet Me with devotion and call Me the 'Pure Lily of the Trinity', and the 'Resplendent Rose of Paradise', I will show forth in your person how great is My power with the Omnipotent Father, with what means are given to Me to effect the salvation of souls through the Wisdom of My Son, and with what overflowing bounty the sweetness of the Holy Spirit fills My Heart! At the hour of your departure I will appear to you with radiant beauty, and I will pour into your soul heavenly sweetness and consolation."

*

†

*   *   *   *   *   *   *

"Do you love Me? Then give yourself to Me. I am
your God, without whom you cannot draw a
breath or even think of Me. You are Mine. I have
given you life and you are completely dependent
upon Me. My little one, I Love you."

*

"I am a Furnace of Love! The love in your heart
for Me is only a spark of the Great Furnace of
Love which is My Heart. That tiny spark has
been enkindled from My burning Love, and
your spark turns towards the Fire out of which
your spark was born. Cast your spark back
into the Furnace of My Heart, that it may be
united with the Love which burns there for you."

*

"You must be tried and cleansed by fire. Do not
be frightened. The Fire of which I speak is the
Fire of My Love. It is a real fire, for it warms,
it enlightens, it purifies, and it consumes, but
it is invisible. Plunge yourself willingly into the
flames of My Sacred Heart."

*

"How great is My Love for you! It is everything
to you — everything Good. My Love is your
Strength! My Love is your Courage; My Love is
your Rest; My Love is your Wisdom; My Love is
your Comfort; My Love is your Happiness; My
Love is your Life; My Love is your Salvation.
Love Me in return, it is so little that I ask of you."

*

"I Love you and I will assist you in loving Me.

"I have waited for you to give yourself entirely to Me. Now you have given Me not only the deed to your house, but the key as well. The house is Mine now, and I can enter at will.

"Since the house is Mine, I will defend it, of that you can be assured. My banner flies from its turret, My forces surround its walls, and I will do battle along with you. The enemy will lay seige to the house, but you shall never be vanquished; I promise you that. You must fight with Me in the battle. Don't expect Me and My forces to fight for you without any effort on your part. Fight at My side fearlessly.

"At times you will be wounded. Then come to Me; I will bind up your wounds and heal them for you. Do not at such times hide yourself and try to nurse your own wounds. You need not be ashamed of wounds received in battle; they are to be expected, neither should you refuse to fight because of the wounds. I am your Physician and I will dress your wounds so that you may once more return to the battle.

"I shall conquer the enemy, for Mine is the deed, Mine is the key, Mine is the house, and Mine is the victory; you do not need to be afraid."

*

"I Love you. My Heart rejoices by your act of oblation. I want you to know that you are not alone, never alone. I am always with you and I shall always be your protector."

*

"You are not here on earth to be consoled, but rather to console Me."

170

"My foolish little one, do you think that I do not know your weakness? It is precisely because you are so little that I have given you a crown of thorns instead of the cross, for you falter even under the weight of the thorns; the cross you could not bear at present."

*

Dear Jesus, how can people be so disinterested in You in the most Blessed Sacrament, and how can priests leave You?

"How can you? I will answer you. It is because of weakness in most cases. There is seldom any malice in their actions. That is why I Love them so much."

Dear Lord, if that is so, then why do You not show them their errors?

"I will not interfere with their free will. They are free to serve Me or not."

My sweetest Lord Jesus, I do not understand, if they deliberately choose not to serve You, isn't that malice?

"They are weak, and they do not wish to be delivered from their weakness.

Dear Jesus, I still do not understand. If they do not want to overcome their weakness . . . ?

"The devil is always searching for the weak points in a person's character. It is at these points that he attacks. He blinds his victims so that they find it much easier to take the road of non-resistance to him. You should know this from your own experience."

Dear Lord, how can those souls be aided? Surely You do not want them to be eternally lost!

"I ask you souls who love Me to pray for them, to offer My Precious Blood to the Eternal Father on their behalf."

Jesus, You do not need the aid of Your creatures in this matter. Why do You ask for their aid?

"I am your God, and therefore I can do as I Will. It is not My desire to reveal My secrets to you at this time. Let it suffice, that I do permit My creatures to share in the redemption of souls."

*

After Holy Mass, I had a desire to share in the other Masses I could not attend because of duties elsewhere.

"Dear child, you believe that I dwell in your heart, do you not? Well then, I can never be divided, and so whenever the priest offers Me to My Father in the Holy Sacrifice of the Mass, I am being offered in your heart also."

*

Lord Jesus, I am worried because I am at times so drowsy when I visit You in the Eucharist.

"Do you think a lover would be insulted if his spouse were to rest her head upon his breast and because of tiredness confidently go to sleep in his arms? Is a mother saddened because her baby goes to sleep in her arms?"

172

"You cannot press Me to your heart without yourself being pierced by the thorns, the nails, and the lance, without yourself being defiled with the filth that covers Me, without yourself being subject to the jeers and the scorn that are My lot. Remember that, and do not be surprised when it happens to you."

Dearest Lord Jesus, how can I leave the Heaven of Your presence and go out into the world? I desire to stay here at Your Feet.

"Child, I left Heaven to come to earth for Love of you. Can you not do the same for love of Me?"

*

"You do not know what degree of holiness My Saints had when they received special favors from Me. When the lives of Saints are written, their weak points are frequently forgotten or omitted. Only the highlights of their lives are presented to you. You cannot tell from that how many times the Saints fell, how great a struggle they endured, how often temptation and daily vexations found them weak and yielding. You also do not know how many there are who are not Saints and to whom I manifest Myself.

"Did Judas who betrayed Me not hear My voice? Did hearing My voice keep Peter from denying Me? Did not John, My beloved Apostle, run away at first when I was arrested? These men lived with Me, ate at My table, and listened to My voice.

"You can render Me great homage by attending to your duties, no matter what they may be. Offer them in loving reparation to My Sacred Heart."

173

I still do not understand, dear Jesus. What You say is beautiful and sounds so very easy, but how can it be done? I feel so utterly helpless.

"Love knows no barriers; no key can lock It away. Love removes all obstacles and overcomes with little difficulty all that attempt to hinder It. When Love is enclosed within the heart of one of My children, It strains to escape, melting, as it were, the lock of the heart-tabernacle, in order to diffuse Itself among others. The more It reaches out to others, so much more does It fill the heart that imprisons It."

Dearest Lord Jesus, I want to love You more. I am grateful to You for Your condescension in drawing me this way to Yourself, but I am afraid of thinking that I am someone special. Please protect me from myself.

"When a demonstration of the power of the magnet is given, tiny splinters of worthless iron are placed beneath the magnet to show how the magnet draws them to itself. Those bits of iron have no value except insofar as they prove the power of the magnet. Your value lies only in the fact that you glorify Me by proving My Power when I draw you to Myself. Let Me draw you then, and do not resist Me."

*

"My child, who do you think you are? I tell you that you are nothing and less than nothing. Were you capable of understanding the abyss of difference between Me, your God, and you, My sinful creature, you would not be able to lower yourself enough."

174

"If you draw near to Me, you will suffer. To suffer with Me and in Me is a far greater joy than any pleasure of earth without Me. Any earthly pleasure enjoyed without Me is a far greater suffering than the greatest pain shared with Me."

*

"Your little sufferings are very precious to Me; I want you to offer them to Me. They shall one day form part of the crown that I am preparing for you. In Heaven there are many different kinds of crowns. Some of My Saints have a single large precious gem in theirs, or a few large gems, but there are many other Saints who have countless small gems, very brilliant, but very tiny. Do you not understand that the cumulative value of these many small gems are equal to, and even surpasses at times, the value of the large ones?

"If a workman were to dig out of a mine, a large and valuable diamond, and rush to present it as a gift to his sovereign without removing from it the dirt and dust, and without polishing the stone, do you think his sovereign would be insulted by the gift? Would he not rather treasure it at its true value and have it cleaned and polished himself? I do the same with your offerings, to which the dust of your sins still clings."

*

"I have given you My consolation, and your desire to embrace Me in a surge of love that you experience is commendable and pleasing to Me. Remember that I am a crucified King. My Head is surrounded by thorns, My Hands and Feet pierced with nails, My Heart pierced with a lance, My Body a festering sore, covered with Blood, and My Face is defiled with filth, spittle, dirt, and sweat.

"My child, in order to atone for the infidelity of priests, it is necessary that you and other souls love Me very much. You must make Me the center of your life, devoting your body and soul, your heart and will completely to Me in love. You must take the place in the world of My defective priests."

Dear Jesus, how can this be done?

"Just as it is the duty of My priests to bring Me down to earth and place Me in the tabernacle for the good of souls, so you must become, a portable tabernacle, housing Me and carrying Me out into the world. You, who receive Me daily in Holy Communion, are My tabernacle in whom I reside in the world. The priest not only encloses Me in the tabernacle, he also opens the door and takes Me out to give Me to the people. You must not only carry Me about in the tabernacle of your heart, but you must also give Me to those persons with whom you come in contact. Thus will you take the place of those disloyal priests by bringing Me to souls who might never come to Me in a Church."

Lord Jesus, how can we give You to others? How can we open the door of the tabernacle?

"All virtues are keys to the tabernacle of your heart. The most perfect key, the one that best fits the lock and opens the door most quickly, is love.

"Give Me all those souls you love, and you will thus give Me to those who are starving for My Love."

"I will teach you how to make every action of yours a special act of love dedicated to Me. In the past you have made only a general intention. Now you must make the intention specific before every act."

I will frequently forget to make such an intention.

"No, you will not forget. A long formula is not needed for this. Before every act, before entering or leaving a room, etc, simply say: 'Jesus,' or 'Jesu,' and I will accept it as a dedication."

*

"To suffer for My sake, you need not bear great physical, mental, or spiritual crosses. Little annoyances, disappointments, and discomforts can be offered to Me in the same manner as your duties. Simply say: 'Jesus' whenever you make an error, or are cold. I will accept the suffering as borne for My sake."

*

"Do not hesitate to rest. This too, can be an act of love for Me. It will strengthen you for the work you must do."

*

"One who dies a martyr's death must lead a martyr's life. A martyr is one who is a witness to Me. If you lead a martyr's life, you must be a witness to Me before the whole world. In every detail of your life, you must proclaim Me to those with whom you come into contact. All who come to you, must come to Me through you. Those who see you must be able to say: 'There is Christ.' You must be a witness to the fact that I am in the world with My creatures, and that to love Me, and belong to Me, is not

177

unhappiness, but supreme joy. It is therefore necessary that you be pleasant, that you laugh and smile and sing, that your whole appearance speaks of joy. Avoid all things which could make loving Me seem unattractive. Be a witness to Me with your life.

"If you, O soul, only knew how much I Love you! You would be consumed if you would look into My Sacred Heart and see the flames of Love; if you could see how you are surrounded and submerged in those flames. I said once that I had come to cast fire upon the earth and that I want it to be kindled. O let your heart be kindled by My flames of Love. How very little you love Me in return! You are far from perfection. You are filled with pride and uncharitableness, yet My Love for you causes Me to endure untold pain and humiliation. O give Me some love in return."

*

"Only the eyes of love can pierce the veil that hides Me in the Blessed Sacrament. Even faith is not sufficient to pierce the mystery of the Holy Eucharist. Look with the eyes of love, for the eyes of love will gaze where the eyes of faith would not look.

"The Holy Eucharist, which is the 'Bread of Life,' may well be called the 'Breath of Life' for the soul, for not only does It nourish the spiritual life as food nourishes the body, but It is the very air in which the soul must breathe to survive. Without It the soul cannot survive. The reception of the Holy Eucharist is indeed a necessity to the soul."

*

"You are nothing but dust. I am your God and I have created you to give Me honor and glory. Have you never seen a ray of brilliant sunlight streaming through a haze of dust, and noticed that the minute particles, reflecting the light of the sun, sparkle like tiny gems? Similarly, when a soul is bathed in the brilliant light of My grace, it gives out a brilliance that is not its own. So it is with you! Why should you be proud? You are still dust. The only cause for any goodness you have, is the fact that you reflect the glory of Him who sheds the sunlight of His Love upon you."

*

Jesus asked me to give Him my heart and I replied: Take it, dearest Jesus.

"No, I do not want to take it, I wish you to give it to Me as a gift freely given."

Lord, my heart is so cold!

"You can still comfort Me, for your heart is not as cold as you may think. It is cold only by contrast to My Heart. The closer you approach the great, flaming Furnace of My Sacred Heart, the colder the tiny spark of your heart's love appears to be."

*

"Do you love Me?"

My Jesus, You know that I love You.

"Do you love Me enough to be crucified with Me?"

Lord Jesus, I am afraid to answer that, lest I be like Peter who boasted that he would die with You, and then out of fear, denied You three times.

"I did not ask Peter if he would be willing to be crucified. He spoke on his own initiative, but I am asking you. Answer Me! Do you love Me enough to submit to crucifixion with Me?"

Yes, my Lord Jesus! With Your help, I gladly submit to crucifixion with You.

"I wish to embrace you with the flames of My Love. Fire consumes that which it embraces, and if you are plunged into this Furnace of Love, you too, will be consumed. Will you submit to this embrace?"

My dearest Jesus, I desire to be plunged into, and consumed in the Furnace of Your Sacred Heart as a victim of Your Merciful Love.

"If you souls refuse to cast yourselves into the flames, your salvation is not thereby impaired, but you deprive Me of honor which should be Mine, and you deprive yourselves of many graces you would otherwise receive. Your imperfections are removed only by great labor and effort, and your inclination to sin remains strong.

"You souls who do plunge yourselves into My Sacred Heart are not thereby assured of salvation without any personal effort. You must cooperate with My grace which is given in greater abundance; this grace will aid you to fight temptation."

*

"The pain of loving Me is terrible, but the pain of not loving Me is far worse."

"You are the least worthy, the least capable, the least courageous, and the least cooperative soul that I could have chosen for this work. You are as nothing in My sight. Why, then, do you think that I have bestowed this grace upon you? It is simply because in using you to confound satan, I am more honored than if I used someone suited to the task. By My working with you, and in you, satan is more humiliated than he would be were I using a proper instrument. For this reason he despises and detests you.

"What honor have you given Me? You have promised Me reparation; you have given me only lip service. You have been selfish and lax in your service, and your lack of courage has led you to relax your efforts on behalf of My priests. You have loved Me but little; you have turned your back on My graces many times; you have refused Me the honor which is Mine.

"It is because of your pride and selfishness, that many of My priests have fallen into error. Reparation for the sins of priests is the most difficult task of all, for when a priest is unfaithful, he wounds Me more deeply than Religious or anyone else, so the task of repairing this evil is far greater.

"How much you have wounded Me by your refusal to accept the opportunities I have given you to make sacrifices, and perform penances on behalf of My priests! Yes, I am giving you the opportunity to continue this tremendous task."

*

"In spite of your unworthiness I Love you."

"I desire to be loved by you, not with the love of friendship, but with the love of a lover for the Beloved."

*

I had offended Jesus, so I wept and begged His pardon.

"You were forgiven even before you asked for forgiveness."

*

"Suffering is not to be sought for its own sake, but only as a means of ascending to Me upon the cross.

"Pray and sacrifice yourself for souls. I Love them and I want them to be saved, but so many pay no heed to Me. The time is so short; there is so much evil in the world; so few love and serve Me."

Yes, my dearest Lord Jesus, but there are many priests, Religious, and lay people who love You!

"That is true, but in proportion to the whole, they are few indeed. Had it not been for them I would have destroyed the earth long ago. Until now, these fervent souls have caused My Mercy to overcome My Justice."

*

"I give you My Heart. My Heart is surrounded by thorns, pierced with a lance, broken by man's ingratitude. My Heart is on fire with Love. My Heart is filled with Humility."

*

My dearest Jesus, I love You!

*

"My dear child, it is My desire that you be set on fire by My Love, which is indeed the Holy Spirit, and that you in turn, spread that fire to others. I desire you to become a living torch of love. A torch does not burn of itself, although it may seem to be all aglow with flame; it is rather that which is placed upon it as fuel which burns. This great Fire of Love which I desire to kindle in you is a free gift from Me. Will you offer yourself to Me to be set on fire in this manner?"

My Jesus, I desire to be set on fire with Your Love.

"This Fire of Love is, as I have said, a free gift. It cannot be earned. I give it to whomever I will. It is not a reward for virtue. It is a sign of My merciful Love.

"I came to cast this Fire of Love upon the earth. It is a searing, burning pain to the soul which is enkindled by it, but just as continual cold will numb the pain of coldness, so will this Fire numb the suffering soul, only to flare up again with redoubled pain.

"The initial pain of the Fire of Love will consist in your relishing nothing and no one but Me. All earthly things will be like ashes to you. You will find neither joy nor peace except in Me.

"If you only knew how much I Love you! Do you love Me?"

Jesus, You know that I love You.

"Tell Me that you love Me."

I love You, Jesus.

"Say to Me: 'My Jesus, I love You.'

"It pleases Me that you love Me, even though beside My Love for you, your love for Me is but a thimbleful. Still, you make My Heart rejoice by it. You give Me great joy by coming to visit Me out of love.

"Bow your head, for I am going to bless you in a very special manner.

"I give you My blessing, by placing upon you My wounded Hands. I give you My Peace in the name of the Father, who caused these Hands to be wounded, in the name of the Son, I Myself, who bear these Wounds, and in the name of the Holy Spirit, who entering your heart, shall give efficacy to these Wounds.

"With the thumb of My right Hand I trace upon your forehead the cross, the symbol of My Love. Invisible though it is to you, the cross shall be an indelible sign that I have pledged to enkindle the flame of My Love in your heart.

"Be at peace, My dear one. Be at peace. Upon the cross which I have traced on your brow, I place My kiss, the kiss of peace, the chaste kiss of your God and your Beloved Spouse. I Love you."

My Jesus, I love You. Help me to recall often what You have taught me. Thank You for the grace You have given me. Help me to be more grateful. Help me to be a flame of Your Pure Love.

The Eucharist

"Behold Me here imprisoned in the Eucharist for Love of you, and let Me tell you how this imprisonment is a daily renewal of My Passion. All day I am left here alone, except for a few visitors. The only company I have consists of those who clean this Church. I await, then, your visit, but when you come, you sometimes scarcely speak to Me, thinking only of yourself, and excusing yourself from the small penance I ask of you because of a slight indisposition. You have sorely disappointed Me, for I expected great love from you, whom I Love so much. Will you not comfort Me? I am your Prisoner of Love!

"At the beginning of My Passion I saw in the garden of Gethsemane all the sins of mankind, past, present, and future, and I seemed to share in those sins. The revulsion was so great that I sweat drops of Blood. Here in the Eucharist, this agony continues, for I see Myself in the midst of sin and the consequences of sin. From My prison here in the tabernacle, I behold My children inflicting injustices upon their fellowmen; I see wars, killings, impurities, and thefts. My suffering is intense, and My agony is renewed.

"In Gethsemane I looked for comfort from My friends, but they slept. They did not at first flee, they remained nearby and slept. Here in the Eucharist, I endure the same loneliness. Many souls not caring about Me slumber in their indifference, although I desire to enter their hearts. It is painful to be ignored by those who should know and love Me.

"In My Passion, I was dragged from one court of 'justice' to another. There I was falsely accused of crimes of which I was innocent, and My reputation was dragged to the depths. In the Eucharist I am falsely described by those who hate Me, in order to destroy, if possible, in the hearts of those who love Me, their faith in the Holy Eucharist.

"At Pilate's house I was scourged. What pain I experienced as those scourges ripped and seared My Flesh! It was a punishment for criminals and outcasts which was administered to Me. Here as the Prisoner of Love, I am scourged by the tongues of those who speak uncharitably of their neighbor. When I am placed in Holy Communion upon such a tongue stained with the blood of a ruined reputation or a slandered soul, it is as if the scourges once more cut My Body. Yes, from you too, I have suffered this scourging.

"The crowning with thorns and the mockery followed. Do you know how sharp and painful the thorns were? They were pressed into My temples; an excruciating agony. In the Eucharist I again suffer the crowning and the mockery of My Kingship whenever I am visited or received by those who render Me only lip service, and then go out and break My Heart by disobeying Me in their daily lives, or who question My authority as expressed by My Holy Church.

"I was presented to the crowd so that they might choose between Barabbas and Me. How it hurt Me when they chose him! Today in the Eucharist, My Heart suffers untold agony when souls prefer their own pleasure and ease to Me. There are countless

The Eucharist 2

souls who pass the door of the Church without even thinking of Me, or if they do think of Me, decide against visiting Me in order to pursue their own interests. Some souls prefer to sleep or recreate rather than attend Holy Mass of obligation. Some are present in body only, but withdraw their minds and hearts from Me to fix them on other objects or persons they desire more.

"You, at times, prefer your own comfort to Me. Your wandering thoughts and comfortable postures while at prayer, and your coldness to Me when I come to you in Holy Communion, are all forms of choosing Barabbas.

"The road to Calvary was a painful one for Me. I was kicked and jostled, thrown to the ground, covered with Blood, mud, and filth.

"In the Eucharist I again suffer the crowning. The sacrileges perpetrated against Me are numerous. At times the Communion Hosts are ground underfoot, defiled, and made an object of ridicule. At times it is a sin-stained heart that oppresses Me when I enter it, as the cross weighed on My shoulders en route to Calvary.

"I was crucified! Exposed naked to the rude gaze of those who jeered at Me, I died in unspeakable agony. My Life in the Eucharist is a continual crucifixion. I see Myself once more exposed to the scorn of My enemies. The indifference of those I Love is like a spear in My Heart. I am fastened to this prison by nails of Love; Love for all mankind; Love for you, Love even for those who ignore me or hate Me.

"For you I endure this life of loneliness. Yes, I permit you to share it with Me, and My Heart rejoices when you come and spend time here with Me. So that you do not leave here discouraged or downcast, I tell you that in spite of your failings, I Love you. Love for you keeps Me in the Eucharist, Love for you brings Me to your heart in Holy Communion. You are very dear to Me! I understand your difficulties and temptation, and I will help you to overcome them. Your efforts to do My Will pleases Me, and I will draw you ever closer to My Sacred Heart.

"Be at peace. Love Me. It is all I ask.

"In the Blessed Sacrament I still suffer torment in My Mind and Will, in My Body, and in My Heart. Although I am imprisoned in the tabernacles, My eyes pierce the veils that hide Me, so that I see My subjects who are present in the Church, and also those who are not there. Those souls who should be present at the Holy Sacrifice, but do not attend, outrage My Will by setting their will against Mine, by disobedience.

"The mental anguish which I endure when My Authority and Wisdom are questioned is beyond description. Those who come into My Eucharistic Presence through force or fear of punishment, and remain there just long enough to fulfill the minimum obligation, cause Me great mental pain.

"My Mind is tortured also by those souls who do not understand My wishes, because they do not want to. Even among My chosen souls, there are those who wound Me thus.

The Eucharist 4

188

"My Sacred Body, which is truly present in the tabernacle, still suffers from the treatment that It receives. I suffer, indeed, the pain of being imprisoned, and I am unable to move without the assistance of My creatures.

"My Body suffers from the insults of physical assault upon the Sacred Host.

"My Body suffers when the Eucharist is kept in unclean mouths, but It suffers more if It is given into an unclean soul. What shall I say of the sufferings of My Sacred Heart?

"The coldness and indifference of mortals whom I Love, for Love of whom I annihilate Myself, pierces My Heart and causes Me untold anguish.

"Those souls who receive Me merely to fulfill an obligation, not because they want Me or love Me, break My Heart with their thoughtlessness and lack of love. Though My Passion is over, let it be remembered that I am God, and that time means nothing to Me. The past, present, and future are one before Me, therefore I endure these torments now, which seared My Mind, My Body, and My Heart during My earthly pilgrimage.

"Love Me, comfort Me! My agony continues and I desire others to share it with Me.

"It is not only on the cross that I draw mortals to Myself, but also in the Sacred Host. When I am lifted up at Holy Mass or Benediction, I draw hearts as a magnet, but many refuse to be drawn! My Heart is broken because so few love Me.

"See, My Love is so great that My Heart is filled by It, and It must be given to souls or else It bursts My Heart and escapes only to be wasted."

O Jesus, I am unworthy to receive Your grace.

"My child, that you are unworthy is irrelevant, for I Love you and that is why I give graces to you. Just as a lover is blind to the defects of his beloved, and sees in her only what is to be desired, so do I Love you. Love Me in return."

The Eucharist 6*

*

"What agony for Me to thirst for the salvation of souls, to hunger for their complete surrender in love! Dear child, will you satisfy My hunger and My thirst?"

Dearest Jesus, if You help me, I will gladly do everything I can, to satisfy Your ardent desires.

"Then pray for the conversion of sinners, make sacrifices for them, give them a good example, lead them to My Sacred Heart. Ask My Mother Mary to help you; ask all My Angels and Saints to help you. That will help much to quench My thirst."

*

"Love Me; bring My Love to others, that they may be spared My wrath."

Dearest Lord, I want to, but how shall I do it?

"Preach My Love by your example, by your life. It is the duty of those who know Me and love Me to carry Me out to the world."

My Jesus, how should we love our neighbor?

"As I Love you. How do I Love you? My dearest child, I Love you to folly, sparing Myself nothing. What have you done? You complain that I have abandoned you, but it is not so. It is rather you who have abandoned Me. Those who love Me do not abandon their devotions, prayers, and mortifications simply because it is hot, or because they are weary, or because they are slightly ill-disposed. Did I say that I would suffer only so much? Did I say that I would suffer only the crowning, but not the spitting; only the scourging, but not the nailing; only the pain, but not the humiliation?

"I know what weariness is; I know also what disappointment is; I know what discomfort is, and because of it, I do not ignore you.

"What you call My abandonment of you is actually your fleeing from My advances. You are afraid to accept My talking with you because of what it costs you; you are unwilling to return love for Love. For this reason you cannot meditate, for you are afraid that I shall speak with you."

*

"When you drink, pause for a moment and offer it to Me, saying: 'My Jesus, I offer You this glass of water, begging You to share it with me, that it may be a refreshment for You as well as for me.' In this way, I will, as it were, be drinking from the same glass as you, and you will give Me great pleasure. Drink slowly, and you will find yourself far more refreshed than you have ever been."

Dearest Jesus, I wish that I might die so that I could be with You and no longer have to contend with the world's problems.

"Do you wish to die? Are you not willing to contend with your problems for such a short time in order to prove your love for Me? Soon I shall call you to Myself."

*

"My child, I, your God, so humble Myself before you as to beg for your love. I, your God, plead for you, a mere creature, a mere speck of dust in My sight, to love Me, to serve Me, to give yourself to Me unreservedly. Can you refuse Me?"

O my Jesus, I love You! I beg You not to plead for my love, for that does not seem proper for You, my God.

"I have done many things for Love of you that did not seem proper for God. Just as I told Peter that he would have no part of Me unless I washed his feet, so I now tell you: unless I plead for your love in order to move your heart to love Me, you would not be able to share My Love."

*

"Dear child, love Me, not in words alone, but in deeds. Give Me proof of your love. Rejoice when you are ignored, when you are ridiculed, when you are despised. Be glad when you are made, as you express it, a 'door mat'. Let others walk over you and trample you into the dust. Be grateful to them and bless them for doing so, thus making you resemble Me, thus proving your love for Me."

*

"Dear child, remember that you are human. You are not an angel; neither are you confirmed in sanctifying grace. You are weak and inclined to sin. Do not be discouraged when you sin or refuse My grace through cowardice. Aim at perfection, yes, and regret your falls and do penance for them, but do not become discouraged or expect more from yourself than I do.

"It is not possible for you consciously to think of Me all the time. That doesn't mean you don't love Me. As a human being you must frequently concentrate on work you are doing, but it does not keep you from loving Me, even though you are not aware of My being in your thoughts.

"I know that you must think about many things. I placed you in the world; I do not expect you to think consciously only of Me. I would be unjust were I to do so, since I have not made it possible. Do you call me unjust?

"When a couple are in love, is it just for a woman to resent the man's thinking about his work and not about her every moment? Does his concentration and attention to his job mean that he loves her less, merely because he does not at every moment have a mental image of her? Then do you think Me less just than My creatures?

"If I were to occupy your thoughts at every moment, you could not live. When such a time comes that nothing else holds your attention, when your thoughts are so filled with Me that no other image can gain entrance, I shall come for you and take you to Myself."

"Though I lavish graces on you, I will not force you to use them. Graces are of no value to you unless you use them."

*

"Give Me your heart. Let Me rest in it."

My dearest Jesus, my heart is small and poor. My heart is an unworthy and unsuitable place for You to rest.

"I understand, but offer Me your heart through the Heart of My Holy Virgin Mother Mary. When I see your unworthy heart encased in the Immaculate Heart of My dearest Mother, I shall be ravished by it and deem it the most beautiful resting place in the world. You can give Me no greater pleasure than by offering Me your heart enveloped in the Heart of most Holy Mary. Seeing your heart thus offered to Me awakens in Me a deep Love for your heart, and I lavish upon you My choicest graces and blessings."

*

"There is not room in your breast for two hearts. My Heart will fill it completely. I will take your heart and I shall transform it, removing all that is opposed to Me, filling it with love and humility, surrounding it with thorns, piercing it with a lance. When I finally return a heart to you, it will be identical with Mine. Guard My Heart well. You have now even more reason for avoiding sin, because you are capable of inflicting so deep a wound upon My Heart. You have now even more reason for saying and meaning: 'Jesus, Meek and Humble of Heart, make our hearts as unto Yours.' "

*

"Repeat these words after Me and ponder them carefully in your heart:

Lord Jesus, King of my soul, my Father, my Spouse, my God, I surrender myself from this moment forth into Your most Holy Hands. From henceforth, I shall have no jurisdiction over myself, but I shall be governed by You.

Whatever You ask of me, I shall give; whatever You permit to befall me, I shall gladly submit to it. Whether joy or sorrow, honor or dishonor, comfort or pain be my lot, I shall be equally happy, for all are gifts from Your Divine Bounty, and I shall praise You and love You for all.

My dearest God, the only reason for my existence is to give You honor. Under the guidance of Your Holy Virgin Mother Mary, I give myself to You forever and irrevocably to be Your slave. All I have, all I am, all I ever hope to be is Yours. Do whatever You will with me, only give me the grace to love You and to serve You faithfully forever."

*

"Every wound made in your heart is one more avenue by which I may enter into it."

*

"You must not complain. Since all you do will be done for Me, you must take care that it is done in the best possible manner."

*

"Do you love Me? See, I give you My Heart. I entrust to you My most priceless treasure. Guard It well."

*

195

"I am a worm and no man."

"A worm is one of the lowliest creatures. It crawls along the ground unnoticed and uncared for except to be scorned by those who see it. If such a creature is crushed or wounded, little attention is paid it. No one sympathizes with it or does anything to help it.

"In My Passion I also was a worm. I was not even considered worthy of sympathy or notice. I was deserted in My pain and agony. When attention was paid to Me, it took the form of scorn, ridicule, and hatred. Finally, when I was crushed beneath the weight of My sufferings, I became an object of repugnance. Worms receive no gratitude from mortals for the service they perform in turning the soil. I, also, receive no gratitude for the service I perform.

"In order to bait fish, worms are pierced on hooks, and by eating the worms the fish are caught. My Body, also is eaten, but not to the destruction of those who eat, but rather to their salvation.

"Pity Me, your Jesus! I Love you! I have reduced Myself to such a lowly state for Love of you. For Love of you I endured sufferings during My earthly life, from My Incarnation to My Death. Now, for Love of you, I am in the Holy Eucharist. My Love has reduced Me to less than a man, yes, to less even than a worm, for a worm can crawl from place to place, but I, in the Holy Sacrament, must wait upon the whims of men to carry Me wherever they wish."

*

"I am the King of Martyrs!"

"I am indeed, the King of Martyrs! I am their King by virtue of the fact that the martyrs gave their lives for Me, and also by virtue of the fact that I suffered martyrdom and thus, I am the Chief of martyrs, their true Leader and Lord, who would ask nothing of them that I would not submit to Myself. My martyrdom was far greater than that of all the martyrs together. Not only My Passion, but also My entire Life earned for Me the title: 'King of Martyrs'.

"No martyr has received a crown without first having loved and served Me before being called to martyrdom. There is a martyrdom of daily duty which is bloodless, but it is nevertheless excruciating. Such a martyrdom is most pleasing to Me.

"As King of Martyrs, I fashion after My own Heart, those whom I chose for martyrdom. I demand their surrender into My Hands, so that I may mold them as I please. Surrender yourself into My Hands, so that I may do what I will with you. Are you willing to do this?"

I placed myself in spirit before my crucified King. I kissed the wound in His side, on a crucifix.

Jesus, I willingly surrender myself into Your Hands.

"Whenever you kiss My image, I, in turn, kiss you; whenever you press My image to your heart, I, in turn, press you to My Heart; whenever you think of Me, I, in turn, think of you. Indeed, you are always in My thoughts, but at these times I think of you with a special Love and devotion. I am truly your King, but the majority of My subjects despise, reject, or ignore Me as if I did not exist.

"I am despised because of My poverty. I am despised because I demand that My subjects, too, be poor — if not actually, at least insofar as they are willing to give away their last coin, their last possession, if I ask it of them. I am despised because I am Humble, because I am Good. I am despised because My Life is a reproach to all who lead dissolute lives. I am despised because I demand obedience and sacrifice.

"I am rejected because I interfere with the comfort of My subjects. I am rejected because I will not tolerate in My subjects the accumulation of wealth, power, or ease, to the detriment of their souls. I am rejected because I come nailed to a cross, naked, wounded, covered with filth and Blood.

"The greatest pain to Me, a true martyrdom, especially in My Eucharistic Life, is that I am ignored. Some, indeed, ignore Me because they have not been told about Me, but many in their pride deem Me unworthy of their notice.

"Think of My agony as I hang upon the cross, all Wounds and Blood for Love of mankind, and they pass by and do not even look at Me or give Me one glance of pity or of love.

"I am God, yet I am King! My Heart is broken and My Love is ignored."

I am the King of Martyrs 2*

"My Banner!"

"You souls who would imitate the Humility of My Heart and be enrolled under My banner, must resemble Me in every way. My Kingdom is, indeed, not of this world. The subjects of this world are clothed in satins and silks; My subjects are clothed in rags which barely cover their nakedness. The subjects of this world are jeweled with gold, silver, and precious stones; My Blood is the only jewel that adorns My subjects.

"The subjects of this world are gathered before a throne resplendent with wealth; My subjects are prostrate before My cross, which is My throne; those among My subjects who are most stripped of the earth's possessions are the wealthiest in My sight. The subjects of this world revel in sensible delights and pleasures; My subjects find their peace only in sharing My sufferings. The subjects of this world bow before a king whose crown is of gold; My subjects love their King who is crowned with thorns. My subjects are the humble: those who would rather serve than command, those who would rather love than receive praise. The subjects of this world are armed to do combat with all who disturb their ease and comfort; in My Kingdom there is only one weapon of war, a spear, which cannot be used to harm others because it is embedded in My Heart.

"I am your King. I am your God. Give yourselves to Me. Help Me to spread My Kingdom of Love until all mortals are enrolled under My banner, that banner which bears the seal of the King: a Broken Heart."

"My Love!"

"My Love for you is eternal. I loved you even before My Incarnation, before Moses, before Abraham, before Adam, before the creation of the world. I loved you from all eternity and I will continue to Love you for all eternity. Even after your earthly life is over and you have been forgotten on earth, My Love for you will go on, for as God, I am Eternal, and My Love for all mankind and for each person is likewise eternal.

"My Love differs from yours. My Love is Pure, unstained by any thought of Myself. Your love is nearly always governed by motives involving your own well-being or pleasure. I Love you solely for your own good, and this is true even though the love you give Me in return glorifies Me. The glory which I receive from your love is incidental, and is not My reason for loving you. I would Love you even if you never return My Love. My Love is constant. It never varies. I do not Love you more at one time than at another. The degree of My Love for you is eternally the same. You, on the other hand, love much at one time and little or not at all another time, depending on circumstances and on your disposition.

"Your deficiencies are not your fault. Many of them arise out of the fact that you are weak, but you should earnestly strive to love Me to the very best of your ability. What I have told you of My Love should move you to make Me some return of love for Love. Pray for the grace to love Me. Ask My Mother Mary to assist you, for She, of all creatures, Loves Me best."

"My Heart is a Flaming Furnace of Love!"

"I shall teach you to love Me; I shall inflame your heart with My Love. My Heart is a great searing, unquenchable Flame, a roaring Fire, a consuming Torch. What you consider to be your love for Me is but a reflection of My Love for you. My flaming Heart of Love can consume the one who contemplates It. Behold, I am God, and My Love is the Love of God. If you wish to love Me in return, cast yourself willingly, gladly, eagerly, into the Fire of My Love. The Fire will indeed, completely consume you, and the act of consuming will cause you unspeakable torment, but unless you do cast yourself therein, you cannot love Me as you desire. My Heart is a Furnace of Love, whose intense flames purify all those who are plunged into It. As gold is purged of all impurities when it is immersed in the flames of the furnace, so too, are you souls purged of your imperfections who are plunged into the Fire of My Sacred Heart.

"There are few souls who actually want to be plunged into the Furnace of Love because the pain of purification is so great, and the fear of losing their identity weighs heavily upon them. Only you souls who plunge yourselves into the flames are ever completely engulfed in them, for I will force no one to do it. Many souls, even saintly souls, never go farther than the door of the Furnace, where indeed, they are seared by the Fire of My Love, and thus purified in part. I invite you and all souls to plunge yourselves into the abyss of My Love, but it must be, nevertheless, a voluntary act on your part.

Flaming Furnace of Love 1

"My Heart's flames of Love enlighten you, who are engulfed in them, with a wisdom you could not otherwise acquire. You will have a greater perception of the deceits of satan, and you will become more keenly sensitive to what gives Me pleasure and what displeases Me.

"These flames of Love sanctify you, who are submerged in them, for they transform your soul until you truly resemble the God in whose image you were created.

"You can satisfy My Hunger by plunging yourself into My flaming Heart. You must expect pain if you do. You know how painful fire is when it burns your flesh, but this mystical Fire of Love is far more excruciating than physical fire. You will not experience its pain at once, but you must expect it and rejoice when it comes. You do not need to wait. The door of the Furnace is open. Stand before It in spirit and look upon Its flames.

"Come, are you ready to step into the Fire of My Love?"

O sweetest Jesus, I place one hand in Yours and the other into the Hand of Your Holy Virgin Mother Mary. I will, with Your grace, plunge myself into the Furnace of Your Sacred Heart. I have no reason to be afraid! You are everything to me. I want to be close to You and to please You at all costs. Jesus, I am all Yours. I desire to be consumed in the flames of Your pure Love.

"So be it. My dearest child, My flaming Love envelops you."

Flaming Furnace of Love 2*

✝

*　　*　　*　　*　　*　　*　　*

"I am a King."

"I am a King because I am God. I am a King, and I have no need of subjects; My Kingdom is Myself. My royalty extends from the bosom of the Godhead over all creation. My royalty extends over the Angels who are in Heaven, whom God created, not from necessity, but from His Goodness, in order that they might celebrate His glory. My royalty extends over all mankind who are upon the earth, and who belong to Me by My title of God the Creator. This royalty is inherent in the very essence of things: by the very fact that Angels and mortals are creatures, He who created them is, and must be, their Master.

"I am a King also on another title: because I am the Savior. The world had existed for four thousand years, and during that time mankind was in slavery. They had rejected the royalty of God the Creator, who made them free, and had fallen under the yoke of satan. Nothing is more frightful than this slavery of mortals. The Light had disappeared from before their eyes, and the darkness in which they walked was the darkness of death. Their strength was but weakness. Never would they have shaken off the yoke of slavery to sin. The Mercy of God cried aloud to Me, and I came to the aid of mankind.

"I came to deliver mankind from their master, satan, and to put Myself in his place; I showed them what they had lost by departing from God,

I am a King 1

203

by showing them that I had come to bring them: the Savior.

"You mortals called Me because you saw your wretchedness, and I came. I am with you. The Mercy of God sent Me to you. My Charity has drawn Me towards you. You had nothing but the darkness of hell; I am the true Light; walk in the brightness of this Light.

"From the beginning you have had nothing but trouble, discord, suffering, and chains. I am Peace, Calm, Happiness, and Freedom. Your king was satan; you must take part with Me against him and vow an everlasting hatred to him. You rejected My sovereignty as Creator; you must accept it again, and acknowledge Me as King; you must acknowledge Me as God the Creator and God the Liberator.

"I am a King! My royalty is unlike the royalties of this world. I reign not only over bodies, I reign over souls, wills, and hearts. I am a King, a Conqueror King, whose conquests are neither the cities nor the empires of earth, but the souls and the hearts of My children. I am a King! I impose a tribute, but it is not gold or silver. The only tribute I require are the vows, the prayers, and the adoration of My children.

"I am a King! I have given a code to My subjects; it contains My laws. They are comprised in two articles: the first is the love of God, the second is the love of neighbor. In everything else I have given My subjects liberty, provided God and neighbor be loved.

"I am a King! I have a sceptre in My Hands and a crown on My Head. My sceptre is My cross on which I died to save My subjects; My crown is a crown of thorns, which reminds Me of all I suffered to acquire My sovereignty over souls.

"I am a King! I have servants and soldiers. All My subjects are at one and the same time servants and soldiers: they are My servants, by maintaining the dignity of Christians which I have given them; they are My soldiers, by striving against sin and the devils.

"I am a King! I have rewards for all the servants and soldiers who are of My Kingdom. I am an everlasting King; the reward I give is a participation in My royalty.

"Behold how great and glorious is My royalty! Is there, can there be, any other like it?

"Before I had appeared in the world My royalty was already announced. The holy prophets had proclaimed to the world, a thousand times, My royalty. Before I had appeared in the world, Angels were sent from Heaven announcing that I was to reign eternally over the House of David. Thus both earth and Heaven announced Me King before My birth.

"After My birth, the Angels of Heaven sang glory to God, whose Son I am and whose Kingdom I have come to establish; peace to mortals who have lost it and who will find it again in My royalty.

"After I was born in Bethlehem, a new star appeared in the sky, and its brightness summoned the kings of the East to My cradle. These kings hastened on their way, and prostrated themselves before Me to acknowledge Me as their Sovereign.

"After My birth, kings, like Herod, already tremble at My Authority; they pursue Me, and I baffle their plots; they fall, and I remain standing.

"I manifest Myself to souls, and though they do not know Me, I give them My Law. I labor for their salvation, I redeem them; I give them My Supernatural Life, I die upon the cross. In giving My Life, I do not lose My royalty. I establish it on an immovable foundation. Behold the immortal title which the cross bears:
'Jesus of Nazareth, King of the Jews.'

"Then I could with truth call Myself King of all souls in the world whom I have saved. Then I could call Myself King, and King of kings. Then I beheld all peoples, all nations and their kings come to bend their knee before Me.

"Happy are you souls who shall acknowledge Me as King, who shall submit to My Law, pay Me the tribute I require, who live and die proclaiming that there is no other King but the Son of Man.

"Happy are you souls who shall acknowledge Me as King, for I will give you an eternal reward, even a participation in My royalty."

The Catholic Church

"Religion is the union of all the duties which the creature owes to the Creator. Here are the marks by which the True Religion can be recognized, the Religion which has been given by God Himself: It is One, Holy, Apostolic, and Universal. The Religion which I gave to the apostles is the True Religion and alone includes all these.

"Religion did not begin with Me when I came on earth, but originated in Heaven. In the beginning God made man; He placed him in the garden of delights, and man acknowledged God as his Creator and the Creator of all things. Adam knew God and adored Him.

"The Jewish Religion was a symbol and figure of the Christian Religion, which I was to establish, which had been promised to Adam, expected by the Patriarchs, and announced by the Prophets.

"Everything concerning My advent was foretold: My birth of a Virgin, the place of My birth, My hidden Life, My public Life, My death, and My Resurrection.

"The Catholic Church is One: one in faith of the One God, One Redeemer, and one Baptism. It is one in Its morality which has but one precept, the love of God and of neighbor. It is one in Its duration; It is the only Religion which has traversed so many centuries, the only one which has remained unshaken, ever strong and full of vigor, the only one which is to abide even to the consummation of the ages.

"The Catholic Church is Holy: It is a Holy Religion, for It unites mortals to God and separates them from the things of earth; It is Holy for It teaches them to shun evil and practice virtue; It is Holy for It possesses the Sacraments: those powerful bucklers for the defense of virtue; they are deadly weapons against evil and sin.

"My Church is Apostolic: I sent My apostles to transmit It to all souls in the world, who charged their successors to spread and preserve It; it is easy to ascend from age to age up to the apostles, into whose hands, it will be found, I deposited My Church; I was sent by My Father.

"My Church is Universal: in all countries of the world Christians are to be found, souls who have one Faith, one Law, and the same Sacraments.

"My Church is Divine. I instituted It, I the Son of Man and also the Son of God. It is Divine; nothing can overcome It, neither persecutions of tyrants, nor the persecutions of other religions, nor the passions of mortals, nor the continual assaults of satan. What religion has produced heroes like the Catholic Religion? What other religion has so transformed the most timid women and the weakest children? Nowhere would it be possible to find a courage greater than their courage. Death has had no terrors for those who practiced this Religion; they have gone to meet it, they have welcomed it with open arms, they have blest God amid the most frightful torments, and not a complaint escaped their lips.

"I am the Church!"

The Catholic Church 2*

"I am the Light of the World and the True Sun of Justice!"

"I am the Light of the world! I will give you some idea of that Light which I came to bring to mankind. My Light not only illumines the eyes of the body, it illumines also the soul, the mind, and the heart; you, who once clearly behold this Light will never desire any other, because It suffices you and never leaves you at any time in darkness.

"My Light produces in your soul operations like those in the bosom of My Father in Heaven. In the bosom of My Father, My Light produces the Intelligence of the Divinity, regulates the Acts of the Divinity, and inflames the Divinity with its fires, eternally uniting the Three Persons together.

"My Light produces intelligence in mankind and regulates their acts. My Light inflames their hearts with its fires, to unite them closely to God.

"Happy are you who receive My Light, who walk by the guidance of My Light, and desire no other light but Mine; you will have the true Light, the Light which will never fade away, which for you will never suffer an eclipse, but will continue to enlighten you so long as you do not close your eyes to it.

"God the Father is Light, God the Son is Light, God the Holy Spirit is Light. I am the Center of these Three Lights; by Me these Three Lights form but One Light.

I am Light 1

"I am the Brightness of Eternal Light, the Splendor of Eternal Glory, not only in My Divinity, I am so also in My Humanity. I united all the Divine Light in My Body and Soul which I took at My Incarnation. By the Power of My Divinity, My Body and Soul retained the Light, to the great astonishment of earth and Heaven. Heaven saw the Light even as it exists in My Father, but mortals on earth had their eyes veiled, therefore they were unable to discern it.

"Three of My disciples saw Me transfigured in Light for a few instants, but I had to close their eyes to every other material and earthly sight, in order that they might behold only My Person and My glory.

"This is how mortals would behold Me if they were just, if they were pure, if they were united to Me. From the first moment in which they came to the use of reason, they would behold Me rise before their eyes like a sun, full of glory and majesty. This Sun would be without rising, meridian, or setting. This Sun would be ever before their eyes, and their gaze would be always fixed on it. Thus, to mortals there would be no darkness, but always Light; by this Light they would perceive, not the beauties of earth which pass away, but those of Heaven which never pass away.

"The Light of this Sun would have for souls so much brilliance and splendor that their eyes would be, not dazzled, but all penetrated therewith; they would attach themselves to it as a child clings to its mother.

I am Light 2

210

"How few are they who seek My Light, who walk in the brightness of My Light, and delight themselves in Its splendors! You know why the number is so small! It is because I am the Light, I am Virtue, I am the Sun. I am not of sin and iniquity, I am not of injustice, which separates from God, but of Justice, which unites to God.

"Appropriately the Son of Man is likened to the sun which enlightens the world, for I am the true Sun which sheds Its beams of Light upon souls, blesses them with its vivifying heat, and governs them by its movements. I am the Sun of the world, the supernatural world, the world made for eternity. I am the image of My Father, far more than is the material sun which enlightens you, for it is the image of God only in the minds of mortals, while I am the real, true, and eternal image of My Father.

"I am not only the Light and heat of the world, but the Sun full of action which made the world and gives it supernatural life.

"Four thousand years after the creation of mankind, I, who am the Light, I, who am Eternal, who subsist in the Godhead, I, who am the Light of God, was pleased to unite and incorporate Myself with My Humanity, in order to manifest by this Humanity, the Sun of eternal Justice. I came into the world of souls to enlighted them. I came, not only to display My Light, to restore Justice, to recall mankind to God, but I also came to make them sharers of My heavenly throne, partakers in My Justice and partakers of My Divinity.

"The material sun enlightens and sustains life; the True Sun of Justice, which is the Son of Man, transforms souls into Its own Light and imparts spiritual life to them. The material sun scorches when it approaches too near the earth; the True Sun of Justice, who is the Son of Man, transforms souls into Itself as It is more nearly approached.

"The material sun is reflected in the ocean, but always appears distinct from that which reflects it; the True Sun of Justice, who is the Son of Man, not only is reflected in the Christian soul, but inhabits it and transforms the soul into Itself.

"Yes, I am the True Sun of Justice; from the inaccessible heights of My Father I descend into the depths of the souls of mortals; from the splendors of the Godhead, I descend into the darkness of humanity, to communicate to them, all that belongs to Me. Even as My Father, by His eternal Generation, communicates to Me both His Life and His Existence, so also, by My temporal generation, I communicate My Divinity and My Light to My children.

"I establish Myself in the world as a legitimate Conqueror in the realm which I have won; I supply and perfect the created beings by giving gifts and communicating My Uncreated Being. This communication, this establishing, this gift of My Light to My creatures, is not for time only, but for eternity. I give with a willing Heart; what I give, is given forever. My Holy Light is incorruptible. I am able to give My Light, and I give It for eternity; in Heaven there will never be, as there never has been, any other light but My Light.

"Who will ever be able to comprehend how precious to souls is the Light of the True Sun of Justice?

"The sun which shines in the heavens is so beautiful, so vast, so swift in its movements, so regular in its course, that it is impossible to sufficiently admire this work of the Creator.

"How far more admirable is the True Sun of Justice! Its beauty is the beauty of God, Its vastness is the immensity of God; the swiftness of Its movements baffles the calculations of every created mind; Its course is invariable; It reposes in the Divine Will, which does whatever It pleases.

"The sun which shines in the heavens surpasses all inanimate creation, but no creature will ever surpass the True Sun of Justice, which is the Son of God!

"The sun which shines in the heavens is very necessary to the world, for it enlightens, vivifies, and makes it fruitful. What would the world of souls become without the True Sun of Justice? It would become darkness and death.

"The sun which shines in the heavens is so enchanting, that no one is ever weary of beholding it, but the blind do not enjoy its light.

"What beauty can exceed the beauty of the Sun

of Justice? What misery is equal to that of the sinner, poor, blind creature, who does not behold My Light?

"The sun which shines in the heavens is for time; it has had a beginning and it will have an end. The True Sun of Justice is for all eternity; It shines for the soul. It has never had a beginning and It will never have an end.

"Let the sight of the Light you now behold keep you ever attached to the center from which It emanates: the Sun of Justice, which is Myself. No longer should you have eyes but for this Light, no desire but for the heat of this Light, and no food but that of this Light.

"Pity the poor sinners who walk far from Me in darkness and in death. Attach yourself to Me. I will be your Light and your Life; I will one day also be your Recompense.

"As God made you upright to look up into heaven, resemble not those unhappy souls which, like animals devoid of reason, do not raise their looks on high, but keep them ever fixed below by their thoughts, inclinations, desires, and affections. The earth is beneath your steps that you may tread it underfoot. Heaven is spread before your eyes that you may gaze upon it without ceasing. I desire to be your Heaven; in this Heaven I will make My Sun to shine, and My Sun will enlighten you by Its Light, will warm you with Its heat, and clothe you with Its brightness."

*   I am Light 6*

"I am a Priest Forever."

"'The Lord has sworn, and He will not repent: You are a Priest forever after the Order of Melchisedech.'

"These words are addressed to Me. I am this Priest forever after the Order of Melchisedech; it is I who was anointed with the Oil of the Lord, and consecrated King and Priest by My Father in eternity. I went up to Calvary to fulfill My office of Priest, by offering to My Father the sacrifice of My Life, as a Sacrifice of sweet savor, alone capable of appeasing Him.

"I was at one and the same time both Priest and Victim. Being both Priest and God, I addressed Myself to God, and offered Him as Victim, a God immolated to His glory. This Sacrifice of Calvary I renew every day, by the ministry of the priest in the Holy Sacrifice of the Mass, which is a representation of the Sacrifice of the Cross. There I offer Myself, no longer in a bloody manner, as on the cross, but it is nevertheless a true Sacrifice which is offered, and I am still there as Priest and Victim, Sacrifice and sacrificed, God immolating and God immolated. It is still the same Victim which is offered to God, for He is the only Victim which is pleasing to Him, the only One for which He asks, the only One which He is willing to accept.

"What abundant gifts of grace you, O soul, and all Christians may derive by assisting at Holy Mass, in person or even only in spirit! You can offer to the Eternal Father, the Victim of the altar, to glorify Him, to honor Him, to love Him more and more, and attach yourself to Him more and more, to satisfy more perfectly for your sins and iniquities, as well as for the sins and offenses of your relatives, friends, and of all those for whom you are particularly bound to pray.

"You can offer to God, the Victim of the altar, to thank Him for all the graces He has given to you, to thank Him for your relatives, to thank Him for the Catholic Church, for the Saints, and for Holy Mary.

"You can offer to the Eternal Father, the Victim of the altar, to beg of Him the graces which are necessary for yourself, for your relatives, your friends, and for Holy Church; you can beg the alleviation and deliverance of the souls of your friends who are still in purgatory.

"Finally, you can have a share in the Victim who is offered, and attract Him to yourself either by receiving Holy Communion or by a Spiritual Communion.

"The priesthood after the Order of Melchisedech gives you the continuation of the great benefits of redemption. This priesthood, in its plenitude, resides in Me. I handed the priesthood down to My apostles; My apostles and their successors transmitted it, and will continue to transmit it even to the end of time, to those who shall be chosen by My Father, that the Holy Oblation may be offered through all the earth, even to the consummation of the ages."

I am a Priest 2*

The Holy Eucharist

"While I am all Love for souls in the Eucharist, many of them have nothing but coldness for Me. I sometimes pour forth My Heart into yours; sympathize with It, since I have admitted you into the number of My friends and confidants.

"While My Heart burns with Love for souls, what indifference they show! I make them hear My voice, not precisely in My own Person, but by My servants and by My grace: they despise My servants and they despise My grace. I seek them, and they hide themselves; I run after them, and they run away from Me; My threats and My promises they ignore. Why, then, do some souls act thus? What have I done that souls should treat Me so? Of what do they complain? What do souls find in Me that displeases them? A person is not forsaken without some reason.

"As for you, My child, since you know My Will, love Me, unite with My servants, outdo them in love, if you can. Repair in some manner the indifference of others.

"I have manifested My strength in the Sacrament of Love. Don't you think that it requires all the strength of the Love of a God to abide ever in this Holy Sacrament, notwithstanding the sacrileges, the outrages, the irreverence, and the insults which I meet with therein every day and every hour? Don't you think that I needed all the strength of the Love of a God to institute this Sacrament? I did not hesitate for a moment. You must not imagine that I had not a perfect knowledge of all the outrages which I would receive therein: I knew even the least word, the slightest thought. I knew the contempt and the offenses against My Father and against Myself; of these I should be more sensible than of every other sin. No matter: this did not stop Me! If one soul was to profit by this Holy Sacrament and find its salvation therein, I still would have instituted It, even though all other souls would have despised and outraged Me.

"I saw an infinite amount of good this Sacrament would produce; so many who were sick would find in the Eucharist their remedy and cure; many who were weak would find strength; many sinners would find the seal of their reconciliation and their sanctification; many just persons would find their consolation and new graces to sanctify themselves yet more.

"The sight of so many feeble persons who would seek support in the Eucharist, so many sick who would come to find relief, and so many souls who would not be saved without this Sacrament made Me institute It, notwithstanding all the outrages and all the insults I would receive therein. Do you think it did not need all the strength of the Love of a God? Did it not need the Love of a God to do such a thing, without ever repenting?

"This little Host is most august in Holy Religion, for It contains God Himself, all My Perfections, all My Merits. One who receives Holy Communion can say: 'I possess in my heart Him whom Heaven and earth cannot contain; all the Merits

The Holy Eucharist 2

218

of My Savior; in truth, I possess everything Good.'

"The power of God appears in the mystery of the Eucharist, almost as much as in that of the Incarnation. In the mystery of the Incarnation a God leaves, as far as He can do so, the bosom of His Father; He descends from the height of His glory and magnificence into the womb of a Virgin, and conceals His Divinity by taking on human nature, but in this Sacrament He conceals His Divinity and Humanity under the appearance of a piece of bread.

"I am in a thousand Hosts as much as in one; I am equally present in all the places where there is any consecrated Host, and yet I am only One. Even though there were a thousand million Hosts, all would receive Me whole and entire, together with an abundance of graces, each one according to his or her dispositions. May it not then be said, that in this Sacrament of My Love, I have made My power appear?

"What Love I have for mankind! I was not content with taking their form and living among them, teaching them the way to Heaven by My words, teaching them the conduct they should pursue after My example, and dying for them, I still could not bear to leave them.

"As My Love is insatiable and cannot be satisfied except with Love, as My Heart is consumed with Love and cannot quench Its thirst except by loving more, therefore I instituted this Divine Sacrament in order to be ever near mankind, to aid them and strengthen them.

"The prophet had good reason to say: 'God has shown forth to His people the power of His work.' How? 'By giving them the Eucharist!' I am the Recompense and the Inheritance of the children of God. All My children are called to receive this Inheritance.

"I am not in My Sacrament only for some, in certain special places, or for a certain time, but for all, throughout the whole earth, and as long as the world shall endure. I will show forth this Sacrament to all generations as a manifestation, ever ancient, ever new, of the power of God.

"The power of God is manifested, moreover, in this Sacrament by the benefit It confers and the good effects which It produces in souls. There are many who would testify to the truth of what I say!

"In this Sacrament of My Love, I have opened the treasure of My Mercy. All the Mercy and Goodness of God are in this Sacrament; in that Host are all the Perfections of God, all the Virtues, and all the Graces, since God who resides therein is the Author of Grace; He is the God of Virtues and Grace, Love and Mercy.

"In the Holy Eucharist, God loves to show Mercy. God is present in the Eucharist through His Goodness and Compassion. Much praise would be bestowed on one who should have stripped himself of his goods in his friend's behalf, and gone into exile with him. Since I have died for all mortals, I have chosen to dwell with them in their exile, that I might console them, fortify them, sustain them, and provide for their wants by giving them what is needed. Who has come to Me, praying with faith, hope, submission, and perseverance, and has not been heard?

"I say to you in truth: if mortals are so weak, so deficient in virtues, it is because they do not ask enough. The greater number come to My House, say a few prayers with a certain degree of fervor; others repeat prayers with their lips while their minds are wandering and distracted. How can you expect that a jealous and Just God should receive and listen to such prayers?

"Who, being in affliction, has come to the Holy Eucharist with holy dispositions, and has not been relieved? It is especially for those who are weighed down by the burden of the law that I am present in the Eucharist, for I have said: 'Come to Me, all of you who are burdened, and I will refresh you.' I invite not only the just, but also sinners, provided they sincerely desire to renounce their sins, for I am in the Holy Eucharist as on a throne of Grace and Mercy, to receive those who shall present themselves. I ask them to renounce their sins and their criminal habits. I am ready, if they are willing to grant Me what I ask of them, to make My graces and blessings fall abundantly on their heads, to pour down upon them all the compassion of My Heart, to give them all My Love, to take them in My arms like wandering sheep which have returned to the fold, to surround them with My solicitude, as a mother does for her sick child, and to devote Myself wholly to them that they may be Mine forever.

"Is it not a manifestation of the immensity of My Mercy thus to abide among My children under the Eucharistic Species every moment of the day and in all places on the earth? Is it not an unfathomable mystery of Divine Mercy, this abasement by which the Son of God places Himself wholly at the disposal of mankind, with all that He is and all that He has?

"What regret will thousands feel in their hearts one day for not having profited by My Mercy in this Sacrament of the Eucharist, when they might have done so with such ease!

"Have you ever understood as you do now the grandeur of the Eucharist?"

O Divine Teacher, thank You for revealing the secrets of Your Eucharist. Thank You for the Holy Eucharist!

"What draws you to the Eucharist?"

Lord, Your presence in the Eucharist attracts me. I experience the sweetness of Your Mercy and the kindness of Your power over me. The attraction is irresistible. I am like the thirsty deer which pants after water from a spring, and I find it in You. I am a poor forsaken child. I want to pour forth my heart into You. I am an exile who waits on the road to meet with a friend who will speak to me of my native land, and I find You here every day to speak to me of Heaven. My Jesus, You are everything to me. O my God, I now understand the truth of the words of the prophet: "How lovely are Your tabernacles, O Lord of Hosts."

The Holy Eucharist 6*

"I am the Way, the Truth, and the Life!"

"I am the Way: those who follow Me shall not go astray. I am the Truth: those who believe in Me shall not be deceived. I am the Life: whoever is united to Me by charity abides in My Life!

"I am the Way. Time leads to eternity by three ways, but two of the ways are not Mine. In Me there is but one Way, very different from the other two, because It alone has been traced by My Divine Hands.

"I wish to make these three ways known to you, and to distinguish from among them the one which belongs to Me, and which those who desire to come to Me must follow.

"The first way is wide, easy, and well trodden. This path was traced by satan in the earthly paradise, and the sinner, who is the slave of satan, walks in this way. It is bordered with flowers, but these flowers conceal thorns which cause death, which are the product of hell. Mortals enjoy themselves there with a wild honey which seems sweet to their taste, but which, in truth, acts as poison to those who eat of it, and leaves them without life. The end of this way is the eternal abyss.

"The second way is less wide, less easy, and less agreeable. It is not traced out by satan, but suggested by him, in order to entice mortals afterwards into his own way. The flowers with which this way is covered are smaller than the first way and less plentiful; their thorns also, which are less sharp and dangerous, do not penetrate to the heart and do not cause mortal wounds. Those persons who walk in this second way preserve their life, if they do not leave it to enter on the first way. They walk onward, and find at the end of it purgatory and its torments, transitory indeed, but terrible and dreadful.

"The third way does not resemble the other two in any manner; it is very narrow, very difficult, and little trodden. It was I who traced it on Calvary, and the Christian soul, who is to Me another 'self', walks along this road. It is covered with thorns, but these thorns shelter flowers which come from Heaven, the perfume of which delights the soul, and heals the wounds caused by the thorns. These wounds, far from being mortal, remove all that is corrupt in mankind, and leave untouched everything that is good.

"Those persons who walk in this way find nothing with which to refresh themselves in their fatigues except a most bitter wormwood, but when they have had their fill, the bitterness is changed into sweetness.

"I am the Way; I have placed the flowers under the thorns, I have changed the bitterness into sweetness, and I give Heaven after the journey is finished. I am the Conductor along this narrow way. I guide those souls who are willing to pursue it, either Myself in person or by those persons whom I appoint for this task, but I am the principal guide.

"I am the Truth. Truth is one, truth is firm, truth does not deceive, truth never yields: it endures eternally. The opposite of truth is falsehood, as the opposite of good is evil; falsehood calls itself truth, and evil calls itself good, in order to combat what is good and true. The grace of God assists the reason of mortals, permitting them to distinguish with certainty both good from evil and truth from falsehood.

"I am the Truth. The manifestation of this eternal truth is contained in these words: 'I AM WHO AM.'

"Falsehood is satan. The first manifestation of falsehood is contained in these words of satan: 'i will exalt myself and become like God.'

"I am the Truth; I enlighten the narrow way. The devil is falsehood; he lures souls along the wide way.

"The conductor along the way which is wide, smiling, pleasant, and strewn with flowers is satan; he promises goods, pleasures, and happiness to those who follow it; he promises them life; satan is falsehood, he will give them only misery, pain, afflictions, and eternal death.

"It is I who conduct along the narrow way; I promise goods that are eternal and not transitory; I promise eternal happiness and not that of time; I promise the life of Heaven and not that of earth; since I am the Truth, I will give eternal goods: eternal happiness and life in Heaven.

I am the Way, Truth, Life 3

"I am the Life. Those persons who walk in the wide way find death. Those who walk in the narrow way find Life. Those who attach themselves to satan, go into the place of eternal malediction; those who attach themselves to Me, go to My Father who blesses them with eternal Happiness.

"Natural death is the separation of the soul and the body. When the soul is separated from the body, the body is without life, but the soul still preserves life; I am the Life of the soul. Separated from Me the soul is dead.

"You souls who keep very close to Me to the end of your journey shall possess Me forever. I shall have been your Life on earth, and I shall also be your Life in eternity. I shall be your Recompense, your Happiness, and your All. With Me you will have everything, even though you shall have lost everything on earth in order to possess Me.

"Some pay little attention to the way they follow, to satan whom they have chosen for a guide and to what awaits them at the end of their lives. Since eternal salvation or damnation depends on the way which is followed, what is more important, and what is more essential?

"My child, walk always in My way; fear neither thorns, nor afflictions, nor anything whatever that may vex you therein; keep your eyes ever fixed on the torch of truth which I lighted on Calvary; repose in Me; I shall be ever with you, and shall eternally give you Life."

*   I am the Way, Truth, Life 4*

"O Christian, you are a Priest."

"You, O Christian, like the priest, are My other Self; consequently, you are a priest also, seeing that you resemble Me and I am a Priest forever. Your priesthood, as a Christian, is but a participation in Mine, which is given to you by Baptism, whereas the priest is the very reality of My priesthood, which is given him by the Sacrament of Orders.

"Baptism gives you spiritual life; all life comes from God and should return to God. This return of yourself, who have received life to Him who gave it, is your sacrifice, and this sacrifice requires a sacrificer: a priest. Every Christian is a priest. Every priest offers a victim. The victim which you as a priest-Christian offer to God is yourself: your body, your soul, your faculties, all that is in you! Every victim that is immolated requires a temple, a place consecrated for sacrifice. Your heart is your temple!

"There must be one to whom the victim is offered. You offer yourself as a victim to God. You unite your life to the Life of God, to transform your life into the Life of God. Immolation is not annihilation, it is not a complete destruction. You, O Christian, are daily dying to yourself, but you do not completely destroy yourself by your immolation. You do not annihilate yourself by your death; by your immolation and your death you go to God; by your immolation you discard all that is in you to receive all that is in God; by your death you exchange your own life to live the Life of God; your immolation and your death effect a complete transformation.

"The Life of God cannot come into mankind except by the destruction of the human life; this is why you, O Christian, like the priest, immolate your life in order to receive into yourself the Life of God. You, being a priest, immolate your life which is material, gross, earthly, animal, and carnal; you sacrifice this life every day, and the more you sacrifice yourself, the more, even here on earth does your life become pure, celestial, spiritual, holy, and divine. The sacrifice does not annihilate your life, it transforms it. When the immolation of yourself becomes perfect, complete, consummated by death, the sacrifice is finished. It is I who operate in you this sacrifice and immolation, as also the transformation which is produced by this sacrifice and immolation, because God the Father does not will to accept this offering or give a participation in His Life except through Me. In offering the sacrifice of which you are yourself the victim, you unite yourself to Me, and I will offer you to My Father, offering Myself with you. My Eternal Father will accept you and communicate to you His Life, as He has communicated It to Me in Its entirety.

"By your priesthood you become like Me. I offer Myself to God continually. I am at one and the same time, the Priest and the Victim of My Sacrifice. It is the same with you. You offer yourself continually to God. You are at one and the same time, the priest and the victim of the sacrifice which transforms your life into the Life of God. You are a priest, and you offer yourself to God in sacrifice.

"A priest also offers Me to God. He takes and offers Me, not only at the moment of My Sacrifice on the altar during Holy Mass, but also at every moment of the day in the Sacrament of My Love, wherein I am, and wherein I continually abide in the state of Victim in the tabernacle. The priest offers Me to My Father to satisfy His Divine Justice, to thank Him for the benefits He has granted him, to ask new graces of Him, to acknowledge His sovereign dominion over all things, and present to Him a worthy Victim.

"O Christian soul, I offer you to God My Father, and you offer yourself. My Father receives you, the victim, which I offer to Him. You, as a Christian, also offer Me to My Father, and He also receives the Victim you offer to Him.

"It is Baptism which gives you a participation in My Priesthood, and makes you a priest. It is Baptism also which makes you a child of God, the brother or sister of the Son of Man, and co-heir of My heavenly glory.

"This marvel is wrought by the power of the Most High, who comes to invest you who are baptized. The Holy Spirit descends into you, and at that same moment the work is consummated. God, by Baptism, comes to generate you in the womb of the Church; He deposits you in Her, and gives you life in Her as in the womb of a mother. He confides you to Her, and says to Her: 'This is My well-beloved child; in this child I have placed all My contentment.' Do you know what contentment I have placed in the Christian? It is sanctifying grace, a participation in My Holy and Divine Life, a participation which makes you a child of God and entitles you to call God your Father.

"You are a child of God by adoption. The children of one and the same father are brothers and sisters to each other; I am, therefore, the Brother of the Christian, and the Christian is My brother or sister by the very fact that God has adopted them for His children. To increase and perfect this brotherhood I became man and was born of the Virgin Mary, in order that, being the Brother of all mankind, because God had adopted them for His children, I might be their Brother also in My Humanity. My Mother Mary adopts all mortals for Her children at the moment of Baptism. This adoption is not to last only during time; you are related to Me not only while remaining here below, for the gifts of God are perfect. Since God adopts you on earth, it is for eternity. You Christian souls are My brethren! You will come to dwell with Me and to partake of My royalty and My glory in Heaven. You will come to find happiness in My Father forever, and after My example render everlasting glory to God.

"O Christians, such is your dignity! God imparts to you His Life by taking you from the life of sin and giving you His grace. I make you Christians My brethren. I call you My friends; I call you to My glory in Heaven. Your Christian character will never be effaced. Happy are you who preserve this character with the beauty and the glory which God has attached to it. You shall shine like bright stars in the Celestial City, where you will receive your eternal reward." You are a Priest 4∗

✝

"People are accustomed to measure the virtue of a soul by the graces which I grant it, but they are not correct. Does your virtue, for example, merit the great graces which I have granted you? You have no virtue, you have no merits, you have nothing! You would have your sins, but they exist no more, for I have forgotten them for all eternity. Why then so many, many graces for you in particular? It is because I am free to do good to whom I Will. The little ones are My weakness; that explains everything! No one can accuse Me of injustice. Since I am a King, I am free to bestow My royal favors on whomever I will."

*

"You must know that what would constitute a fault in great souls is not one in little souls, and you are so very small! I have made you good! I Love on your behalf, and so I count your entire day as one continuous act of love.

"Remember always that My strength will never fail you. Of all the virtues which I grant you, I endow you in particular with My strength, for you are weakness itself!"

*

"You and I will not go to purgatory; we will pass from the cell to Paradise!"

*

"Love Me! I thirst for your love just as a parched man thirsts for fresh water from the spring!"

*

"Love Me on behalf of each one of My creatures, of each heart that exists."

231

"The devil one day swore he would ruin you, and I vowed I would save you. The devil also swore he would ruin all souls, and I vowed I would save them. I will save souls through the triumph of My Mercy and My Love. Yes, I will save souls through My merciful Love!

"The distress which reigns in the world at the present time is not the work of My Justice, but of My Mercy. Fewer sins are being committed since money is scarce, and many more prayers are being raised to Heaven by people in financial straits. Do not think that the sorrowful conditions on earth do not move Me. I Love souls; I wish them to be saved; in order to achieve My end, I am constrained to be severe, but believe Me, I act out of Mercy! During times of abundance, souls forget Me and are lost; in times of distress, they turn to Me and are saved."

*

"I desire to be loved by innocent hearts, by the hearts of children, by hearts who will give Me all their love!"

*

"For one act of love from you I would create Heaven."

*

"When you love Me continuously, I enjoy heaven in your heart."

*

"The desires of your heart please Me so greatly that, if I had not already instituted My Divine Sacrament of Love, I would institute It for Love of you, in order to have the pleasure of abiding in your soul!"

*

"Love Me. Love Me alone! Love is everything, and so you will be giving Me everything. I desire to have you and all My creatures serve Me out of love. Do not avoid some fault for fear of My chastisements. I desire to be loved; I crave your love and the love of all My creatures. When you come to love Me, you will no longer offend Me. When two persons really love each other, they never offend each other. That is precisely the way it should be between you and Me, your Creator."

*

"Only Divine Love can make apostles out of apostates, immaculate lilies out of soiled ones, and 'Trophies of Mercy' out of revolting and vicious sinners! Ask of Me, your only Love, the triumph of My Love over you and over each soul who is now on earth, or who will ever exist until the end of time. By means of unceasing prayer, prepare for the triumph of My Sacred Heart and of My Love throughout the earth."

*

"You must never forget that I always am, and Love to be, Kind and Merciful towards My creatures. The Mercy which I exercise toward poor sinners in their life on earth, consists in heaping benefits on them."

*

"Have confidence in Me. Trust Me always. You must have a blind confidence that I will fulfill all the great promises which I have made you, for I am Kind, immensely Kind and Merciful. I do not desire the death of the wicked but that the wicked turn from their evil ways and live in Me."

"My Father, who has given Me the souls, is greater and more powerful than all the demons! No one can possibly snatch souls from My Eternal Father!

"If the 'good thief': Dismas, in addition to all his sins, had also committed all your faults, do you suppose I would have changed My Verdict?"

No, Jesus, You would have said just the same: "Today, you shall be with Me in Paradise!"

"Well then, some evening I will say the same words to you!"

*

"Your poverty is limited, but My Love has no limits!"

O Jesus, that You could Love the white and spotless lilies, I can believe, but that You should Love me, that I cannot understand!

"If you will remember that I did not come for the just but for sinners, you will understand at once."

*

"'God is Charity; souls who abide in Charity, abide in God, and God in them.' I am Love; as long as you remain in Love, you remain in Me and I also in you. Even when I am silent and you no longer hear My voice, remember always that as long as you love Me, I am in you and you are in Me! Is it not true that you desire to love Me alone and always? I will therefore always remain in you and you in Me!"

*

"I am Merciful!"

"Which are the more perfect souls: those who are always crying and telling Jesus that they are imperfect, are constantly committing faults, and are unfaithful to their resolutions, or those who are always smiling at Jesus, doing what they can to love Him, but do not worry over their involuntary imperfections so as not to lose time, because they are intent solely upon continuing to love Jesus?"

Lord Jesus, I choose and prefer the latter.

"Do what you can to love Me, and when you realize that you have been unfaithful to Me, offer Me a more ardent act of love, and then take up once again your 'song of Love'. I, your Jesus, am not a tyrant; since I forgive an entire lifetime of crime in return for one act of love, then tell Me, how is it possible be that I would notice some useless thoughts on which you had dwelt involuntarily? It is a futile lament and a loss of time to keep repeating to Me; 'Look, Jesus, what I have done; how faithless I have been.' On the contrary, a more ardent act of love enriches your own soul and delights Mine! Do not give the least thought to your involuntary imperfections!

"Believe Me, you will be no less dear to Me if your weakness permits you to be untrue to your promises. My Heart is won more readily through your wretchedness than through your virtues! The soul who said: 'Lord, be Merciful to me a sinner', went away from the Temple justified. The sight of a humble and contrite soul is irresistible to Me.

"Remember always that I Love you and always will Love you dearly, no matter what fault you may unwillingly commit. Never harbor the least doubt that I might not carry out My promises because of some infidelity of yours; never! You would be wounding My Heart deeply if you did. Remember that only I can fully understand your weakness; only I know human frailty in its entirety. You must never, never, never commit that fault of doubting that I would keep My promises because of your unfaithfulness! Promise Me that, won't you? Do not offer Me that insult, for you would cause Me great suffering!

"The enemy will make every effort to shake your blind faith in Me, but you must never forget that I am, and always will be, exclusively Kind and Merciful. Understand My Sacred Heart; understand My Love, and never permit the enemy to gain entrance into your soul, even for an instant, with a thought of diffidence; never!

"Believe Me, I am always Kind and Merciful! I am always a Parent to you! Imitate the children who, at every little scratch of the finger, run at once to mother to have it bandaged. You should always do the same. Remember that I will cancel out and repair your imperfections and infidelities, just as the mother will always bandage the child's finger, whether it is really hurt or only seems so. If the child's arm or head were hurt, how tenderly would the child be cared for and bandaged by the mother! Well, I do the very same with regard to your soul when you fall, even though I may do it in silence. Lack of confidence wounds My Heart and makes Me suffer."

I am Merciful 2*

236

"I am limitless Love and infinite Goodness! My Heart is Gentle. Everyone knows that I am Holy, but not all know that I am Gentle."

*

"You think you do not deserve the joy of Heaven because you are doing nothing. What does the catechism say? You have been created to love Me, to serve Me, and to be happy with Me for all eternity. Do you not love Me? Do you not serve Me? Well then, you are entitled to the glory and joy of Heaven! I give you Heaven not only out of Love, but out of Justice."

*

"Trust in Me. Trust always in Me. If you only knew how much pleasure that gives Me! Grant Me this solace to trust in Me even in the shadow of death. Never have fear of anything! Trust solely, completely, and always in Me! When darkness envelops your soul, then repeat with even greater ardor: 'Jesus, I behold You no longer, I hear You no longer, but all my trust is placed in You.' "

*

"Tell the little souls, tell everyone of My ineffable condescension! Tell all souls in the world how Good I am. As a Parent, I desire only love from My creatures. You may speak of it, and tell of My extreme Mercy and My limitless parental condescension."

*

"Whether you are working, eating, drinking, or sleeping, do everything with a great deal of love. Love is what I look for in every work. Fix all your attention upon your task of the moment, so as to accomplish it with all possible love."

*

237

"Be at peace. Do not make Me out to be a severe Person! I who sent the raven to awaken St. Francis of Assisi who was sleeping late one morning, because he had little sleep during the night, can also grant permission to you, one of My creatures, to support yourself or sit down in choir because you are suffering. Don't you understand that I am Goodness, Mercy, and Indulgence? Many persons represent sanctity by austerities, scourgings, and chains, but it is not like that. Sacrifice and penance do enter into the life of a Saint; sacrifice and penance are not the whole of a Saint's life. The soul who gives itself to Me with generosity, is the most fortunate being on earth, for I am Kind, altogether Kind.

"Never lose sight of the fact that I, whom you behold dying on the cross at the end of My mortal life, am the same Person who for thirty years shared the life which is common to all men, in the bosom of My own family. I am the same Jesus who all during My three years ministry sat down to table with mortals and joined in their banquets, and I was Holy, the Holiest of men. Do not misrepresent Me in your need, but remember that I am always Kind; to you I am and ever will be parental Tenderness.

"I prefer an 'Act of Love' and a Communion of love to any other gift which may be offered to Me. The 'Act of Love' which I ask of you is 'Jesus, Mary, I love You! Save souls!' This 'Act of Love' is better than the discipline; I thirst for love. Do not think that in order to reach Me it is necessary to live an austere, penitential life."

*

"It would be impossible to formulate a more perfect 'Act of Love' in fewer words than: 'Jesus Mary, I love You! Save souls!' It contains all: love for Me, love for My Mother Mary, and love for souls whom I came to redeem. This 'Act of Love' includes all souls: the souls in purgatory, the innocent, the suffering, the sinful, the dying, and even your own poor soul.

"Do not lose time! Every 'Act of Love' means a soul!

*

"If you are of good will and desire to love Me and make the 'Act of Love' from the moment of your rising until you fall asleep at night, be it well understood that I will perform incredible things for you. I will speak for you; I will act for you. Since you believe Me to be Omnipotent, you must also believe Me to be capable of granting you this continual 'Act of Love'. In order not to lose time, you should have the intention to renew all your promises everytime you pronounce an 'Act of Love'. If you fall, rise again; if you have forgotten, then start anew. An 'Act of Love' is useful for everything, at anytime, and under every condition!

"It matters little that the devil and your passions unleash in your soul every possible attack; do not mind thunder, storm, and lightning. Say: 'I want to continue undismayed my 'Act of Love' from one Communion to the next; that is my duty, my sole duty!' Forward! Nothing else!

"As a little fish will die outside of water, so also will you die outside the 'Act of Love'! Bid

239

farewell forever to all that is earth and creature, and head for the open sea with the unceasing 'Act of Love'! Forward! Toward the Eternal Shores!"

*

"What more beautiful prayer do you want to offer Me than: 'Jesus, Mary, I love You! Save souls'? Love and souls! What more beautiful prayer could you desire?"

*

"You think you do not know how to pray? What prayer is more beautiful and more acceptable to Me than the 'Act of Love'!

"Do you know what I am doing in the tabernacle? I am Loving the Father and I am Loving souls; that is all; no sound of words, nothing. Only silence and Love! You should do the same! Gaze upon the tabernacle and love Me."

*

"The 'Act of Love' fills every void and lays low all pride."

*

"Yes, an unceasing 'Act of Love'! That alone and nothing else, for love is everything, and in the practice of love all other virtues are practiced."

*

"Love is sanctity. The more you love Me, the more you will become holy! Remember that love, and only love, will bring you to the highest degree of sanctity! Remember that love and only love will bring you victorious to every summit! You love as soon as you cease to think of your own self interests."

*

Jesus, Mary, I love You! Save souls!

"Your 'Act of Love" will save souls!"

"As you close the door of your cell, for solitude is so beautiful, you must also close every door to the senses. Let us always live in intimacy, you and I alone. Close the entrance to every thought, to everything. Just the two of us alone, always. If you are in Me and we are one, then you will bring forth much fruit and will become strong, for you will disappear like a drop of water in the ocean; My silence will pass into you, also My Humility, My Purity, My Charity, My Gentleness, My Patience, My Thirst for Suffering, and My Zeal for souls whom I wish to save at all costs! All that is Mine is yours: not only all My Virtues but all My Words, My Thoughts, and therefore also My Sufferings and My Love!

"Since you desire to love Me and to save souls for Me, dwell in Me always, at work and during recreation. Do not leave Me for an instant! Then you will bear much fruit. Look at Saint Peter. He had been fishing all night long and had caught nothing; together with Me, he pulled in his nets filled with fish almost as soon as he had cast them into the water. It will be the same with you if you never leave Me for an instant. Whenever you receive from Me an inspiration to mortify yourself, throw out your net in response, and you will haul it in filled with souls, souls whom you will not know until you reach Heaven.

"Behold Me crowned with thorns. Imitate Me in a very real manner by not permitting another thought to enter your mind. In that way souls will be brought to salvation and you will free to love.

"Thoughts which come to you without your desiring them, do not make you unfaithful. I leave you to struggle against useless thoughts, for it is meritorious for you.

"Do you desire useless thoughts? Surely you don't. Then everything is to your merit. When you desire only to love Me, then everything that obstructs your love becomes meritorious. Do you understand? Not only are undesired thoughts meritorious for your soul, but it is also profitable for many other souls. Offer Me these undesired thoughts at every instant with this intention: 'For You, O Jesus, and for souls'. I will transform these thoughts which come to you from morning to night, and which hinder your love, into graces and blessings for souls.

"Now that all your thoughts are Mine, give Me also all your words; I desire them all. I desire a continuous silence. I wish you to belong entirely to Me. Have no fear, I will take the responsibility for your thoughts and for your words as well, that is, I will see to it that you will be able to keep these two promises. Are you content? Will you trust Me? I wish you to think of Me alone and not to speak unless you are questioned. Then I will always give the answer, and you must not be astonished at the replies which will be pronounced by you, for it is I who will be giving them.

"Be silent always. Be miserly even with necessary words. Instead, give everyone a smile in exchange, and always keep a smiling countenance. What is it that keeps you from loving Me? It is useless thoughts and being inquisitive about others!"

Your 'Act of Love' 2*

242

"My little victim, does not My thirst for love and My request for reparation for your brothers and sisters tell you everything? Yes, I have given you everything; now you must give Me everything; all your love, your every heartbeat, in one unceasing 'Act of Love'. I desire nothing else!

"Only by your unceasing 'Act of Love' do you give Me everything, everything for yourself, and for your brothers and sisters.

"I wish you to show Me your generosity and fidelity by renouncing every thought and word, so as never to interrupt your 'Act of Love'. You must love Me always and accept all the consequences, but never interrupt the 'Act of Love'! I know that this will gradually consume and immolate you. That is what it means to be a victim of Love!"

*

"To suffer for the love of Jesus and of souls, is a joy!"

*

"Love is a Fire. Permit it to consume you quietly. Love in peace."

*

"Behold the Blessed Virgin Mary at the foot of the cross. She suffers, yes, but what dignity in Her suffering! She is in anguish, but not one lament! She does not become despondent or discouraged. She accepts and suffers! She offers it all up with calmness and strength, even to the 'consummatum est'. That is the way I wish you to suffer."

*

Jesus, Mary, I love You! Save souls!

"If you will obliterate yourself and will not permit any outside thought to enter, then I will be thinking within you; if you will not speak, then I will speak within you; if you will stop following your own will, I will act within you; it will not anymore be you who lives but I in you."

*

"Transform everything disagreeable that you meet with into little roses; gather them with love and offer them to Me with love. I delight in gifts which you offer with all possible love. Then even your trifles become precious to Me.

"I do not demand heroic acts from you, but merely trifles; only they must be offered with all your heart!"

*

"Do you wish to do penance for your sins? Then love Me! Love shall be your penance! With love you can make reparation for the horrible sacrileges committed by mankind; with love you can suffer, with love you can immolate yourself and can consummate the sacrifice! Everything through love, and only through love."

*

"Just as I have taken on the responsibility for your thoughts and words, so also for your continuous 'Act of Love'. You must remember that when you are conversing with Me or when you are writing or meditating, the 'Act of Love' continues. I credit you with it just the same, even though your heart is obliged to keep silent at those times."

*

Jesus, Mary, I love You! Save souls!

"You must do your utmost to offer Me the unceasing 'Act of Love', but when you fail, I will make it good for you. Have no fear, I am always Kind!

"Why is it, that I do not permit you so many vocal prayers? It is because the 'Act of Love' is more fruitful. One 'Jesus, Mary, I love You! Save souls!' repairs a thousand blasphemies!"

"What would you like to give your Mother Mary during Her novena of the Immaculate Conception? Offer Her a continual 'Jesus, Mary, I love You! Save souls!' With that you will be giving Her everything!"

*

"Not only is your cell a sanctuary where you can always find Jesus, the Sacred Heart, or the Crucified, but you should be a tabernacle wherever you may be. Just as you do not wish anything but the continual 'Act of Love' to enter into your cell, so too you must not permit anything but the continual 'Act of Love' to occupy you, no matter where you may be or in what work you may be engaged."

*

"Even if good thoughts may creep in, there is always a bit of self-love, of complacency, and it is easy to see how they will spoil the 'Act of Love'. If you will have complete trust in Me, that I am attending to everything and will continue to do so, and if you will not permit even one other thought to enter, then your 'Act of Love' will possess a virginal purity.

"If I confirm you, through grace, in the virginal

purity of love, you must not think that it will cost you no further effort to love Me. Oh no! Confirming you in grace does not preclude that struggle and effort will not be needed!

"The unceasing 'Act of Love' procures for you virginity of heart, virginity of body, and virginity of spirit."

*

"While you are loving Me, the enemy cannot enter with a bad thought, because all your faculties are absorbed in loving, but if you cease to love, he can do so very well. You therefore must always love!"

*

"Let Me do everything! You will see that I will do everything, and do it well, and you, My little victim, will become fruitful in love and in souls!

"I delight to work in your soul. I love to do everything Myself, and from you, O soul, I ask only that you love Me."

*

"Think no longer about yourself, about your perfection, on how to attain sanctity, about your defects, or your present and future troubles. No, I will see to your sanctification. You must henceforth think only of Me and of souls; of Me to love Me, of souls to save them!"

*

"Follow Me with an unceasing 'Act of Love', day by day, hour by hour, minute by minute! I will attend to everything else! I will provide everything!"

*

Jesus, Mary, I love You! Save souls!

†

"Who could be happier than you, My Christians?
You have the same Father as Mine, the same
Mother as Mine, and I am your Brother."

*

Jesus, we are all alone.

"Say: 'My Jesus'. Don't you prefer to be called
'My N . . . '?"

*

"When you say: 'Sacred Heart of Jesus, have
Mercy on us' with love, I grant more grace than
for a long prayer that you repeat mechanically."

*

Thank You my Jesus, for all the Hosts I have
received since my first Communion.

"They are yours forever. A Host received is
eternally given. This is the treasure of the elect."

*

"All that is Mine is yours. Tell Me that you share
everything with Me; tell Me often."

*

"Say: 'Eternal Father, I offer You my Jesus living
in my life and dying in my death; I offer You
His Heart in each one of my heartbeats.' "

*

"Everything I say to one of My children, regarding
My Love, is for all of them."

*

"If I did not allow you to be tempted, where
would your victory be? Instead of being unhappy
you should be glad. Say to yourself: 'Now is the
moment to win.' "

"If you suffer alone, you are poor, but if you unite your sufferings with Mine, you are rich."

*

"Try to avoid the smallest faults. This is your work, since you have been called to holiness, and holiness is the absence of any willful faults. It is a work of love."

*

"Has it never occurred to you that this or that grace was given to you because of some prayer said for you, or some priest's blessing, or what your parents won by their efforts, or because of My Divine Compassion, or the Goodness of My Mother Mary? Don't ever get the idea that the cause is any goodness of your own or anything in yourself."

*

"What if I created you only to console Me and to give Me a refuge in your heart where you sing Me the hymn of love? Why shouldn't I have a home on earth? Must I still have no stone on which to rest My Head? Open to Me! Hurry and open wide the doors of your heart, My dear little one."

*

"You have much more cause for loving Me than your first parents. I was their Creator and Benefactor; I gave them light, whereas I am your Savior and Redeemer, your tender Victim, your only Love. I do more than visit you. I dwell in you. You partake of Me as Food. I never leave you unless you drive Me away. Find within yourself heart-melting words of love."

*

"Make everything tidy and attractive remembering that I am the Master of the house."

"You are coming to the end of your life, sing your hymn of thanks to Me every day, because I gave you this life. It was a free gift, you understand? I foresaw all your ingratitude. I gave it to you with the thought of all the happiness that I am preparing for you. Oh, My children, you are My extravagance of Love."

*

While I was digging around the hydrangeas:
"Be one with Me in My toil as a carpenter. It is not what you do that matters, but the way you love Me while you work. Love is oneness. Give Me the spectacle of a soul engulfed in its Savior, and this will be My joy."

*

"When you were little you wanted someone to take your hand when you crossed the street. Ask Me often to take your hand, because you are always little. Don't ever think that you can do anything good without Me."

*

"Do you love our solitude? I want you to know that if you leave My Eucharistic Presence for some social duty, you please Me just as much, for you find Me in every work of love. A day will come when you will never leave your Savior and God."

*

"Even by your ordinary actions you can make amends for ingratitude and save sinners. I saved souls while I was sweeping the workshop."

*

"What merit would there be in loving Me after you had seen Me? This is the test of life. Pass through it victoriously."

*

"I love children. It is I who give them delicate thoughts and feelings: complete trust, docility, a thirst for Jesus, candor and purity, absolute surrender and the forthright glance. You must keep the same sentiments with you right through life, for they come from Me, and I so love to find them again. Find your child-soul again and give it to Me."

*

"Today I ask you to keep your mind in a state of simplicity, your thoughts rising like candle flames toward My Power, Majesty, and Love, for I am your Father and your Spouse.

"Even if you don't see the results of your prayers or efforts, don't let this hold you back. Just keep in mind that I know everything, and place yourself once more in the Hands of your Redeemer. Remember this: I will be for you what you want Me to be. If you treat Me as a stranger, I will be only a judge; if you trust Me, I will be your Savior; if you live in My Love, I will be your Loving Spouse, the Being of your being."

*

"The grace which the Holy Spirit gives is not just for His Feast. It is forever. He does not take back what He has given. How could Love ever take away His gift? Ask Him! He will heap on you grace upon grace."

*

"My little child, all My merits are yours. They are for all My children. You are My heiress."

*

"There is a way of ceasing to think of your little anxieties: just think about Mine."

"Tell Me that it doesn't bother you to go along beside Me. What you do cheerfully for Me pleases Me more. I do not want to impose on My friends, and so, I am overjoyed when you express your ever-new happiness to be with Me.

"I am not an exacting Master. I am the fullness of Love. Give yourself with open arms. You know how little children leap to be caught and lifted up into the arms of their father."

*

"Don't you know that because of My Compassion a single act of perfect love atones for a whole lifetime of sin? Don't you know that one humble and tender look from you pierces My Heart with love? Don't you know that I am sensitive to every cry of your heart?

"My desire is to have you come nearer. You may even invite the Angels to help you in your upward climb. I have so much to say to you, so much to give you. Come nearer, always nearer."

*

"My presence! Do everything: work, pray, think, and talk, just as though I were with you, for I actually am there. Don't you find this infinitely wonderful? When you wake up, I am with you; when you rest, I am with you. You can truly say: 'Jesus never leaves me alone'. This is what makes solitude divine."

*

"Do you at last believe with all your heart that I created you in order to make you eternally happy? It was out of pure Love that I made you, not for My own interest, but for yours: to give you infinite Bliss."

251

"I gave you everything, even My Mother Mary."

My Jesus, I love You!

"Say it again, so that it may chime once more in My ear. Prolong its vibration like music. I never shall become weary of listening. Tell Me why you love Me and how this love began; tell Me all that you want to do for My Love. Of course, I know all about it, but to hear it from you is a joy to Me, as a story ever new."

*

"Don't get the idea that it is the greatest number of prayers that touches your God. It is the way you speak to Him. Be irresistible in love, abandonment, and humility. When you ask Him for bread, He will not give you a stone, but a double portion. When you tidy your house, think that it is Mine and you will make it more beautiful. My friend, when you prepare your meals, think that it is to honor Me, and when you rest your body, think that it is My Body. This is the reality, since all that you have is first mine, isn't it? You will see Me everywhere. I will be your Host and your Guest, the One who receives and the One received; the One who has taken your heart and asks the free gift of it. Two lives in one!"

*

"Sometimes you think that you are wasting time, that love in you is feeble, when all the time it is increasing. To desire to love is love itself. All these efforts of yours to love Me more, only add to the sum of your love in the eyes of the Divine Compassion."

*

"I stand at the door waiting even before you call Me. Do you remember this or that danger you escaped? You may have thought that it all happened by luck. Nothing happens by luck; never lose sight of My watchful, kindly Providence. Thank Me for My invisible care. My Love wants to plan for you and does everything for your good."

*

"Multiply your sacrifices. Two or three a day are not many, but united with Mine — can you imagine what a fortune that would be? To pray is itself a sacrifice — like the smoke rising toward Heaven from the holocaust. You can pray by working and you can pray by singing to Me. You can also pray by just looking at Me in silence, in a silence laden with the love that is worth more than whole rosaries that you would recite mechanically. These are ways of approaching your Savior and God who is waiting for you!

"If you did not come, how could I give you My grace that is like a burden upon Me? What a happy day, when it has been spent so near, within My Light. I am like someone suffering from cold, who, without a word, awaits the tender pity of some passer-by, hoping to receive alms. It is not so much the gift that will fill Me with joy, as the gesture of the heart. You can understand My agony on seeing the indifference and hatred souls have for Me, right to the end of the world. Think about My sweat of Blood.

"You are the one who passes by. You pass by in life. Cover Me with your love, all of it. I want to be your NOW. I want to be you, your breathing and the beating of your heart right to the very last. Even if after that final heartbeat, your soul has not yet been liberated from your body, I want your last thought to be for Me.

"Try to understand the demands of Love. You see, I paid for everything on the cross."

Lord Jesus, I am so poor in love.

"Take My Love, since you know that It is yours, for It belongs to all My children. Offer It to the Father, with full assurance of your power over Him, and then ask, ask, ask!

"My little children all down the ages, clothe yourselves with your Brother Jesus, as Jacob clothed himself to resemble his brother Esau; then the Father will give you the heritage of all His Treasure. I will be full of joy at having paid with My tears, the blows I received, and My Blood. O My little children, you are My very own."

*

"Thank Me for your nature, even with all its faults and failings, for this can be a source of merit for you."

*

"All during the month of the Rosary, call My Mother: 'Our Lady of Love' and say: 'Our Lady of Love, give me love.'"

*

In the bus I was saying my prayers mechanically as I was eyeing the pedestrians and the stores.

"Are you praying? Are you offering this to Me? Are you making fun of Me?"

254

"Suppose someone were to ask you: 'What are you doing at this moment?' You could answer: 'I am loving my God.' Even if the whole universe were to stand still, it would be a event of little importance compared with a soul striving to love Me.

"To make reparation, to comfort Me, and to thank Me, is loving Me. To glorify Me, to ask for My grace, and to please Me, all these are ways of loving Me. Love Me just for the sake of loving. That's what the Saints in Heaven are doing, and would you believe that it is forever the story of My Passion which is perpetually renewed! Take all these concerts of praise, all these transports of love, and offer them to Me in the Garden, in order to veil the assualts of the powers of evil from Me.

"Pray for all centuries, all peoples, all sinners. There is infinite treasure in My sweat of Blood. What have you to fear? Give My Blood to all souls in the world, that It may give them life.

"My dear little child, so full of weakness and poverty, I am counting on you to help your elder Brother."

*

"You are only an instrument, but be that; be always ready to serve Me. Serve Me, not yourself. You are dependent on Me. I am your Employer. Thank Me for wishing to make use of you. Are you not happy with your Employer? Could you ever say that I don't look after you? You have experienced the delicate little touches of My Tenderness and you have seen it also in the

255

details of your life, for nothing is too small for My watchful Love. You have learned to recognize Me in all circumstances too. This pleases Me so much. It is really I, your Christ, who comes to meet you so often."

*

"Begin anew every day as though it were the very first. You are forever at the beginning. Do not be afraid, for I am with you.

"I would like you to tell Me where you have failed and to explain yourself to Me. It brings out your confidence in Me. What else would you speak to Me about if not of your poverty. It's the case of the beggar at the rich man's door. If only you had seen the joy of those I healed on the roads of Judea. They left Me singing the praises of God.

"Sing every day in your heart and make Me known to others through joy. You want to make Me known, don't you? Since satan uses others to act for him, why shouldn't I? Since I live in you, don't you see how simple it would be to express Myself through you? Your life is Mine."

*

"Your body belongs to Me. Take care of it because it is Mine. Do your work because it is My work. Rest, to rest Me, and when you speak to your neighbor, that is My public life."

*

"Don't have a care in the world unless it be the fear of offending Me."

*

"They brought Me the sick and crippled. Isn't your love for Me both sick and crippled? Didn't I know how to raise the dead to Life?"

"If you could only see My Splendor, My Power, and My Tenderness in the tabernacle! If you could only see the guard of honor formed by My Angels burning with zeal. What reverence, what a sense of nothingness you would feel! You would see the utter unimportance of everything that is not love. You would realize too, that nothing could possibly give you more joy than to give Me joy. You would not want to cease looking upon Me. I am Heaven!

"Heaven is inside the tabernacle. Adore Me with all the Heavenly Hosts. Love Me with them. Sing praise! You can never overdo it, since all you have is what I have given you, and all My merits are yours for the taking.

"Do you realize that if it were necessary, I would begin all over again? Find a new way of praising Me every day. Keep on exploring My hidden treasures. You can never come to the end of them.

"Discover, until fires undreamed of are kindled within you. You can say: 'It is You, Lord! How blind I am! The best of me is always You.'

"Even while you are talking to Me, I continue to heap blessings upon you, for My Heart is filled with them, and to give eases It of Its burden. It takes a mere nothing from you to make My Heart overflow. If you only knew!

"Wake up to your power over Me. Get to know Me a little better. Stammer out your words of love. I will complete them.

"Have you seen the great sun dancing in tiny mirrors? Who can bear its dazzling brilliance? What is a mirror without the sun? What are you without Me? I am the Light of the world!"

*

"How can you make progress all by yourself? Let yourself be carried in stronger arms, just as you did when you were little. Don't be ashamed of being weak and imperfect. Be smaller still; I will Love you even more. Don't lose sight of the path of spiritual childhood. Cultivate your confidence; let it blossom as a flower. You can trust Me, can't you? Look back! Don't you find that I am worthy of it? My friend, don't put any limit to your feelings for Me. I put no limit to My feelings for you. Come to Me, little by little, your heart will be on fire at the moment of death. Find a sweeter name for death. Call it: 'the meeting', and even now, though you cannot see Me, you will stretch out your arms to Me. Oh, the charm of an impatient heart longing to be enfolded in Mine."

*

"Remember this: as one lives, so one dies. If during these moments before our 'meeting' your heart is full of Me; if zeal for My Kingdom consumes it; if you are thirsty for My glory, you will pass on to our 'meeting' with a thought of love. It will be your true Birthday: born to Life Everlasting. I am Life, I, your Jesus."

*

"You know one of the names Jesus gives Himself: a 'Lamb', a 'Poor Lamb of God'. Don't you like that Name? It speaks of the Gentleness of My Heart."

"My little child, you may be sure of this, that even though I am no longer seen on earth, your neighbor is there. I am your neighbor! Your desire to love Me, to receive Me, to serve Me, and to give Me rest, as in the home of Martha and Mary, may be realized in what you do for others. How ready you would be to smile at everyone if you could only see your Jesus in them. Remember this and don't economize your kindness. It is I who will receive it all. I have a thousand ways of responding to those who try to please Me.

"Isn't your life on earth drawing to a close? Don't you need to warm your heart more often in the secret place of the Most High God? When someone is about to make a last voyage to a particular country, doesn't that person live through it all in anticipation, holding the far horizons to his or her heart?

"Look forward to your departure to Heaven, since it is to take you to your Beloved. Say to Him: 'It is time we saw one another. When will You unveil the sweetness of Your Face for me? Have I not been traveling long enough in the desert? May I not leave this cold and barren earth to throw myself into Your arms? Enliven my desires. Hasten my steps. No longer can any earthly tie hold me back. Let my soul escape from its body as a bird from its cage, so that the breath You have given me may be lost in Your Divine Being.'

"I will listen to your voice, for I too am at work in you, preparing for our 'Meeting'. You will ask: 'Where is my Beloved?' I will be there all the time, since I am everywhere.

"Wait for Me in silence. Offer yourself to the Father enfolded in My Merits. Implore the Holy Spirit to give you love, and abandon yourself forever as I did on Calvary."

Lord, I should very much like to take Mary Magdalene's place on earth, because she had such a great love for You.

"Offer Mary Magdalene's love to Me. It is yours by the Communion of Saints, for all time is present to Me. You find it difficult to believe in this Treasure that your God devised for you. Accept it in all its magnificence, even though it is beyond your understanding. Believe it! All that I have thought out for My children is for their good, not for Mine. Humble yourself in faith and love as Mary Magdalene did. Tell Me often in secret, of all the ways in which you have grieved My Heart. Be deeply sorry. You know how My Heart listens. If your heart is moved as you confess, what do you think My Heart must feel?

"O, My child, may love lift you above your usual ways. Like Mary Magdalene, learn to be a new person, even giving up your all.

"The sacrifice most pleasing to Me is a contrite heart. What deeper pain could you have than to have little love? Take all the love of the Saints and give it to Me as though I were receiving it for the first time. Ask Mary Magdalene to help you, for she loves Me so much."

"Here I am. I was waiting for you. When My children receive Holy Communion in the morning, I wait during the day for their little visit of thanks. Haven't I deserved it? Just think what it means to receive Communion. How heartless not to say: 'Thank You!' I gave all of Myself to My little children. Whoever wants Me may take Me, and those who receive, receive all Heaven, for Heaven is your Jesus. Don't take such an immense favor for granted. Think of each Communion as a first Communion.

"You were wondering how to use those moments when you wake up in the night. Speak to Me of love, ardently desiring your next Communion. Stretch out the desires of your heart to Me. Call Me by the gentlest names, even when you are half asleep. Be stirred to your heart's depths as you yearn for My Host-presence, prepared for you since the Last Supper. Today's Communion is different from yesterday's and tomorrow's; the grace I give is always unique."

*

"Picture Me as a Living Being! I Love you more than you could ever imagine, even in your greatest desires. Keep before you the thought that I, who gave My Life for you, am waiting with infinite yearning for the moment of our 'meeting'.

"Picture Me often this way, as a real Person, not just someone near you, but actually in you; One whose presence never leaves you."

Lord, I want to die for the salvation of souls.

"My child, resemble Me as much as possible. Say

261

to yourself, 'I will do this or that like Jesus.' In this way you will grow and come closer to Me.

"Do you know that while I was on earth, the tenderness between My Mother and Me was so great that we had only one Heart? Try to be like Her by making your will one with Mine, for I am your Great Friend.

"Be ever ready to help others right to the very limit of your strength. You remember with what Love I gave Myself. In My public life, in the midst of so many people all crowding around through self-interest, I seldom met with love. The people came to Me through selfishness, yet My tenderness reached out to each one of them.

"Imitate Me! Bargain with Me for souls! Don't complain!

"You cannot think of Me all the time, but in the morning say: 'Everything will be for You, my Great Friend.' From time to time during the day, repeat a little phrase such as: 'This is for You, my Jesus.' It will warm your heart and bring balm to Mine.

"If you have failed in something, say: 'My dear All, I could have been more faithful today. Please forgive me.' When you humble yourself sincerely, without your knowing it, I press you to My Heart, burning with Love. That is what you call grace, and My grace is sufficient for you."

*

"In the Host, My Heart is beating as It did on earth, as It does in Heaven. There is only One Heart of Christ. Believe without the shadow of a doubt in My presence here before you, and comfort Me by bringing your heart close to Mine. Look how alone I am in this empty church. I knew it would be like this, yet I instituted My Eucharist. I would feed even a single soul. Speak with the Host as with your most gentle and intimate friend. The Host is listening to you, and you may be sure that you are most dearly Loved. Breathe freely! Relax! Leave the earth. Enter the realm of the Spirit. Let yourself be carried away. Do you want to come? Tell Me about your impatience to join Me and your faithfulness to Me. You are Mine. How could you keep yourself to yourself?"

*

"I always forgive, if you tell Me of your neglect and feel truly sorry for it. I am not one who spies on faults and failings, ready to be severe. I am all Goodness. See how easily little children come to Me. Keep your heart childlike and come. Try to understand My Love better, and give yourself to It wholly."

*

"If you have to make sacrifices to reach Me, don't worry about them. I am in you. I will shoulder their weight. If you find no words to express your love, keep silent and I in you will speak to Myself. If you can't keep your thoughts on Me, come back to Me as soon as you notice this, gently, without bitterness against yourself. Since I can put up with you, you can surely put up with yourself."

*

"I ask My children for the most ordinary actions: eating, drinking, sleeping, working, your whole day united with My actions of the past, your actions clothed in My Merits. There is nothing difficult about this; it heals you of your usual poverty and wraps you in the richest garment. Couldn't you try something so simple?

"Acquire the habit of gazing at Me as I gaze at you. Don't you love to look at your Great Friend? It is like a caress. Always it is Power, like My words, like My Eucharist! Everything about Me is power. Life-power! Isn't that a joy? Doesn't it give wings to your love in a greater understanding of the Divine Being?

"If you only knew who God is, and how much He deserves to have you study His unsearchable Riches, His Generosity, His extreme Goodness, His Love; always His Love, for Love is the essence of His Being.

"When you have entered into the Love of My Sacred Heart, you will stay There. You will make It your home. My Heart is where you belong.

"From My Heart, as from a lofty balcony, you will see life, your neighbor, and service for God's glory from a new viewpoint, that will completely change your usual petty opinions.

"When the Saints lived on earth, they saw things differently from others, and that is why they seemed to lead strange lives. They did not have the same view."

*

"Ask Me for everything you have lost through neglecting to harmonize with My grace. Ask humbly, with confidence, and My Compassionate Heart will give it to you, because with Love nothing is impossible and My Love is victorious. I will help you pick up those dropped stitches of your life. You will have light that you have missed.

"Don't ever give way to the distress that keeps you aloof from Me. Be sure that My Goodness is infinitely greater than the sinfulness of My children. If you did not count on Me for help, to whom would you turn? Hope and trust to the utmost in Me, and you will honor Me. I will answer every time you call."

*

After I had received Holy Communion Jesus said: "I am praying to the Eternal Father for you."

My Lord Jesus, since You are praying to the Eternal Father for me, please tell Him what You would like me to say to Him!

*

"Are you ready to understand that joy can serve Me as well as trials if you give them to Me, if you live them for Me? If you recognize joy as My special gifts, you can love Me more because of them! Am I not free to bestow happiness where I wish and as much as I wish? Sometimes you like to prepare a lovely surprise and your whole heart is joyful at the pleasure the gift will give. Can you imagine My joy when you thank Me for making your cup run over? I never come to the end of all My gifts. Doesn't everything belong to Me?"

"Ask St. John the Apostle to help you. Today is his feastday. Although I left him on the day of My Ascension, he went on living with Me to the end of his life on earth. Ask him for the tender faithfulness that won so much light for him."

*

"Don't be alarmed when your imagination gallops. It is your will that concerns Me. I died to make your will Mine. Do you want to give it all to Me? Don't just treat Me as the guest of your great moments, but as the Beloved you never leave. As often as you think of yourself you find Me, because you are always before My Face."

*

"You cannot compute holiness like a column of figures. One act of love with absolute abandonment and trust can make you a saint even at the moment of death, and how this honors Me! I am like Samson; I lose My power as Judge when you tell Me of your faithful love, not because your love is so great, but because it is the greatest you have to offer Me. It touches Me and I am ready to bend to your will and make it My own."

*

"You are worried about the passage from this life to the next? It is the greatest proof of love that you can give Me, so be happy. Offer your death to Me now with complete detachment, ready even for heroism. Say: 'Even if I did not have to suffer death, I would choose it in order to be more one with You.' In this way, you will give Me the greatest glory a creature can give the Creator. O precious death of the Saints, that echoes even in the Heavenly Courts of the Father's Home!"

*

Lord Jesus, I thank You. You seem to go to all lengths to fill my cup of joy to the brim at the end of my life, don't You?

"Isn't that My special task? I am Fullness! Everything exists in Me, and those who possess faith, drink deep. You must believe and hope. Oh, this great virtue of hope! Practice it often, so that it will increase in you.

"The more you expect, the more you receive! Then expect even the impossible and you will have it.

*

My Jesus, I desire that You would be happy in my heart.

"Your desire pleases Me and gives Me great honor. You make reparation for yourself and you make reparation for the ingratitude of so many others. Do they think of Me with a little affection even once a year? Do they accept the thought of My Love for each one of them? When will they realize that time, the span of earthly life, is too short, that I need all eternity to Love them? How long will it take them to learn that this present life of theirs is not their goal, but only a means given them to earn Heaven?

"If you could only bring all the people around you to Me! Try to tell them that I Love them and how much I Love them. My Love is so great that I will forgive them everything from the moment they repent. Bring them to Me and I will enfold you with them."

*

"Unforeseen events, such as moving from one place to another, variable weather, rough weather: that is life. Come what may, remain steadfastly in My Heart. Keep your eyes fixed on Me as you ask Me for advice or as you tell Me that you love Me always. Remember that nothing happens without My permission, so be very serene. There is nothing like serenity for convincing people of the good."

*

"Which of us is waiting the more impatiently for the moment of Holy Communion, you or I? Yes, I know that you are thinking about it and preparing for it; you are coming out of a sense of duty, but I am coming out of pure Love. Ask Me for this love as though I were a merchant."

My Jesus, what shall I give you in payment for all You have given me?

"Your gratitude is payment, which will burn as a flame. What I give you will surpass your poor little means and awaken new feelings within you; feelings you thought to be beyond your power to experience."

*

"I give you the treasures I have received from My Father. Give to other souls exactly what I have given you."

*

"Love Me with My Love!"

*

"To see a Christian is to see Jesus!"

*

"I illumine the nothing that you are, so that you may have a clear picture of your nothingness."

"Do you think of yourself as one not yet born? Your real birth is your entrance into heavenly Glory. Prepare for it. Make everything ready. Recall the life of the humble caterpillar crawling on the earth. Consider next its secret, hidden life within the chrysalis, and at last, marvel at the butterfly with its magic-colored wings, flying free in the clear blue.

"O rejoice at the thought that you will soon be born to fullness of life."

Lord, I am so very little. I have only what You have given me.

"Ask for more! Ask better! Although you are very far from holy perfection, ask Me for it unceasingly, in order that it will bring you nearer to Me. How many blessings you miss by not asking for them!"

*

"You must not be afraid of aiming at perfection, since I am with you and I have lived It, and since it gives Me great joy to look after you. You see you are not alone; you have Me."

*

"Never mind if you have not kept your word, or if you have fallen lower than yesterday. If you despise yourself and tell Me so in sorrow, you need not be afraid to believe that you are in My Heart — this Heart, so Great and Good, so unlike the hearts of mortals.

"From time to time, be glad to be counted as nothing; to look at all that you lack, at the good that you failed to do; to see the faults you did not want to commit, but committed after all. You may be sure, My child, that you don't see them all. I alone know the number and the weight of all your faults, yet, I Love you; I am Love.

"You know that your spiritual house is not firmly built and that its only foundations are in Me. When it topples, I take the debris and build a new temple more beautiful than the last, because you have humbled yourself. Think of this; it will help you to take pleasure in humiliations. Was I not intimately acquainted with humiliation during My entire life on earth?"

*

"When the moment of death comes for My friends, you believe, don't you, that I come gently to take souls into My Kingdom? You would do the same if you were taking someone into one of your beautiful homes. You would want to feel the joy of their surprise, wouldn't you? How could I, your God, who Love more and possess more, fail to be interested in the passing of My friends from time?

"Nothing that you may possibly have imagined of the Love of My Sacred Heart comes anywhere near the reality. Remember that I want your joy so much that I came down to earth to know suffering. When I see you suffer, and suffer for Me, I gather each of your sufferings with great Love, as though yours were greater than Mine, and had a value that My Heart would like to make infinite. This is why, when you allow Me to do so, I merge your life with Mine."

*

"Have you thanked Me for all I did for you, for mankind, for the Angels, for My Mother Mary? What a concert of blessings, My child! Gather them all as though they were yours, and join in the 'Symphony of Thanksgiving'. Sing your part in the choir of numberless voices, and I will know it from all the others. Are there two voices alike in the whole world? Are you not struck by the diversity in human creation? In Heaven too, each Saint differs from the other, and if you are enchanted by the variety of colors in your garden, you may be sure that Paradise flashes with a myriad of many-splendored things, all for My glory. There too, I know the voices, for I know all souls. My children, I atoned for all of you and I know My redeemed ones."

Lord, who will teach me to thank You and what words I should use?

"Use the most simple words which come straight from your heart. Say them to Me at Mass. Say them again after your Communion when we are only one. Once more it will be I who give them to you. How much I desire to act for Myself in you. Can you believe that? I feel at home, and I feel you are Mine."

*

"Keep going blindly. Take delight in knowing nothing about the future for the sole purpose of seizing an opportunity of abandoning it to Me. I know how to lead the blind by the best paths. When you, as a blind person, know that you are My child, won't you be glad of your infirmity, since it is your power over My Heart?"

*

271

Lord, I am ill.

"Use these discomforts for My Cause. Unite them to My sufferings. Offer them within My sufferings. I will make them fruitful. What better fruit, what fruit more urgently needed than those of the mission that will soon take place in your parish? Use your body and mind for it. Ask Me to shower new grace upon everyone: the aged and the active, women and children. When you ask in the name of the Son, believe that the Eternal Father grants your request. Keep on asking and I will keep on giving. While Moses prayed on the mountain with his arms raised toward Heaven, the Israelite armies fighting on the field were victorious, but when he grew weary of asking, the Israelites were forced to retreat. Stretch out your arms to God, for your brethren."

*

"My child, ponder more often on the value of the present moment, the danger of going back over the past, and the uselessness of gazing into the future. Just live the little moment that you hold in your hands."

*

"If your wealth were unlimited, wouldn't your gifts be fabulous? My treasures are boundless. As a friend who is fearful of burdening another with too great a sense of gratitude, I offer them to you so delicately, that you take them for granted without always appreciating their value."

*

"Do you realize how many sinners you can save in a single day? Think of My dazzling power, riches, and generosity. Who could hinder Me from giving gifts to you souls if I wish to do so?"

272

"I always make My Home among you. You see My House: the Tabernacle! I wait for all of you. In the world you have a day called 'open house' when you receive guests. Every day is an 'Open House' for Me. Nothing is lacking in My Home; you know that, don't you? At My 'Open House' you have the banquet, the spirit, the affection, and the gifts of My graces. You don't have to wait to be received. I am the One who waits. I know some who have never come. I don't mean who have never come to Me to confess their sins; I mean that they have never come to greet Me.

"Other souls come for certain ceremonies, but without the slightest thought that I am there waiting for them. They leave as they entered. Nothing in them has been stirred. My eyes follow them sadly, with My sadness of Gethsemane.

"You souls who come every day to My House, speak to Me of those other souls, so that before they come for the last time carried in a coffin, they will give Me their living bodies, their faculties, their entire being. With what warmth I shall receive them and respond to their trust!

"I have another temple which is your soul in a state of grace: a state of Me-in-you, since Grace is your Christ. Who can ever know the joy it gives Me to be loved there, even if your love is feeble! Do you know what it is to feel at home in a soul, to be the One waited for, the most loved, the most understood, the Head of the household? I am always ready to fulfill the desires of one who lives for Me alone.

"Beloved friend, be ever joyous and ready to please Me, eager to listen to Me, eager to deepen the love that you find so fleeting, poor, uncertain, and fragile, so fearful of falling into the same faults as yesterday. Let us close up all the portals of our home, so that we shall no longer hear the howling of the wolves. Let us forget the earth and its little things, and in the innermost sanctuary, which is within your own heart, let us speak our language of love, without words."

*

"You remember the person who offered you a handsome gift and said: 'Thank you for the honor you give me by accepting it.' You were pleasantly surprised. I offer Myself to you. I say: 'Thank you for the honor you give Me by accepting Me.' Humble yourself. Be filled with gratitude."

*

"Win souls, work for souls! Prayers, yes, but also sacrifices. Few of you think of this. Many laugh at it, and yet it is the money that buys and redeems. Do everything with gladness. Be joyous in love.

"How fleeting and small the earthly sacrifices are! Do you know that the Saints in Heaven would envy you? Their time of sacrifice is over.

"You realize that without Me, your life is empty. Meet Me more often. Enter into your Savior-God. This solitude of ours is of such wealth that even the Angels envy it, for the Angels have never received Holy Communion.

"Don't lose any time, since you told Me that everything was for Me."

"When you are at My Feet praying or meditating, why not be one in spirit with all the pure in heart who are praying and meditating? You are not a little church all by yourself. You are part of the great activity of Christ. In isolating yourself you break the chain; be linked together with other fervent people and aware of My desire for the pure of heart to be one. You remember My seamless robe?

"Become humble enough to lose yourself in everyone else and eager enough for merits, to seek to benefit by the merits of your brothers and sisters in Heaven, in purgatory, and on earth, since I permit this. I am the Father who has found a way to help His children get rich quickly. Having explained this to them, I wait for them to profit by it, for I suffer more than they do from their poverty. You don't see how poor you are. You should be careful to cover your clothing with someone else's garment in order to be pleasing in My sight.

"Do you want to think more often of this daily union with all My Christians in the world at this moment? Unite yourself to the suffering ones, the persecuted, the abandoned, those in exile and in prison, those who are martyred for My name's sake, the souls in ruined bodies who continue to bless Me, to serve Me and to call Me with all their love, right to their very last breath. Unite with them so that you may lose nothing of all this. Try to grasp the fact that these new treasures bring you ever nearer to Me. This is your goal: to reach Me. I am so eager to have you, that I stoop down, stretching out My Hands to you. Don't turn away. It's the proud who refuse a free gift. I desire you to do Me the favor of accepting My help. I will even say: 'Thank you!' "

*

"My Merits are Myself. My Merits never come to an end. They are fitted to everyone's needs. They only multiply as you take them."

*

Lord Jesus, the cold was intense and to honor You I did not light my fire.

"What a small deprivation, if in exchange you bring back sinners to Me!

"You do not feel yesterday's cold any more, and you cannot feel the cold of tomorrow, so it is only the present moment. What is a moment of discomfort in exchange for the salvation of souls who will praise Me eternally? You too, will know their joyous gratitude, but you will give all the glory to My Compassionate Heart, since you know that without My help you have done nothing."

O Lord, I have only little things to offer You, since I am ill.

"A little thing with great love is a big thing."

Lord, live in me. I need You, but you do not need me.

"Yes, I do need you, My Love needs you."

*

"Take great care of your love, since it is I."

"If you are weary, rest, but take this rest in My Heart. In no other place will you find the same love. I am Eternal Rest! I bought it with pain, when I gave Myself up. I have earned everything for you. Since it is for you, don't be afraid to accept. Don't be so timid and heedless. Offer My Merits to the Father, just as though they were your very own. How few make use of them! How few desire them! My Merits are there for the taking, all of them.

"If a man had sent out an invitation to every passerby to come to a sumptuous feast which he had gone to great trouble to obtain, would he not be wounded in the depths of his heart if, instead of eagerly accepting his invitation, people ignored it with contempt?

"If those persons who called themselves his intimate friends came only on rare occasions because of their forgetfulness (forgetfulness is a wound to Love), don't you think that this very generous man would be deeply offended, and that he would have every right to close his door?

"I am this Generous Man. My Banquet is free to all, even to the end of time.

"Come, all of you who have not yet felt the tenderness of the invitation, and bring your friends too; bring all of them. Come, take My riches; give them to the poor in confidence, the poor in desires, the poor in vision, for they think they are rich. The more you give, the more munificent your part will be.

"You don't ask Me for enough. Why are you so timid? Why don't I hear your voice? Don't you yet understand the joy I have in making your cup run over? Even if you don't understand, try to go deeper into the reality. Some explorers travel on the run, while others stop to study the details. Explore the boundless needs of My Heart in order to satisfy them. You will find that I am waiting for your requests on a bigger scale. Let your requests be humble, but powerful, contrite, but full of assurance.

"Be My delivery messenger, standing by until your arms are filled. My Angels will carry the gifts from door to door, but it must be you who procure them. I am waiting for you to lift the sinners from the mire again and again. The missions need your help. My priests need your help to persevere in My likeness; all the people in your time need your help, so that they will desire to be intimate with Me at every moment. Have I not deserved it? Have I not suffered more atrociously than words can describe? If you could only know! At least remember this: a word of love pays Me. When you bring your life close to My Life, to Heaven and the Eucharist, I will carry you in My arms and cover you with My merits.

"Let your way of asking be warm and long, joyous as though you already had the answer, loving because you are sure that you are Loved. Be generous and charming since you are full of My gifts. Do not tremble, but be daring, because it is in the name of Jesus that you are asking."

*

"Even when you are doing the most ordinary things, I am with you, because while I am the Greatest, I am also the Humblest, and nothing is ever deadly dull to Me. What is most obscure and despised only attracts Me more. Don't be afraid that I will leave you at certain moments; I Love you all the time."

*

"Do you know what you mean to Me? You were My reason for living and dying on this earth. It is you, little one, who tore Me from the splendors of My Father to go the length of human shame.

"When I look at you I see My horrible sufferings again and all the inventions of My Love, even before you were born. Now that you have received the breath of God and His likeness, what are you going to do for Me in the few days that remain for you on earth? Are you going to awaken your little heart to a new life so that it turns towards Me, or will you keep to your ordinary little trial flights without ever showing Me other upsoarings, warmer and more direct?

"I lived so strenuously for you. You can then understand, can't you, how much I desire the loving response of your life? I have an absolute need for the return-sacrifice of your body, and much more, of your faculties that you received from Me. Your desires can move your heart and make you act for Me. You can keep Me in your thoughts and desires; they are proof to Me of you. Your thoughts and desires can lead you to heroism and enable you to put Me on as clothing, that fits you in every detail.

279

"When your thoughts of confidence reach Me, I show Myself, joyful, thankful, and generous.

"I did not leave you during the thirty-three years of My Life on earth, nor will I leave you throughout eternity. I am your Globe. If you burn, it is in My fire. Your footsteps are Mine. I am your breathing. I ask you never to leave Me deliberately; I ask you to stay with Me to your last moment on earth, to the moment of our 'meeting'."

*

"Expect the Infinite, in other words, expect Me. What else would you expect but Love? Don't look for more, for in Love is everything good. Give thanks and give yourself."

Lord, I find nothing in myself worthy to offer You.

"Have I not told you that I am a collector of miseries? I am like one who mends china and is only happy when practicing this art on the thousand and one fragments of some beautiful object. I am like a painter who takes pleasure in touching up the colors of a faded canvas. I am a Surgeon who has put together broken limbs. Nothing, no one is beyond My care. It is all free. I am paid when My people pay attention to My Commandments and say with childlike tenderness: 'Thank You, dear God.' Is that too difficult?"

*

"Understand this: When you say: 'Lord, I love You,' you can go no farther, for you have said everything; you can only repeat.' "

†

*　　*　　*　　*　　*　　*　　*

The Sacred Heart of Jesus

Once as I was praying before the most Blessed Sacrament, Jesus disclosed to me the marvels of His Love and the inexplicable secrets of His Sacred Heart. He opened to me His Divine Heart.

Jesus: "My Divine Heart is so inflamed with Love for mankind, that, being unable any longer to contain within Itself the flames of Its burning Charity, It must be manifested to them in order to enrich them with the precious treasures which I reveal to you. My Sacred Heart contains all the Graces, Sanctification, and Salvation necessary to withdraw them from the abyss of hell."

I saw this Divine Heart more brilliant than the sun and transparent as crystal. This Heart has Its adorable Wound and is encircled with a crown of thorns which signify the pricks our sins cause It. It was surmounted by a cross which signifies that from the first moment of the Incarnation, when the Sacred Heart was formed, the cross was placed in It. From the very first moment this Heart was filled with all the bitterness, humiliations, sorrow, and contempt which His Sacred Humanity would have to suffer during the whole course of His Life and during His Holy Passion. Our Lord made me understand that the ardent desire He had of being loved by mankind and of rescuing them from the path of perdition into which satan was hurrying them in great numbers, had caused Him to reveal His Sacred Heart to mankind, together with all Its

The Sacred Heart of Jesus 1

treasures of Love, Mercy, Grace, Sanctification, and Salvation which It contains. Jesus did this, so that those who were willing to do all in their power to procure for His Heart: honor, love, and glory, might be enriched profusely with these divine treasures of the Heart of God. He told me that He must be honored with the symbol of His Heart, whose image He wished to be publicly exposed. He wanted me to carry it on my person, over my heart, that He might imprint His Love into it, to fill my heart with all the gifts with which His own Heart is filled, and destroy in my heart all inordinate affection. Wherever the image of His Sacred Heart would be exposed for veneration, He would pour forth His graces and blessings. He showed me that this devotion was as a last effort of His Love, which desires to favor mankind with this loving Redemption. The Sacred Heart will withdraw us from the empire of satan, which He intended to destroy, in order to place us under the gentle freedom of the Empire of His Love. This reign of His Love He would set up in the hearts of all those who would embrace this devotion.

On one occasion, while the Blessed Sacrament was exposed, Jesus, my Gentle Master, presented Himself to me, all resplendent with glory, His five Wounds, shining as so many suns. From His Sacred Humanity there issued flames on all sides, but especially from His most Loving and most Lovable Heart, the living source of the flames. It was then that He revealed to me the unspeakable marvels of His pure Love and showed me to what an excess He had Loved mortals from whom He received only ingratitude and neglect.

The Sacred Heart of Jesus 2

"I feel the ingratitude and neglect more acutely, than all that I suffered during My Passion. If only mankind would make some return for My Love, I would think little of all I have done for them and would wish, were it possible, to suffer still more. The return they make Me for all My eagerness to do them good, is to reject Me and treat Me with coldness. At least you should give Me the pleasure of making up for their ingratitude."

On another occasion, being before the Blessed Sacrament, I received from my God special tokens of His Love. I earnestly desired to correspond to His grace, and of rendering Him love for Love.

"Behold this Heart which has so Loved mankind, that It has spared nothing, even to exhausting and consuming Itself, in order to give them proof of Its Love. In return I receive from the greater number of them, nothing but ingratitude by reason of their irreverence and sacrileges, and by the coldness and contempt which they show Me in this Sacrament of Love. What I feel most keenly is, that the hearts which are consecrated to Me, treat Me with coldness and contempt.

"I therefore ask that the Friday after the Feast of Corpus Christi, be kept as a special Feast in honor of My Sacred Heart. Receive Holy Communion on that day; make reparation of honor to My Heart for all the unworthy treatment It has received, during the time It has been exposed on the altars. I promise you that My Heart shall give Its Divine Love in abundance to

The Sacred Heart of Jesus 3

all those who shall thus honor It, and cause It to be so honored."

This devotion to the Sacred Heart of Jesus will withdraw many souls from perdition and direct them toward salvation. That is why Jesus has such an ardent desire to be known, loved, and honored by mankind. He wants, by means of this devotion to His Sacred Heart, to establish in the hearts of all mankind, the reign of His pure Love.

It is necessary for us to be completely consumed in this burning furnace of the Sacred Heart of our Adorable Master, and never to depart. After we have lost our sinful hearts in the Divine Fire of Pure Love, we must then take from the Fire completely new hearts, that will make us henceforth live new lives, with thoughts and affections entirely new, and that will make us perform all our actions with dispositions altogether new in purity and fervor.

There must remain no longer anything of ourselves, rather this Heart of Jesus must take the place of our own so completely, that our Lord alone will live and act within us and for us. Our will must be so completely taken up by His, that He may be able to act in us without any resistance on our part. The affections, the thoughts, and the desires of the Heart of Jesus, but above all, Its Love must take the place of ours. It is then that His Love will Love Himself in us and for us. It is thus that this Lovable Heart, being all things to us, we shall be able to say with Saint Paul, that we no longer live, but that it is Christ who lives in us.

The Sacred Heart of Jesus 4*

Saint Margaret Mary's Ardent Aspirations
for Holy Communion

Great God, whom I adore veiled under these humble appearances, is it possible that You have so lowered Yourself as to take possession of this contemptible dwelling, so that You might come into my house and remain corporally with me? The Heavens are unworthy to contain You, and You are satisfied with these poor and weak Species of the Eucharist, so that You may be ever with me! O inconceivable Goodness, could I ever believe this, if You did not assure me of it? Could I dare to believe that You desire to enter my mouth, to repose upon my tongue, to descend into my heart? You will it then! To incite me to come, You have promised me a thousand benefits, O God of Majesty!

O God, would that I were all understanding to realize this Mercy, all heart to feel it, all tongue to publish it! What a God of Love must You then be, thus to create me to be the object of Your Love and the subject of Your ineffable Goodness! The Angels never cease to behold You; they desire this favor even while enjoying it. Shall I not wish to possess You? Since it pleases You, O my Amiable Savior, since my wants compel me to desire it, and Your Goodness permits me, I will open to You my mouth and my heart. Come, O Divine Sun! I am plunged in the horrible darkness of ignorance and sin; come, enlighten this obscurity and cause the Divine Light of Your Knowledge to illumine my understanding. Come, O Amiable Savior! You once delivered Yourself up entirely to save me from hell. I have fallen back miserably under the servitude of sin. My dearest Jesus, come once more to break my chains, burst my fetters, and set me at liberty. Come, O Charitable Physician of my soul! You have made me a bath of Your Blood, and in Baptism made me more holy and healthy than I deserved to be, yet I have, through my own fault, contracted a thousand dangerous diseases which bring trouble to my soul. Come, then, and cure me. I need it more than the paralytic whom You asked if he desired to be cured. Yes, my God, I wish it sincerely, but You know the coldness of this desire. By Your infinite Mercy, increase my fervor and desires!

O most faithful, most tender, and most gentle of all friends, come to my assistance! I, whom You Love am faint; dangerous and mortal infirmities oppress me. You know them, O my Savior! You read the depths of my heart. If until now I have been insensible to my misfortune and thoughtless of my danger, now, by Your grace, I complain, I cry out, I feel my wants and implore Your assistance.

By Your incomparable Love, and by Your own words, I entreat You to come and help me. Come, and never permit me to give You reason to leave me again. Come, O Life of my heart, O Soul of my life, only Support of my being, O Bread of Angels, Incarnate for Love of me, delivered up for my ransom, and prepared for my nourishment. Come, support me powerfully; satisfy me abundantly; make me truly live by You, in You, and for You! My only Beloved, if a

Ardent Aspirations 2

body were to be deprived of its soul, how earnestly would it seek the soul, how ardently would it call upon it to return! Have I so little feeling of the union between You and me, that I am not aware that when You are absent I am a body without a soul? My God and my All, come and animate once more my languishing soul, which sighs after You who are the Light of its beauty, the Principle of its motions, and the Source of its life. O Jesus, my Love, I beg You to absorb all created things by the power of Your Love. O Love, more ardent than fire, and sweeter than honey, grant that I may die consumed with the ardor of Your fire, as You have been willing to die of Love for me. O Lord, so wound this ungrateful heart in every part, and pierce it so thoroughly, that it may no longer be able to contain anything earthly or human, but be filled with the fullness of Your Love alone, since it is Yours, and wishes to be Yours eternally. Amen.

Ardent Aspirations 3*

* * * * *

To Jesus in the Blessed Sacrament

It is to honor You as Victim in this Sacrament of Love, that I come to You, O Divine Jesus, entreating You to be pleased to be my Sacrificer, immolating me upon the Altar of Your Loving Heart. As this victim is guilty in every way, I beseech You, O my Divine Sacrificer, to be willing to purify and consume it in the ardors of Your Divine Heart as a perfect holocaust, to give me a new life of love and grace in You! O my Sweet Jesus, only Love of my heart, sweet pain of my soul, and blessed martyrdom of my flesh and body, grant me the favor I ask of You as the Divine Victim: I. May I live and die the little victim of Your Sacred Heart, by an utter aversion for all that is not You. 2. May I be a victim of Your Love, by all the sorrow and desolation of which my heart is capable. 3. May I be a victim of Your Body, by the abandonment of everything which gratifies mine, through hatred of this criminal flesh, which I desire to crucify for the love of You. Amen.

* * * * *

Act of Love to the Sacred Heart of Jesus

O most Loving Heart of my only Beloved, unable to love and glorify You according to the extent of the desire You have given me, I invite all Heaven and earth to assist me; I unite myself to the burning Seraphim in order to love You. O Heart, burning with Love, why do You not set Heaven and earth on fire with Your pure Fire, to consume whatever they contain, that all creatures may breathe only Your Love? Oh, make me suffer or die, or at least change my heart entirely; consume me with Your most ardent heat, that I may love You perfectly.

O Divine Fire, O most pure Fire from the Heart of Jesus, my only Love, burn me without compassion, consume me without resistance. Do not spare me, since I am only fit to burn, and deserve only fire. O Love, O Love of Heaven and earth, come into my heart and reduce me to ashes! O devouring Fire of the Divinity, come and dissolve me, burn me, consume me in the midst of Your pure Fire, which cause those who die in them to live. Amen.

*

Act of Consecration to the Sacred Heart of Jesus

O Adorable Heart of my Amiable Jesus, You are the Seal of all Virtues, and the inexhaustible Source of every Grace. What did You see in me to induce You to Love me with such an excess of Love, while my heart, sullied with a thousand sins, felt only indifference and coldness toward You. The extraordinary testimonies of Your Love for me, even when I did not love You, make me hope that You will accept the proofs I now wish to give You of my love. Look favorably, then, O my Amiable Savior, upon my desire to consecrate myself entirely to the honor and glory of Your Sacred Heart. Accept the donation I make You of all that I am. To You I consecrate my person, my life, my actions, and my sufferings, wishing henceforth to be a victim consecrated to You, already burning, and one day, if it please You, to be consumed entirely in the sacred Fire of Your Love.

I offer You my heart with all the feelings of which it is capable, trusting and ardently desiring that during my whole life it may be perfectly conformed to the sentiments of Your Sacred Heart. I devote myself, Lord, entirely to Your Heart and entirely to You. O my God, let Your Mercies be great toward me! God of Majesty, what am I that You should deign to accept the sacrifice of my heart? It shall henceforth be all Yours, no other being shall divide its affections with You, for they are not worthy to do so. From now on, O my Amiable Jesus, be my Father, my Friend, my Master, and my All. I wish to live only for You. Receive, O Amiable Savior, the sacrifice made by the most ungrateful of creatures to Your Sacred Heart, in reparation for the offenses I have incessantly committed in corresponding so little to Your Love. I give You little indeed, but at least I give You all that I can give, and whatever I know You desire of me; I consecrate to You my heart; I intend never again to deprive You of it.

O Adorable Savior Jesus, teach me perfect forgetfulness of self, since that is the only way to find the entrance I so much desire into Your Sacred Heart. Since henceforth I shall do everything for You, grant that whatever I do may be worthy of You. Teach me what I should do to attain the purity of Your Love; give me this love, and let it be an ardent and generous love. Give me that humility without which it is impossible to please You. Perfectly accomplish in me Your Holy Will, in time and throughout all eternity. Amen. Act of Consecration 2*

*

Our Lord has revealed to me treasures of Love and favors for those who consecrate and sacrifice themselves to procure for His Heart all the honor and glory in their power; treasures so great as to be beyond expression. This Amiable Heart has an infinite desire to be known and loved by Its creatures, in whom It wishes to establish Its Kingdom, in order to provide for all their wants, since It is the Source of every Blessing. For this reason It desires to be addressed with great confidence. It seems to me that there is no more efficacious means of obtaining what we ask, than by doing so through the mediation of the ever-blessed Sacrifice of the Mass.

Act of Reparation to the Sacred Heart of Jesus

Most Adorable and Amiable Jesus, You are ever full of Love for us, You are ever concerned about our miseries, You desire to impart Your treasures to us, and even to give Yourself to us. Jesus, my Savior and my God, by an excess of the most ardent and wonderful Love, You have placed Yourself in the state of Victim in the adorable Eucharist, where a million times a day You offer Yourself in Sacrifice for us. What must be Your feelings in that State, when, notwithstanding all this, You find in the greater part of mankind nothing but coldness, forgetfulness, ingratitude, and contempt! Was it not enough, O my Savior, to have chosen the most painful way to save us? You could have testified Your excessive Love at much less cost! Was it not enough to have abandoned Yourself for a time to that cruel Agony, to that tremendous Sorrow, caused by the sight of our sins with which You were loaded? Why will You still expose Yourself day by day, to all the indignities of which the blackest malice of mortals and devils are capable? My God and my ever Blessed Redeemer, what are the sentiments of Your Sacred Heart at the sight of all this ingratitude and all these sins? With what bitter sorrow must Your Heart have been overwhelmed at so many sacrileges and outrages!

My heart is affected with extreme regret for all these indignities. I am prostrate and annihilated before You, to make reparation in the sight of Heaven and earth for all the irreverence and insults which You have received upon our altars since the institution of this Adorable Sacrament.

With a humbled and broken heart, a thousand times I ask Your pardon for all these indignities. Oh, that I were able, my God, to water with my tears, and wash with my blood, all the places where Your Sacred Heart has been so awfully insulted, and where the marks of Your Divine Love have been received with contempt! Oh, that I could by some kind of homage, humiliation, or annihilation, repair so many sacrileges and profanations! Oh, that I could for one moment be the master of the hearts of all mortals, to repair in some way, by the sacrifice I would make of them to You, the forgetfulness and insensibility of all those who have not known You, or who have known and loved You so little!

O my Amiable Savior, what covers me with still greater confusion, and should make me grieve the most, is that I have been among the number of these ungrateful beings. You see my heart; You know the sorrow I feel at my ingratitude, and my regret at seeing You so unworthily treated. You know my earnest desire to suffer anything and do anything to repair these offenses. Behold me, then, O Lord, with a heart broken with sorrow, humbled and prostrate before You, ready to receive from Your Hand whatever You shall exact from me in reparation for so many outrages. Strike, O Lord, strike; I will bless the hand which shall inflict upon me so just a punishment. Oh, that I were a proper victim to repair such injuries!

Oh, that I could water with my blood all those places where Your Sacred Body has been thrown upon the ground, and trampled under foot. Happy I

Act of Reparation 2

would be if I could, by every possible torment, repair so many outrages, so much contempt and impiety. If I do not deserve this favor, at least accept the sincere desire I feel for it.

Eternal Father, receive this reparation that I make You, in union with the prayer made by this Sacred Heart upon Calvary, and the prayer which Holy Mary made at the foot of Her Son's Cross. In consideration of the prayer which His Sacred Heart offers You in reparation, pardon my many acts of irreverence. By Your grace render efficacious the will that I have, and the resolution I make, to omit nothing in my power in order to love ardently, and to honor in every possible way my Sovereign, my Savior, and my Judge, whom I believe to be really present in the Adorable Eucharist.

Eternal Father, I intend henceforth to show by my respect in the presence of the Blessed Eucharist, that I believe my Jesus to be really present. I will make my profession of singularly honoring His Sacred Heart. It is also in this same Heart that I wish to pass the remainder of my life. Grant me this one favor: that at the hour of my death, I may render my last sigh in the Sacred Heart of Jesus. Amen.

Act of Reparation 3*

*   *   *   *   *   *   *

Promises of our Lord Jesus Christ
to Saint Margaret Mary, in favor of persons
devoted to His Sacred Heart.

1. "I will give souls devoted to Me all the graces for their state of life.

2. "I will establish peace in their families.

3. "I will bless every house in which the picture of My Heart shall be exposed and honored.

4. "I will console them in all their difficulties.

5. "I will be their Refuge during life and especially at the hour of death.

6. "I will pour abundant blessing upon all their undertakings.

7. "Sinners shall find in My Heart a Fountain and a boundless Ocean of Mercy.

8. "Tepid souls shall become fervent.

9. "Fervent souls shall rise speedily to great perfection.

10. "I will give to priests the power of touching the hardest hearts.

11. "Those who propagate this devotion shall have their names written in My Heart, never to be blotted out.

12. "I promise you, in the excessive Mercy of My Heart, that My all powerful Love will grant to all who receive Communion on the first Friday of the month, for nine consecutive months, the Grace of final penitence; they shall die in My pleasure after receiving the Holy Sacraments; My Divine Heart shall be their safe Refuge in this last moment."

The Abyss of the Sacred Heart of Jesus is suited to every disposition of the needy and suffering soul.

The Sacred Heart of Jesus is an Abyss where everything may be found. It is especially an Abyss of Love, in which every other love should be swallowed up: self-love with its evil effects, which are human respect and the desire of exalting and satisfying ourselves. In burying these evil inclinations in the Abyss of Divine Love, you will find all the Treasures necessary for your needs.

If you, O soul, are in an abyss of privation and desolation, this Divine Heart is an Abyss of all Consolation, in which we must lose ourselves without desiring to feel Its Sweetness.

If you are in an abyss of dryness and weakness, bury yourself in the Heart of Jesus Christ which is an Abyss of Power and Love, without being eager to taste the Sweetness of this Love until He wishes to give it to you.

If you are in an abyss of poverty and deprivation of everything, bury yourself in the Heart of Jesus. It is filled with Treasures. It will enrich you, if you permit It to do so.

If you are in an abyss of weakness, of failings and miseries, go frequently to the Heart of Jesus. It is an Abyss of Mercy and Strength. It will relieve and fortify you.

If you, O soul, are conscious that you are filled

with pride and vain self esteem, bury these quickly in the deep humiliations of the Heart of Jesus. That Humble Heart of Jesus is the Abyss of Humility.

If you find yourself in an abyss of ignorance and darkness, the Sacred Heart of Jesus is an Abyss of Light and Knowledge. Learn especially to love Him, and to do only what He desires of you.

If you, O soul, are in an abyss of infidelity and inconstancy, the Divine Heart of Jesus is one of Constancy and Fidelity. Bury yourself in His Heart; you will find in the Sacred Heart, a Love which is constant in loving us and helping us.

If you feel, as it were, buried in death, go to the Heart of Jesus. You will find in the Sacred Heart an Abyss of Life, and you will draw from It a new life, a life by which you will regard everything with the eyes of Jesus Christ; you will act only as He prompts you; you will speak only with His tongue; you will love only with His Sacred Heart.

If you are in an abyss of ingratitude, the Heart of Jesus is an Abyss of Gratitude. Draw from His Heart all that you need. Offer His Heart to God the Father for all the benefits you have received from Him, and beg Jesus to supply gratitude for you from His abundance.

If you find yourself overcome with agitation, impatience, or anger, go to the Heart of Jesus which is an Abyss of Sweetness.

Abyss - Sacred Heart 2

If you are in an abyss of dissipation and distraction, you will find in the most Sacred Heart of Jesus an Abyss of Recollection and Fervor which will supply everything, which will repair your heart and imagination by uniting them to Him.

If you find yourself plunged in an abyss of sadness, bury the sadness in the Sacred Heart of Jesus, which is an Abyss of Heavenly Joy, and the Treasury of all the delight of the Saints and Angels.

If you are in trouble or in anxiety, the Divine Heart is an Abyss of Peace, and that Peace will be communicated to you.

When you are in an abyss of bitterness and suffering, unite them to the Abyss of the infinite Sufferings of the Heart of Jesus; you will learn to suffer with Jesus, and to be contented to suffer.

When you are in an abyss of fear, the Heart of Jesus is an Abyss of Confidence and Love. Abandon yourself to His Heart. In His Heart you will learn that fear should yield to Love.

Finally, everywhere and in everything, bury yourself in this Ocean of Love and Charity. If possible, never depart from It. May we only be penetrated with the Fire by which the Sacred Heart of Jesus is inflamed for God and mankind, as the iron is aglow in the furnace, or as a sponge cast into the sea is filled with its waters.

* Abyss of the Sacred Heart 3*

Consecration to the Sacred Heart of Jesus

My Lord Jesus, I, N . . . give and consecrate to Your Sacred Heart, my person and my life, my actions, penances, and sufferings, not wishing to make use of any part of my being, for the future except, in honoring, loving, and glorifying Your Sacred Heart.

It is my unchanging will to be entirely Yours, and to do everything for Your Love, renouncing with my whole heart whatever might displease You. I take You then, O most Sacred Heart, as the sole Object of my love, as the Protector of my life, as the Pledge of my salvation, as the Remedy of my frailty and inconstancy, as the Repairer of all the defects of my life, and as my secure Refuge in the hour of death.

Be then, O Heart of Goodness, my justification before God the Father; remove from me His just wrath. O Heart of Love, I place all my confidence in You. While I fear all things from my malice and frailty, I hope for all things from Your Goodness.

Consume in me then whatever can displease or be opposed to You; may Your Pure Love be so deeply impressed upon my heart, that it may be impossible that I should ever be separated from You, or forget You.

I implore You, by all Your Goodness, that my name may be written in Your Sacred Heart. In You I wish to place all my happiness and glory, living and dying in bondage to You. Amen.

Saint Margaret Mary's method of rendering,
by each action, Homage to the Sacred Heart
of Jesus in the Blessed Sacrament.

O Blessed Virgin Mary, every morning I place
myself under Your protection; I entreat You to
present me to Jesus in the Blessed Sacrament.

O Jesus, I unite my soul to Yours, that You may
preserve me from sin. I unite my heart to Your
Sacred Heart, that whatever is displeasing to You
may be consumed in It. I unite myself entirely
to You, so that You may supply for all my
deficiencies.

I unite my prayer to the prayers which You
make for mankind in the Blessed Sacrament,
and then I offer to God the prayer which You,
my Divine Savior, offer to repair all the defects
and loss of time of which I am guilty.

O Jesus, at the Holy Sacrifice of the Mass I unite
my praises to Yours. I endeavor to enter into
Your Holy Intention, that You may ever supply
for my deficiencies before Your Father. I will
attentively consider Your obedience to the priest,
whether good or bad, who offers You. You place
Yourself in the priest's hands to undergo a
Mystical Death, without showing any aversion. You
take the nature of man, to be immolated and
sacrificed according to the designs of the priest
who consecrates. To conform myself to You, I will
be prompt to obey. As a victim of immolation,
I will place myself in the hands of my superiors,
of whatever sort they may be, that being entirely
dead to my own will, inclinations, and passions,

they may dispose of me as they choose without my showing any aversion. The violence that I do to myself shall be to honor that which You offer to Yourself by entering into souls sullied by sin; it is an act of which You have so great a horror, that every time You do so, You renew, so to speak, Your mortal agony in the Garden of Olives.

Your Life, O Jesus, in this Blessed Sacrament is hidden from the eyes of creatures, who perceive nothing but the poor appearance of bread. In like manner, I will endeavor to keep myself so hidden, as to have no greater joy than to find myself surrounded by all that is most abject and poor; ever availing myself of the rebuffs and contempt I encounter from creatures, in order to remain buried under the ashes of humility. By this means I will endeavor to comfort You in the contempts, injuries, sacrileges, profanations, and indignities that You experience in this hidden Life, without ever becoming weary or complaining of them. With this view, I will neither complain nor excuse myself, thinking that everyone has a right to accuse me, humble me, and make me suffer, since the love of Your Sacred Heart obliges me to bear everything without saying: "It is enough."

My Jesus, You are ever solitary in the Blessed Sacrament. In the Eucharist You converse with God alone. To be like You, I will be everywhere solitary, conversing interiorly with You alone. My understanding shall have no other desire than to know You, and my heart no ardor or desire but to love You.

Whenever I go to eat, I beg You, my Jesus, to guard me against myself. I entreat You to make the nourishment I am going to take for love of You, a spiritual Communion for me, by which Your grace may be diffused in my soul and nourish it, and that my heart may be watered with Your Love.

At recreation, I will be attentive to recreate Your Heart, O Jesus, by speaking willingly of You, by consecrating all my conversation to the Divine Word. Do not permit me to say anything contrary to Your glory; let me cheerfully accept the humiliations that I may meet there.

O Jesus, when I am oppressed by heat, I beg You, O burning Furnace of Pure Love, to inflame my heart, and all hearts, with Your Divine Fire, that being consumed, we may become a fire of love in order to love You incessantly.

O Jesus, when I suffer thirst, it shall be in honor of the thirst which Your Adorable Heart experiences for the salvation of mankind, and that You may be known, adored, and loved by them in the Sacrament of Your Love.

In taking my repose, I unite it to Your Sacred Heart, O Jesus, which from all eternity existed in the bosom of Your Father. I offer You all my respirations and the movements of my heart, to be, during my sleep, so many acts of love and sacrifice of my whole being to You. I beg You to permit my repose to give me new strength, so that I may serve You faithfully.

St. Margaret Mary's Prayer at Holy Mass

Eternal Father, I beseech You to receive the offering I make of the Heart of Jesus Christ, Your Beloved Son, as He offers Himself to You in Sacrifice. Be pleased to accept this offering for me, with all the desires, sentiments, affections, heartbeats, and actions of His Sacred Heart. They are all mine, since He immolates Himself for me. I desire, for the future, never to have any other intentions than His. Receive them in satisfaction for my sins, and in thanksgiving for all Your benefits. Receive them, and grant me, through their Merits, all the graces necessary for me, particularly the grace of final perseverance. Receive them as so many acts of love and praise which I offer to Your Divine Majesty, since it is by Him alone that You are worthily honored and glorified. Amen.

*

O Heart of Love, I place my trust entirely in You.

*

O Jesus, it is best to give up everything rather than lose the Love of Your Sacred Heart!

*

I understand that life without Your Love, my Jesus, is the greatest of all miseries.

*

O Jesus, it will be sweet to die after having had a devotion to the Sacred Heart of my Judge, my Savior, and my All!

*

I enter into Your Heart, O Jesus, as into a school. In Your School is taught the Science of the Saints, the Science of Pure Love. O Sacred Heart, You are my Love, my Life, my Strength, my King.

†

* * * * * * *

"You are nothing! Apart from Me you are nothingness.

"God alone Is.

"I am your Life. I am as inseparable from you as your breathing, as the breath within your soul. I am so near to you.

"It is I who incline you to be patient, to be gentle. Ask all of Me; ask every day and every morning what is necessary for the day; don't cease to ask for yourself and for the whole human race. It is My joy to answer! I always answer!"

*

"This is love: to clothe others with grace and virtue that will make them pleasing to Me. I clothe you with grace in giving you My Body and Blood!

"My Heart will give you joy, strength, meekness, and love, for I wish you to be joyous and strong, irresistibly loving and very meek."

*

"Do you believe that in the Sacred Host where I seem to be doing nothing, I am working? I work by the immolation of Myself to the Father's Will. I work imperceptibly but efficaciously on souls.

"Many souls who are Mine join their actions to Mine in the quiet way of immolation; there is nothing to be seen, and yet it is the most powerful action. Will you follow Me so far?"

"Do not lose your serenity on account of your work. As a religious, you must dominate the task assigned to you, otherwise you would only be a hired worker."

*

"There are many little troubles in the interior life of a cloister, many sufferings in bearing one another's faults, but what are faults compared with the crimes committed in the world?

"Your real Cloister, without boundaries, is My Sacred Heart; It is your Refuge and your Rest. My Heart is always open; It is always awaiting you."

*

"Am I not enough for you? Is it not sufficient for you to know that your Jesus Loves you?"

*

"How could you love the soul of some sinner who is in need of your sacrifices, if you do not unreservedly love a soul quite close to you, in which I dwell, and which is perhaps greater than your own soul? Such are the demands of the Communion of Saints."

*

"Never appear alone before the most Holy Trinity, but always with Me and with My Holy Virgin Mother Mary. We have adopted you! You have given Me your humanity; I wish to live in you. I pray within you."

*

"The perfect fidelity of one soul makes reparation for many. It is not the quantity of your offerings that honors Me, but the quality of your gift.

"The best gift you can give Me is to receive Me."

"I am Living in the Blessed Sacrament, in the Real Presence.

"I, the Real Presence, am also living in each soul that is in the state of sanctifying grace. Why don't you adore in spirit My Presence in your neighbor?

"I am always your neighbor. Through your neighbor I ask for your help; through your neighbor I give you My gifts. The Holy Trinity is in the soul of your neighbor who is in the state of sanctifying grace. If the Holy Trinity is not in the soul of your neighbor because of sin, help the soul to receive It back by treating the soul as if I were already dwelling within it."

*

"I loved suffering, I the Man of Sorrows; I chose it because it makes reparation for sins when it is offered with love.

"It is love that makes reparation, because that which offends God in sin is the absence of love. When suffering is joined to love, the proofs of love given through suffering are a true reparation offered to God. It is giving God something He does not have in His Heaven.

"I chose suffering so that all My creatures, even the most miserable, like yourself, might have something precious to offer to God."

*

"The time that you have spent in praying and loving, has been the most useful time of your life; then you have obeyed your vocation. All that is done apart from Me, apart from Love, is wasted."

305

"There is an abyss between the Creator and the creature. Your value does not lie in your personal capabilities, however brilliant they may be, but in your capacity to receive your Creator and allow Him to live and shine through you. Be faithful to Me unto death."

"It is I who inspire your desires and encourage your generosity so that they may increase, and in order that I may have the joy of fulfilling even greater desires in you.

"I am as near you as your own breath, and you seek Me so far away in formulas and attitudes outside of yourself!"

*

"There must be victims who mingle their blood with My Blood at Calvary. Reparation is Justice, Order, and Divine Wisdom. Sanctity requires reparation.

"There must be victims who will be witnesses to My Word, in order that it may be transmitted, and that it may be accurately perpetuated."

*

"Do you think that I will abandon you at the moment of death, you who are so miserable that you cannot live without Me? As a mother embraces her newborn child, so will I enfold you in My Love, because you are My tiny child, and I know that you cannot live without Me."

*

"When you waste your time, you do Me an injury; you treat My gifts with contempt; the 'present' I surrender to your love and to your generosity."

306

Victim Souls

"I desire an army of voluntary victims who, in order to save souls, will give Me the help which is refused by worldly souls.

"I desire an army of apostolic souls consecrated to Me by the Vow of Victim, not to expiate the sins of others by extraordinary trials; that is not what I desire.

"I desire a great army of victim souls who will join Me in the Apostolate of My Eucharistic Life, who will bind themselves by the Vow of Victim, choosing the methods which I chose: silence, immolation, and love.

"I desire an army of victim souls who confine their efforts to imitating My Apostolate: for I am the Master and I have been the servant of all.

"The Vow of Victim will give you the strength of greater fidelity to be the servant of all, so that My Spirit may spread and all souls may believe My Words.

"I desire victim souls to be everywhere: in the world and in the cloisters; in every occupation, in every station of life, in the fields and in the factories, in schools and in stores, in families and in convents, in business and in the arts, everywhere, so that their fidelity may bear witness to My Words.

"You souls who offer yourselves as victims are more closely united to Me. The more I Love a soul, the more I desire to associate that soul with My Apostolate. Look at My Saints and look at My Holy Virgin Mother Mary.

"I ask you souls who bind yourselves more closely to Me by the Vow of Victim, to listen to Me more than you speak to Me; to strive to reproduce My Actions, My way of acting. I ask you souls to be before mankind as you are before Me, in a state of poverty that begs, not in a state of spiritual wealth that gives alms of its surplus.

"I ask you victim souls to confine your efforts to spreading My Gentleness and My Kindness which does not dwell on evil, but overcomes evil by good. Be exacting with no one but yourself. You will help souls by your silence. You will also receive the grace which your fidelity and sacrifices will obtain from Me for other souls."　　Victim Souls 2*

*

"Where there is no injustice, there is not the virtue of reparation. There may be other virtues, but not reparation which I practiced by preference in My Apostolic Life and in My Passion, which My Holy Virgin Mother also practiced, which I ask of souls who are dearest to Me, and which I expect of My spouses. It is where injustice exists that you are called to overcome evil by good."

*

"If you suffer, come nearer to Me. I am always waiting for you. I will tell you My secrets which console and strengthen. I Love you and I will take care of you. I wish you to be entirely Mine. You have such need of Me! I will shelter you in the secret places of My Heart; you are My tiny child!"

†

*   *   *   *   *   *   *

"The Eucharist is Light."

"My Son, whose Body is a Sun, because He is One with Me, the True Sun, in such a way that He cannot be separated or divided from Me, as is the natural sun, whose heat and light cannot be separated, so perfect is their union. The sun, never leaving its orbit, lights the whole world and warms whoever wishes to be warmed by it. The sun is not defiled by any impurity on which it shines; its light, heat, and color are united. The Body of Christ in the Eucharist is a Sun. You cannot receive the Body without the Blood, or the Blood or the Body without the Soul of the Incarnate Word, nor the Soul or the Body, without the Divinity of Me, the Eternal God, because none of these can be separated from each other. The Divine Nature never left the human nature, so you receive the whole Divine Essence in the most sweet Sacrament, concealed under the whiteness of the bread. As the sun cannot be divided into light, heat, and color, the whole of God and the whole of Man cannot be separated under the white mantle of the Host. Even if the Host should be divided into a million particles, if it were possible, in each particle I would be present, whole God and Man. When a mirror is broken, the reflection that is seen is not broken; similarly, when the Host is divided, God and Man are not divided, but remain in each particle, nor is the Sacrament diminished in Itself.

"If you had a candle, and all the people in the world would take light from it, your light would not be diminished, yet each person has it all. It is true that everyone participates in this light, according to the substance into which each one receives the fire. Suppose that there are many souls who bring their candles, some small and some large, and light them in the flame. In each candle, whether it is large or small, there is the whole light, that is to say, the heat, the color and the flame; nevertheless it would seem that those with the smaller candle have less light than those with the larger candle. The same thing happens to those who receive the Eucharistic. Each one carries a candle, that is, the holy desire, which is received in this Sacrament. The candle is without light, but it is lighted by receiving the Eucharist. I say without light, because you can do nothing of yourselves, though I have given you the material with which you can receive this Light and feed it. The material is love, for through Love I created you, and without Love you cannot live.

"Your being, given to you through Love, has received the right disposition in Baptism, which you receive in virtue of the Blood of the Word, for, in no other way, could you participate in this Light. You would not be a candle, but wax without a wick inside it, which cannot burn or receive light, if you had not received in your souls the wick which catches this Divine Fire, that is to say, the Holy Faith, which you receive by grace in Baptism, united with the disposition of your soul, so fitted for Love, that without Love, which is your food, you cannot live.

"The soul, united in this way, obtains Light at the Fire of My Divine Love, loving and fearing Me, and observing the lessons of My Truth. The soul becomes lighted according to the material which it brings to the fire. All have one and the same material, in that all are created to My image and likeness. You Christians possess the Light of Holy Baptism; you may grow in love and virtue by the help of My grace, as you desire. You do not change the form I have given you, but you can increase your strength in love and your free will, by using it while you still have time. You can increase in love, by going with love to receive the sweet and glorious Light, which I have given you as food for your service, through My priests; you receive this Light according to the love and fiery desire with which you approach this Light.

"You souls receive the entire Light, in spite of the difference in weight of the candles, because the Light cannot be divided, neither on account of any imperfection of the priest, nor of those who receive It. You personally participate in this Light, that is, in the grace which you receive in this Sacrament, according to the holy desire with which you dispose yourself to receive It.

"Those souls who go to this sweet Sacrament in guilt of mortal sin, will receive no grace, though they actually receive the whole of God and the whole of Man. Do you know the condition of a soul who receives Me unworthily? It is like a lighted candle on which water has fallen, for no sooner has the water touched fire, than it is extinguished, and nothing remains but smoke; so the soul casts the water of guilt within its mind upon the wick of its own candle which it received in Holy Baptism. The soul should have heated it at the fire of true contrition and confession, before receiving this Light with the body and not the mind. The Light, since the soul is not disposed as it should be for so great a mystery, does not remain by grace in that soul, but leaves it, and in the soul, remains only greater confusion, for the Light of Grace is extinguished and its sin increased. Of the Sacrament, the soul feels only the pangs of a remorseful conscience, not through the defect of the Light, for the Light cannot be hurt, but on account of the water that was in the soul, which impeded its proper disposition, so that it could not receive the Light.

"This Light, united with its heat and its color, cannot be divided, either by the scanty desire of the soul who receives the Sacrament, or by any defect which may be in the soul, or by any defect of the priest, anymore than the sun can be defiled by shining on anything foul. The sweet Light of this Sacrament cannot be defiled, divided, or diminished in any way, nor can It be detached from Its Orbit.

"If all souls would receive Holy Communion, the Light and heat of this Sun, the Word, My Only-Begotten Son would still not be separated from Me, the True Sun, His Eternal Father. In this Mystical Body, the Holy Church, He is given to whoever will receive Him. He remains wholly with Me, the Eternal Father, and yet you have Him, whole God and whole Man. If all souls were to take light from It, each would have It entirely, and yet It would remain whole."

"See in what an excellent state is your soul and all souls who receive Me, the Bread of Life. Since you receive Me in this Holy Sacrament, which is a Divine Ocean, in the state of sanctifying grace, you dwell in Me and I in you, as the fish in the water of the sea, and the water of the sea in the fish. I dwell in your soul as sanctifying grace, for since you have received the Bread of Life in a state of grace, My grace remains in you after the accidents of bread have been consumed. See then how you are obliged to love Me because I Love you so much, and, being the Supreme and Eternal Good, deserve your love."

*

"Unite yourself always to Me, for I am the Supreme and Eternal Purity. I am that Fire which purifies the soul. The closer you come to Me, the purer you become, and the further you are from Me, the more purity leaves you. This is the reason why mortals fall into such iniquities, for they are separated from Me, while the soul that unites itself directly to Me, participates in My Purity."

*

"As you desire your will to be one with My Will, you cannot desire other than what I desire; though you desire to come and be with Me in Heaven, you are contented to remain on earth, if I desire you to stay with your pain, for the greater praise and glory of My Name and the salvation of souls.

"When you are suffering, you are also rejoicing, because the enduring of many tribulations is to you a relief of the desire you have for death. You not only endure your sufferings with patience, but you give glory to My Name in bearing much tribulation.

"Were it possible for you to have virtue without toil, you would not want it. You would prefer to delight in the cross with Christ, with its pain, rather than obtain Heaven in an easy way. Why? It is because you are inflamed and steeped in the Blood, where you find the blaze of My Charity, which is a Fire proceeding from Me, ravishing your heart and mind and making your sacrifices acceptable. The eye of your intellect is lifted up and gazes into My Deity, where your affection is nourished and united with Me. This is a sight which I grant to the soul, infused with grace, which in truth, loves and serves Me."

*

"The dignity of the priesthood belongs to the good and bad alike. All priests have the Sun to administer. Good priests illumine and warm their neighbors through their love and with their light. With this heat they cause virtues to spring up and bear fruit in the souls of their subjects.

"I have appointed priests to be, in truth, your guardian angels, to protect you, to inspire your heart with good thoughts by their holy prayers, to teach you My Doctrine reflected in the mirror of their life, and to serve you by administering to you the Holy Sacraments. Priests watch over you and inspire you with good and holy thoughts as does an angel.

"Worthy priests are My beloved children; they shine as a sun in the Mystical Body of Holy Church."

"The devil is the instrument of My Justice."

"The devil is the instrument of My Justice to torment the souls who have miserably offended Me. I also permit the devil to tempt My creatures, not for My creatures to be conquered, but that they may conquer, proving their virtue, and afterwards receive from Me the glory of victory. You should not fear any battle or temptation of the devil that may come to you, because I have made you and all creatures strong. I have given you strength of will, fortified in the Blood of My Son. Neither the devil nor any creature can move your free will, because it is yours, given by Me. You therefore, with free arbitration, can use it as you please. It is a tool, which, if you place it in the hands of the devil, becomes a knife with which he strikes and slays you. If you do not give this knife of your own free will into the hands of the devil, that is, if you do not consent to his temptations, you will never be injured by the guilt of sin in any temptation. You will even be fortified by temptation, when the eye of your intellect is opened to see My Love which allowed you to be tempted, so as to arrive at virtue, by being proved.

"You do not arrive at virtue except through a knowledge of yourself, which is more perfectly acquired in the time of temptation, because then you know yourself to be nothing, being unable to remove from yourself the pains and vexations from which you would flee. You do not arrive at virtue except through a knowledge of Me, and you know Me in your will which is fortified by My Goodness, so that it does not yield to the temptation. My Love permits these temptations. The devil is weak, and by himself can do nothing unless I allow him. I let the devil tempt you and all souls, through love, and not through hatred, that you may conquer, and not be conquered, that you may come to a perfect knowledge of yourself and of Me, and that virtue may be proved, for it is proved only by its contrary."

*   *   *

O God, how do worldly people give You praise and glory, whether they will to or not?

"Worldly people, whether they will it or not, give glory and praise to My Name. They do not do so in the way they should: loving Me above everything. My Mercy shines in them, in the abundance of My Charity; I give them time, and do not order the earth to open and swallow them up on account of their sins. I even wait for them, and command the earth to give them of her fruits, the sun to give them light and warmth, and the sky to move above them. By My Charity and Mercy, I even permit them to use the goods of the earth.

"I often give more to sinners than to righteous souls, because righteous souls are able to endure privation. I take from righteous souls the goods of the world, that they may more abundantly enjoy the Goods of Heaven. In sinful, worldly mortals, My Mercy and Charity shine, and they give praise and glory to My Name, even when they persecute My servants, for they prove in them the virtues of patience and charity, causing them to suffer humbly and offer to Me their persecutions and injuries, thus turning them into My praise and glory."

A Prayer of Saint Catherine of Siena

Thanks, thanks to You, O Eternal Father, for You have not despised me, the work of Your hands. You have not turned Your Face from me, nor despised my desires. You, the Light, have not regarded my darkness; You, True Life, have not regarded my living death; You, the Physician, have not been repelled by my grave infirmities.

You, the Eternal Purity, have not considered the many miseries of which I am full; You, who are Infinite, have overlooked that I am finite; You, who are Wisdom, have overlooked my folly. Your Wisdom, Your Goodness, Your Clemency, Your infinite Good, have overlooked the evils and sins which are in me.

Having known the Truth through Your Clemency, I have found Your Charity, and the love of my neighbor. What has constrained You? Not my virtues, but only Your Charity! May that same Charity constrain You to illumine the eyes of my intellect with the Light of Faith, so that I may know and understand the truth which You have manifested to me.

Grant, O Lord, that my memory may be capable of retaining Your Benefits, that my will may burn in the Fire of Your Charity, and may that Fire so work in me, that I may unlock the door of Heaven.

With all my heart, I ask that these same benefits and favors may be showered on all the members of the Mystical Body of Your Holy Church.

Prayer of St. Catherine 1

I confess and do not deny that You Loved me before I existed, and that Your Love for me is ineffable.

O Eternal Trinity, O Godhead which gave value to the Blood of Your Son. You, O Eternal Trinity, are a deep Sea, into which the deeper I enter, the more I find, and the more I find, the more I seek. My soul cannot be satiated except in You, for I continually hunger after You, the Eternal Trinity, desiring to see You with light in Your Light.

As the deer desires water from the spring, so my soul desires to leave the prison of this dark body and see You in truth. How long, O Eternal Trinity, Fire and Abyss of Love, will Your Face be hidden from my eyes? O melt at once the cloud of my body.

The knowledge which You have given me of Yourself in Your Truth, constrains me to abandon the heaviness of my body, and to give my life for the glory and praise of Your Name. I have tasted and seen with the light of my intellect in Your Light, the Abyss of You, the Eternal Trinity, and the beauty of Your creature, for, looking at myself in You, I saw myself to be Your image. My life was given to me by Your Power and Your Wisdom, O Eternal Father, which belongs to Your Only-Begotten Son. My life, shining in my intellect and my will, is one with Your Holy Spirit, who proceeds from You and Your Son, by whom I am able to love You.

You, Eternal Trinity, are my Creator, and I am

Prayer of St. Catherine 2

the work of Your Hands. I know through the New Creation which You have given me in the Blood of Your Son, that You are inflamed with love of the beauty of Your workmanship.

O Abyss, O Eternal Godhead, O profound Sea, what more could You give me than Yourself! You are the Fire which ever burns without being consumed; You consume in Your Heat all the soul's self-love; You are the Fire which takes away all cold. With Your Light You illumine me, so that I may know all Your Truths. Your Holy Light is above all light, which illumines supernaturally the eye of my intellect, clarifying the Light of Faith so abundantly and so perfectly, that I see my soul is alive, and my soul receives You, the True Light.

By the Light of Holy Faith, I have acquired wisdom in the Wisdom of the Word, Your Only-Begotten Son. In the Light of Holy Faith, I am strong, constant, and persevering. In the Light of Holy Faith, I hope. Let me not faint by the way. This Light teaches me the Road, and for this I say: "O Eternal Father, You have illuminated me with the Light of Holy Faith."

O Eternal Trinity, Your Light is a Sea! The Water of the Sea is not clouded, and causes no fear to the soul, for I know the Truth; It is a Deep which manifests sweet secrets, so that where the Light of Your Faith abounds, the soul is certain of what to believe. This Water is a Mirror into which You, the Eternal Trinity bid me to look, holding it with the hand of love, that I may see myself, who am Your creature, there

Prayer of St. Catherine 3

319

represented in You, and Yourself in me through the union which You have made of Your Godhead with our humanity. Through this Light, I know how to represent You to myself. You are the supreme and infinite Good, Beauty above all beauty, Wisdom above all wisdom; You are Wisdom! You, the Food of the Angels, have given Yourself in a Fire of Love to mankind; You are the garment which covers all our nakedness, and You feed the hungry with Your Bread. O Sweetness, without any bitterness, O Eternal Trinity, in Your Light, which You have given me with the Light of Holy Faith, I have known many wonderful things which You have declared to me. You have explained to me the Path of Perfection, so that I may no longer serve You in darkness, but in Your Light. With Your Light, may I be the mirror of a good and holy life, and arise from my miserable sins.

Why did I not know You? It is because I did not see You with the glorious Light of Holy Faith, and because the cloud of self-love darkened my intellect. O Eternal Trinity, You have dispelled the darkness with Your Light.

Who can comprehend Your Greatness and give You thanks for such immeasurable gifts and benefits? You have taught me many Truths, which has been a special grace over and above the ordinary graces which You give also to Your other creatures. How can I thank You? You permit us to look at our own nothingness and at Your Greatness. You satisfy Your servants. Clothe me with Yourself, O Eternal Truth.

O Jesus, when You were a Pilgrim on earth, You said: "Learn of Me, for I am Meek and Humble of Heart, in Me you shall find rest for your souls." O Almighty King of Heaven, my soul indeed finds rest in seeing You condescend to wash the feet of Your apostles, "having taken the form of a slave". I recall the words You used to teach me the practice of humility: "I have given you an example, that as I have done to you, so you do, also. The servant is not greater than his Lord . . . If you know these things, and do them, you shall be blest." I understand these words which come from Your Meek and Humble Heart; I wish to practice them with the help of Your grace.

I desire to humble myself in all sincerity and to submit my will to those in authority, without ever contradicting them and without questioning their orders. No one, O my Beloved, had authority over You and yet, You obeyed not only the Blessed Virgin Mary and Saint Joseph, but even Your executioners, and now, in the most Holy Eucharist, I see You complete Your selfabasement. O Divine King of Glory, with wondrous Humility You submit Yourself to all Your priests without any distinction between those who love You and those who, alas, are lukewarm or cold in Your service. You are always ready to come down from Heaven at the call of Your priests.

O my Beloved, under the white eucharistic veil, You indeed appear to me Meek and Humble of Heart. To teach me humility, You cannot further abase Yourself. I wish to respond to Your Love, by putting myself in the lowest place, by sharing Your Humiliations, that I may "have part with You" in the Kingdom of Heaven. I implore You, dear Jesus, to send me a humiliation whenever I try to set myself above others.

O dearest Lord, You know my weakness. Each morning, I resolve to be humble, and in the evening, I recognize that I have often been guilty of pride. The sight of these faults tempts me to discouragement, yet I know that discouragement is itself a form of pride. I wish, therefore, O my God, to build all my trust upon You. As You can do all things, deign to implant in my soul this virtue of humility which I desire, and I will often say to You: "Jesus, Meek and Humble of Heart, make our hearts as unto Yours."

*

I am too little to have any vanity. I am too little to use nice phrases to deceive people into thinking I have a great deal of humility. I prefer simply to admit that God who is mighty has done great things in me, and the greatest is that He has shown me my littleness, my powerlessness to accomplish anything good.

It is not because I have been preserved from mortal sin that I lift up my heart to God in confidence and love. I am certain that even if I had every imaginable crime on my conscience, I would not lose my confidence, but would throw myself, my heart broken with sorrow, into the arms of my Savior. I know that all this multitude of offenses would be swallowed up like a drop of water in Your flaming Furnace.

God has manifested to Me His infinite Mercy, and it is in this shining mirror that I contemplate His other attributes.

O Jesus, I beg You only for love without limits. Would, O my Jesus, that for Your Love I could be a martyr! Oh, give me martyrdom of soul or martyrdom of body, or rather give me both.

*

O Jesus, I love You! You come in the Host to unite Yourself to my enraptured soul! Veiled in the white Host, O my Beloved, how Meek and Humble of Heart You show Yourself. You know, O Omnipotent God, my extreme littleness, and You do not fear to come to my lowliness. Come into my heart, O Sacrament that I love! Come into my heart, for my soul hungers for You! O Living Bread of Heaven, Divine Eucharist! O Blessed Mystery that Divine Love has instituted! Come to dwell in my heart!

O Jesus, my Divine Spouse, grant that the robe of my Baptism may never be soiled. Take me from this life, rather than permit that I should sully my soul by committing the slightest deliberate sin. My heart sighs for You! My greatest desire is to possess You. O God of my heart, You are my Possession forever!

*

O Jesus, You are in the ciborium waiting for me. You are burning with desire to come to me. O Jesus, the golden ciborium that You desire above all others is my heart.

O Virgin Mary, change my heart into a pure corporal, to receive that white Host, in which our Lamb without spot hides Himself.

*

O Lord God of Hosts, You said in Your Gospel: "I have not come to bring peace but a sword." Arm me for the combat. I burn with desire to do battle for Your Glory, but I pray You to enliven my courage. Then, with holy David, I shall be able to exclaim: "You alone are my Shield; You, O Lord, teach my hands to fight."

O my Beloved! I know the warfare, in which I am to engage; it is not on the open field that I will fight. I am a prisoner, held captive by Your Love. Of my own free will I have riveted the fetters which bind me to You, and cut me off forever from the world. My sword is love! With it, like Joan of Arc, "I will drive the strangers from the land, and I will have You proclaimed King" over the kingdom of souls.

It is true, You have no need of so weak an instrument as I. Joan of Arc, your chaste and valiant spouse, said: "We must do battle, before God gives the victory." O my Jesus, I will do battle, then, for Your Love, until the evening of my life. As You did not will to enjoy rest upon earth, I wish to follow Your example. Then this promise which came from Your Sacred Lips will be fulfilled in me: "If anyone wishes to serve Me, let him follow Me, and where I am, there will My servant be, and My Father will honor him." To be with You, to be in You, that is my one desire; Your assurance of its fulfillment helps me to bear with my exile, as I wait the joyous eternal day when I shall see You face to Face.

My Vocation is Love

St. Therese of the Child Jesus

To be Your spouse, to be a Carmelite, and by my union with You, to be the mother of souls, should not this suffice me? No, this does not satisfy my desires! No doubt, these three privileges sum up my true vocation: Carmelite, Spouse, Mother, yet I desire other vocations. I desire the vocation of the warrior, the priest, the apostle, the doctor, and the martyr. I feel the need and the desire of carrying out the most heroic deeds for You, O Jesus. I feel within my soul the courage of the crusader, of the papal guard, and I would want to die on the field of battle in defense of the Church.

I have within me the desire for the priestly vocation. With what love, O my Jesus, I would carry You in my hands, when, at my voice, You would come down from Heaven. With what love would I give You to souls! While desiring to be a priest, I admire and envy the humility of Saint Francis of Assisi, and I desire to imitate him in refusing the sublime dignity of the priesthood.

O Jesus, my Love, my Life, how can I combine these contrasts? How can I realize the desires of my poor little soul?

In spite of my littleness, I would like to enlighten souls as did the prophets and the doctors. I have the vocation of the apostle. I would like to travel over the whole earth to preach Your Name and to plant Your glorious Cross on infidel soil. O my Beloved, one mission alone would not be sufficient for me, I would want to preach the Holy Gospel on the five continents simultaneously, and even to the most remote isles. I would be a missionary, not for a few years only, but from the beginning of creation until the consummation of the ages. O my Beloved Savior, I would shed my blood for You even to the very last drop.

Martyrdom was the dream of my youth and this dream has grown with me within Carmel's cloisters. Here again, I feel that my dream is a folly, for I cannot confine myself to desiring one kind of martyrdom. To satisfy me I need all. I would be scourged and crucified as You were, my Adorable Spouse. I would die flayed like Saint Bartholomew. I would be plunged into boiling oil as Saint John the Apostle; I would undergo all the tortures inflicted upon the martyrs. With Saint Agnes and Saint Cecilia, I would present my neck to the sword; as Joan of Arc, my dear sister, I would whisper Your Name at the stake, O Jesus. When thinking of the torments which will be the lot of Christians at the time of the anti-Christ, I feel my heart leap with joy, and I desire that these torments be reserved for me. Jesus, Jesus, if I wanted to write all my desires, I would have to borrow Your book of life, for in it are reported all the actions of all the Saints, and I would accomplish all of them for You.

O my Jesus, what is Your answer to all my follies? Is there a soul as little as mine, weaker than mine? Nevertheless, even because of my weakness it has pleased You, O Lord, to grant my little childish desires. You desire today to grant to me other desires that are greater than the universe.

During my meditation, my desires caused me a veritable martyrdom, and I opened the Letters of Saint Paul to find some kind of answer. Chapters 12 and 13 of the first Letter to the Corinthians fell under my eyes. I read there, in the first of these chapters, that all cannot be apostles, prophets, doctors, etc., that the Church is composed of different members, and that the eye cannot be the hand at one and the same time. The answer was clear, but it did not fulfill my desires and gave me no peace.

Just as Mary Magdalen found Jesus by seeking Him, by stooping and looking into the empty tomb, so I, abasing myself to the very depths of my nothingness, was able to attain my end. I continued my reading and this sentence consoled me: "Strive after the better gifts, and I point out to you a yet more excellent way." The Apostle Paul then explains how all the most perfect gifts are nothing without love; that charity is the excellent way that leads most surely to God.

I finally had rest. Considering the Mystical Body of the Church, I had not recognized myself in any of the members described by St. Paul, but rather, I desired to see myself in them all. Charity gave me the key to my vocation. I understood that since the Church has a body composed of different members, the most necessary and the most noble of all could not be lacking to it; I understood that the Church had a Heart and that this Heart was burning with LOVE. I understood it was LOVE alone that made the Church's members act, that should LOVE ever become extinct, apostles would not preach the Gospel, and martyrs would not shed their blood. I understood that LOVE comprised all vocations, that LOVE was everything, that LOVE embraced all times and places, that LOVE was eternal!

Then, in my excessive joy, I cried out: O Jesus, my Love, . . . my vocation, at last I have found it . . . MY VOCATION IS LOVE!

Yes, I have found my place in the Church and it is You, O my God, who have given me this place; in the Heart of the Church, my Mother, I shall be Love. Thus I shall be everything, and thus my dream will be realized.

Why do I speak of an excessive joy? No, this expression is not exact. It was rather the calm and serene peace of the navigator perceiving the beacon which must lead him to the port . . . O Luminous Beacon of Love, I know how to reach You, I have found the secret of possessing Your Flame.

I am only a little child, powerless and weak; it is my weakness that gives me the boldness of offering myself as a victim of Your Love. O Jesus, in times past, victims, pure and spotless, were the only ones accepted by the Strong and Powerful God. To satisfy Divine Justice perfect victims were necessary, but the Law of Love has succeeded the Law of Fear; Love has chosen me as a holocaust, me, a weak and imperfect creature. Is not this choice worthy of Love? Yes, in order

My Vocation is Love 4

328

that Love be fully satisfied, it is necessary that It lower Itself to nothingness and transform this nothingness, that I am, into fire.

O Jesus, I know it; Love is repaid by love alone; I searched and I found the way to solace my heart by giving You love for Love. "Make use of the riches which render one unjust in order to make friends who will receive you into the everlasting dwellings." Behold, Lord, the counsel You give Your disciples after having told them: "The children of this world are more prudent than the children of Light." As a child of Light, I understood that my desires of being everything, of embracing all vocations, were the riches that could render me unjust, so I made use of them to make friends. Remembering the prayer of Eliseus to his father Elias, I presented myself before the Angels and Saints and I said to them: "I am the smallest of creatures: I know my misery and my feebleness, but I know also how much noble and generous hearts love to do good. I beg you then, O Blessed Inhabitants of Heaven, to adopt me as your child. To you alone will be the glory which you will make me merit, but deign to answer my prayer. It is bold, I know; however, I dare to ask you to obtain for me your twofold spirit."

Jesus, I cannot fathom the depths of my request; I would be afraid to find myself overwhelmed under the weight of my bold desires. My excuse is that I am a child, and children do not reflect on the meaning of their words. If however, their parents are placed upon a throne and possess immense treasures, they do not hesitate to satisfy the desires of the little ones whom they love as much as they love themselves. To please them they do foolish things, even going to the extent of becoming weak for them. I am a child of the Church; the Church is a Queen, since She is Your Spouse, O Divine King. The heart of a child does not seek riches and glory, not even the glory of Heaven. I understand that this glory belongs by right to the Angels and Saints. My own glory will be the reflected glory which shines in Holy Mother the Church. What I ask for is love. I know only one thing: to love You, O Jesus. Astounding works are forbidden to me; I cannot preach the Gospel, or shed my blood, but what does it matter since my brothers work in my stead and I, a little child, stay very close to the King and Queen. I love in the place of my brothers while they are fighting. How will I prove my love since love is proved by works? I, Your little child, will place flowers before You, I will perfume You with their sweet scents, and I will sing in silvery tones the Canticle of Love.

Yes, my Beloved, this is how my life will be consumed. I have no other means of proving my love for You, other than giving You flowers, that is, not allowing one little sacrifice to escape, not one look, one word, profiting by all the smallest things and doing them through love. I desire to suffer for love and even to rejoice through love; in this way I will place flowers before You. I will not come upon one without unpetalling it for You. While I am giving You my flowers, I shall sing, for could one cry while doing such a joyous action? I will sing even when I must gather my flowers in the midst of thorns, and my

My Vocation is Love 6

330

song will be all the more melodious in proportion to the length and sharpness of the thorns.

O Jesus, of what use will my flowers be to You? I know that these fragrant flowers, these fragile, worthless petals, these songs of love from the littlest of hearts will charm You. Yes, these nothings will please You. They will bring a smile to the Church Triumphant. I will gather up my flowers unpetalled through love, and have them pass through Your own Divine Hand, O Jesus. The members of this Church in Heaven, desirous of playing with their little child, will cast these flowers which are now infinitely valuable because of Your Divine Touch, upon the Church Suffering in order to extinguish its flames, and upon the Sun's Church Militant in order to gain the victory for It.

O my Jesus, I love You! I love the Church, my Mother! I recall that: "The smallest act of pure love is of more value to Her than all other works together." Is pure love in my heart? Are my measureless desires only a dream, a folly? If this is so, Jesus, then enlighten me, for You know I am seeking only the truth. If my desires are rash, then make them disappear, for these desires are the greatest martyrdom to me. I feel, O Jesus, that after having aspired to the most lofty heights of love, if one day I am not to attain them, I feel that I shall have tasted more sweetness in my martyrdom and my folly than I shall taste in the Fatherland, unless You take away the memory of these earthly hopes through a miracle. Allow me, then, during my exile, the delights of love. Allow me to taste the sweet bitterness of my martyrdom.

Jesus, O Jesus, if the desire to love You is so delightful, what will it be to possess and enjoy this Love?

How can a soul as imperfect as mine aspire to the possession of the plenitude of love? O Jesus, my first and only Friend, You whom I love uniquely, explain this mystery to me! Why do You not reserve these great aspirations for great souls, for the eagles that soar in the heights?

I look upon myself as a weak little bird, with only a covering of soft, fluffy feathers. I am not an eagle, but I have only the eyes and heart of an eagle. In spite of my extreme littleness, I still dare to gaze upon the Divine Sun, the Sun of Love, and my heart feels within it all the aspirations of an eagle.

The little bird wills to fly towards the bright Sun which attracts its eye, imitating its brothers, the eagles, whom it sees climbing up towards the Divine Furnace of the Holy Trinity. Alas, the only thing it can do is raise its little wings; to fly is not within its little power!

What then will become of it? Will it die of sorrow at seeing itself so weak? Oh no! The little bird will not even be troubled. With bold surrender, it wishes to remain gazing upon its Divine Sun. Nothing will frighten it, neither wind nor rain. If dark clouds come and hide the Star of Love, the little bird will not change its place, because it believes that beyond the clouds its bright Sun still shines on, and that the Sun's brightness is not eclipsed for a single instant.

My Vocation is Love 8

At times the little bird's heart is assailed by the storm, and it seems it should believe in the existence of no other thing except the clouds surrounding it; this is the moment of perfect joy for the poor little weak creature. What joy it experiences when remaining there just the same, and gazing at the invisible Light which remains hidden from its sight!

O my Jesus, up until the present moment I can understand Your Love for the little bird because it has not strayed far from You. I know, and so do You, that very often the imperfect little creature, while remaining in its place, that is, under the Sun's rays, allows itself to be somewhat distracted from its sole occupation. It picks up a piece of grain on the right or on the left; it chases after a little worm; then coming upon a little pool of water, it wets its feathers still hardly formed. It sees an attractive flower and its little mind is occupied with this flower. Being unable to soar as the eagles, the poor little bird is taken up with the trifles of earth.

After all these misdeeds, instead of going and hiding away in a corner, to weep over its misery and to die of sorrow, the little bird looks at its Beloved Sun, presenting its wet wings to Its beneficent rays. It cries like a swallow; in its sweet song it recounts in detail all its infidelities, thinking in the boldness of its full trust, that it will acquire an even greater fullness of love of Him who came to call not the just, but sinners. If the Adorable Star remains deaf to the plaintive chirping of the little creature, even if It remains hidden, well, the poor little one will remain wet,

My Vocation Is Love 9

333

accepting its numbness from the cold and rejoicing in its suffering which it knows it deserves.

O Jesus, Your little bird is happy to be weak and little. What would become of it if it were big? Never would it have the boldness to appear in Your presence, to fall asleep in front of You. Yes, this is the weakness of the little bird. When it wants to fix its gaze upon the Divine Sun, and when the clouds prevent it from seeing a single ray of that Sun, in spite of itself, its little eyes close, its little head is hidden beneath its wing, and the poor little thing falls asleep, believing at the time that it is fixing its gaze upon its dear Star. When it awakens, it doesn't feel desolate; its little heart is at peace and it begins once again its work of love. It calls upon the Angels and Saints who rise as eagles before the consuming Fire. Since this Fire is the object of the little bird's desire, the eagles take pity on it, protecting and defending it, and putting to flight at the same time the vultures who want to devour it. These vultures are the demons whom the little bird doesn't fear, for it is not destined to be their prey, but the prey of the Eagle whom it contemplates in the center of the Sun of Love.

O Divine Word, You are the Adored Eagle whom I love; You alone attract me! Coming into this land of exile, You willed to suffer and die in order to draw souls to the eternal Fire of the Blessed Trinity. Ascending once again to the inaccessible Light, henceforth Your Abode, You remain in this "valley of tears," hidden beneath the appearances of a white Host. Eternal Eagle, You desire to nourish me with Your Divine Substance, yet, I am but a poor little thing who would return to nothingness, if Your divine glance did not give me life from one moment to the next.

O Jesus, allow me in my boundless gratitude to say to You that Your Love reaches unto folly. In the presence of this folly, how can You not desire that my heart leap towards You? How can my confidence, then, have any limits? The Saints have committed their follies for You, and they have done great things because they are eagles.

My Jesus, I am too little to perform great actions, and my own folly is this: to trust that Your Love will accept me as a victim. My folly consists in begging the eagles to obtain for me the favor of flying towards the Sun of Love, with the Divine Eagle's own wings!

As long as You desire it, O my Beloved, Your little bird will remain without strength and without wings and will always stay with its gaze fixed upon You. It wants to be fascinated by Your divine glance. It wants to become the prey of Your Love. One day I hope that You, the Adorable Eagle, will come to take me, Your little bird. Ascending with it to the Furnace of Love, You will plunge it for all eternity into the burning abyss of this Love, to which it has offered itself as a victim.

O Jesus, why can't I tell all little souls how unspeakable is Your Condescension? I feel that if You found a soul weaker and smaller than mine, which is impossible, You would be pleased to grant it still greater favors, provided it abandoned itself with total confidence to Your infinite Mercy.

Why do I desire to communicate Your secrets of Love, O Jesus? Was it not You alone who taught them to me, and can You not reveal them to others? Yes, I know it, and I beg You to do it. I beg You to cast Your divine glance upon a great number of little souls. I beg You to choose a legion of little victims worthy of Your Love!

(signed)

The very little Sister Therese of the Child Jesus and the Holy Face, unworthy religious of Carmel.

My Vocation is Love 12*

*   *   *   *   *

To remain as little children before God is to recognize our nothingness, to expect everything from God as a little child expects everything from his or her father. To be little is not to attribute to oneself the virtues that one practices. Children do not become discouraged over their faults, for they fall often, but they are too little to hurt themselves very much.

*   *   *

Our Lord died on the cross in agony, and yet this is the most beautiful Death of Love. To die of love is not to die in ecstasy. I tell you frankly, it seems to me that this is what I am experiencing.

*

According to my natural inclinations, I prefer to die, but I rejoice in death only because it is God's Will for me.

*

When I am in Heaven, how many graces I will beg for you! I will beg God so much that, if He wanted to refuse me at first, my importunity would force Him to grant my desires.

†

*   *   *   *   *   *   *

God the Father to Holy Mary: "I do not desire those who are written in My memory for eternal happiness to expect honors, inconsiderate praise, and applause of mortals as part of their reward for working in My honor and service during mortal life. The One and only Creator has made them, sustains them, illumines and defends them.

"The malice and sins of mankind are so great, that We are much constrained by the rigor of Justice. Our Goodness and Mercy is greater than all their evil-doing, nor can it extinguish Our Love towards them. We will look with Mercy on the works of Our Hands, which We created according to Our image and likeness, so as to enable them to become inheritors and participators of Our Glory.

"My Dove, I desire You to see the treasures of My Immutable Being and of My infinite Perfections, and also to perceive the hidden gifts destined for the souls whom I have chosen as heirs of My Glory, and who are rescued by the Life-Blood of the Lamb. Behold, how liberal I am toward My creatures that know and love Me. I am True in My Words, Faithful in My Promises; I am Powerful and Admirable in My Works. Take notice, My Spouse, how true it is, that those who follow Me do not walk in darkness. I desire that You be an eyewitness of the treasures which I hold in reserve for raising up the humble, enriching the poor, exalting the downtrodden, and for regarding all that mortals shall do and suffer for My Name."

Holy Mary: "O Lord and incomprehensible God, how can You pursue with such great favors Your most useless and poor creature? How can You in Your Greatness have such loving Condescension toward Your slave, who is incapable of making the least return? You look down on the servant. The Most Powerful stoops to enrich the poor! The God of all Holiness lowers Himself to the dust! I am the little one among the creatures, and least of all deserve Your favors. What shall I do in Your divine presence? How shall I repay what I owe to You? Since You give me being, life, and activity, what have I that is not Yours? I rejoice, O my Beloved, that You possess all Good; without You the creature possesses nothing. I rejoice, that You alone can claim the glory of raising the little one, of favoring the most useless, giving existence to nothingness, for thus You shall become more known and exalted.

"My dearest Lord, You are incomprehensible in Your magnificence, overflowing in Your riches, unspeakable in Your mysteries, faithful in Your promises, true in Your words, perfect in Your works, for You are infinite and eternal in Your Essence and Perfection. What shall I do at the sight of Your magnificence? I acknowledge myself unworthy to look at You, yet I am in great need of Your Mercy. In Your presence all creation is as nothing. What shall I do, who am but dust? Fulfill in me all Your pleasure! Since trouble and persecutions suffered by mortals in patience are so valuable, since humility and meekness are so precious to You, my Beloved, do not consent that I be deprived of such a rich treasure and pledge of Your Love."

God the Father to Holy Mary: "My Spouse and My Dove, I Love You with an infinite Love. I desire of You what is most pleasing to Me and the fulfillment of all My desires.

"You are aware, My Daughter, of the hidden treasure, which is contained in hardships and tribulations so much dreaded by the blind ignorance of mortals. It is known to You that My Only-Begotten, when He clothes Himself in human nature, will teach the Way of the Cross in words, as well as in deeds; He will leave it as a heritage to My chosen ones, He will choose it for Himself and establish upon it the Law of Grace, making humility and patience in suffering, the foundation of that Law, which will be firm and excellent.

"Tribulation is best suited to the present condition of human nature, and much more so, after it has been depraved and inclined by so many sins. It is also conformable to My equity and Providence, that mortals should attain and merit for themselves the crown of glory through the cross, since My Only-Begotten Son is to merit it by the same means in human flesh.

"My Spouse, You therefore will understand, that having chosen You for My delight, and having enriched You with My gifts, it would not be just that My grace should be idle in Your Heart, that Your Love should want good results, nor that You should be excluded from the inheritance of My elect. Hence, I wish that You dispose Yourself for tribulations and sorrows for Love of Me."

Holy Mary: "Lord God and my Highest King, all my faculties and their operations, and my life which I have received from Your infinite bounty, I hold in readiness as a sacrifice to You, wishing that it be fulfilled entirely according to the desire of Your infinite Wisdom and Goodness. If You give me any freedom of choice, I wish only to choose suffering unto death in love for You; I beseech You to make of Your slave, a sacrifice and holocaust of suffering acceptable to You.

"I acknowledge, O powerful and most liberal God, my debt, and that no creature owes to You so great a return as I, nor are they as indebted to You as I, who am so entirely unequal to the task of discharging this indebtedness to You.

"If You will admit suffering as a sort of return, let all the sorrows and tribulations of death come over me. I will only ask for Your divine protection and, prostrate before Your infinite Majesty, I supplicate You not to forsake me. Remember, O my Lord, the faithful promises, which You have made to our ancestors and prophets, that You will favor the just, stand by those who are in tribulation, console the afflicted, be a protection and a defense to them in their tribulations. True are Your words, infallible and certain are Your promises. The heavens and the earth shall sooner fall to pieces before Your words would ever fail. The malice of the creature cannot extinguish Your Charity toward those that hope in Your Mercy; fulfill in me Your Holy and Perfect Will."

*

Holy Mary: "Eternal God, Creator of all the universe, infinite is Your Wisdom and Goodness, incomprehensible in Essence and Perfection. Well do I know that my sighs are not hidden and that You know the wound that pierces my heart. If, as a useless servant, I have fallen short in Your service and in pleasing You, O Life of my soul, why do You not afflict me and chastise me with all pains and sufferings of this mortal life, so that I may not be obliged to endure the turning of Your Eyes from me? I have deserved this treatment through my fault. All punishments would be less than this, for my heart cannot bear Your displeasure. You alone are my Life, my Happiness, my Glory, and my Treasure. My soul counts for nothing. All that You have created lives in my soul only to praise Your Greatness and to acknowledge You as Creator and Lord of all. What shall I do then, if You, my Blessed Lord, the Light of my eyes, the Goal of my desires, the Northstar of my pilgrimage, the Life of my being, and the Essence of my life, fail me? Who will give fountains to my eyes to bewail my want of correspondence to the blessings I have received, and my ingratitude for these benefits?

"My Lord, my Light, my Guide and Teacher of the Way, by Your most exalted and perfect operations, direct my fragile and lukewarm undertakings. How can I regulate my life, if You fail me as my Model? Who will guide me securely through this desert? What shall I do and where shall I turn if You deprive me of Your assistance?"

Holy Mary to Her Guardian Angels: "Sovereign princes and intimate friends of the Highest King, my guardians, by your felicitous vision of God's Divine Countenance and His ineffable Light, I ask you to tell me the cause of God's displeasure. Intercede for me in His Real Presence, that through your prayers He may pardon me, if I have offended Him. Although I am dust, remind Him that I am formed by His Hands and that He has placed upon me the seal of His image; beseech Him not to forget His needy one to the end, so that I may confess and praise His Name. Ask my God to give back to me the breath of Life which fails me at the dread of having lost His Love. Tell me, how and by what means I can please Him and regain the joy of His Blessed Countenance?"

The Angels to Holy Mary: "Our Queen, Your Heart is dilated so that You cannot be vanquished by tribulation. No one is as able as You to understand how near the Lord is to the afflicted who call upon Him. Without doubt He recognizes Your affection and does not despise Your loving sighs. You will find our God a Kind Father; You will find His Only-Begotten a most affectionate Son, looking upon Your affliction."

Holy Mary to Her Guardian Angels: "Will it perhaps be presumption to prostrate myself before my God, asking His pardon for any fault He might find in me? What shall I do? What relief can I find in my anxieties?"

The Angels to Holy Mary: "A humble heart does not displease our King; upon it He fixes His loving regard. He is never displeased by the prayers of those who act in love."

Holy Mary's Prayer when She Presented
the Child Jesus in the Temple

"Highest King, Lord and Creator of all that has being, in Your presence is useless dust, which Your ineffable condescension has favored with grace which I can never merit. I find myself forced onward by the flood of Your blessings to give You thanks. What return can I offer, who, being nothing, have received my life from You, and am overwhelmed by such incomparable mercies and blessings of Your Divinity? What thanks can I render in acknowledgement of Your immense Bounty? What reverence can I offer which is worthy of Your Majesty? What gift can I give to Your infinite Deity, since I am only a creature? My soul, my being, and my faculties, all have I received and continue to receive from Your Hands. A thousand times do I offer them in sacrifice to Your glory. I acknowledge my indebtedness to You. I thank You for having preserved me from the contagion of sin and for having chosen me to give human form to Your Only-Begotten Son, to bear Him in my womb and at my breast, though I am only a daughter of Adam and made of lowly and earthly matter.

"I perceive Your ineffable condescension towards me, and in gratitude for it my heart fails and my life is spent in affections of Divine Love, having nothing else to repay all the favors You have conferred upon me. My heart is now revived and rejoices in possessing a gift worthy of You, since I can offer You Jesus, who is One in Substance with You, Equal in Majesty,

Holy Mary's Prayer 1

343

and Equal in perfection of Your Attributes; He is the Only-Begotten of Your Intellect, the Image of Your Being, the fullness of Your pleasure, Your only and most Beloved Son. This, Eternal Father, is the Gift which I offer, the Victim which I bring You, and this I am sure You will receive.

"Having received Him as God, I return Him to You as God and Man. Neither I nor any other creature, O Lord, can ever offer You a greater gift, nor can Your Majesty ever demand one more precious. It is so valuable, that It will suffice to repay You for what I have received. Having given Him human flesh, I have made Him the Brother of mortals. As He wishes to be their Redeemer and Teacher, it is my duty to be their advocate.

"Father of my Only-Begotten, God of Mercies, I therefore offer Him to You from all my heart. With Him and because of Him, I beg You to pardon sinners, to pour out upon the human race Your Mercies of old and to open new fountains for the renewal of Your Wonders. Rich, O my God, is this Oblation. You can well pour forth Your Mercies upon the human race in return for It: pardoning the sinners that have turned from the path, consoling the afflicted, helping the needy, enriching the poor, aiding the weak, enlightening the blind, and meeting those who have strayed away. This is what I ask of You in offering to You Your Only-Begotten, who by Your merciful condescension is also my Son. In wealth do I return to Your Temple from which I departed poor. My soul shall praise You forever, because You have shown Yourself so liberal and powerful towards me."

Holy Mary: "Dearest Jesus, my Lord and Highest God, in Your royal presence I present myself before You, in my own name and in that of the human race. I bless and praise You. I confess and adore You in the mystery of the union of the Divine and Human Nature of the Eternal Word. The unfortunate children of Adam are forgetful of this blessing of the Incarnation, and those who remember it, fail in giving worthy thanks for it. Remember, O Kind Father, that they live in weak flesh, so full of darkness and passions. They cannot come to You, if You, in Your loving condescension, do not draw them. Pardon the shortcomings of their weak nature and condition. I, Your slave, with all the Angels give You thanks for myself and for all mortals in acknowledgment of this Blessing. I beseech You, with all my soul, to take up this cause of Your brethren and obtain for them the forgiveness of Your Eternal Father.

"My Jesus, favor these unfortunate mortals conceived in sin, who do not recognize their own misfortune, and do not know what they are doing nor what they should do. I beg for Your people and for my own. As You are man, we are all of Your nature, which You do not despise; as You are God, You give infinite value to Your works. You alone are the worthy return and thanksgiving for satisfying our debt, since You alone can pay for what we have received and for what we owe to the Eternal Father, for sending You from Heaven to earth as the Savior of the poor and Rescuer of the captives. Give life to the dead, enrich the poor, enlighten the blind; You are our Salvation, our Happiness, and our Restoration."

The Attributes of God

The Holy Angels speak to the Virgin Mary: "Our God is Beauty, and He contains within Himself all Perfections beyond all desire. He is Amiable without defect, delightful beyond comparison, and pleasing without the least flaw. In Wisdom, He is inestimable; in Goodness, without measure; in Power, boundless; in Greatness, immeasurable; in Essence, infinite; in Majesty, inaccessible; all His Perfections are infinite. God's Judgments are most equitable, His thoughts are unsearchable, His words, most true. God's Works are Holy, and His Mercies are rich.

"Space cannot overreach God, narrowness cannot confine Him, sorrow cannot disturb Him, joy cannot cause any change in Him, nor does He ever fail in His Wisdom, or change His Will. Abundance cannot overwhelm, or want come near Him. Memory adds nothing, forgetfulness takes away nothing from His Knowledge. The beginning gave no origin to His Being; what was, is not past for Him, and time will bring to Him no end. Without being caused, He causes all things; He has no need of anything, but all things need participation in Him; He preserves them without labor, and He governs them without confusion.

"Those who follow God do not walk in darkness. Those who know Him are happy, those who love and extol Him, are blest. He exalts His friends, and at last glorifies them by His eternal vision and conversation. This is the Good which You love and whose embraces You shall soon enjoy without intermission through all His eternity."

Suffering

Holy Mary our Teacher: "My beloved child, I wish you to remember that to suffer and to be afflicted with or without one's fault is a benefit of which one cannot be worthy without the special and great Mercy of Almighty God; moreover, to be allowed to suffer for one's sins, is not only a mercy, but is demanded by justice. Behold, the great insanity of the children of Adam, in desiring and seeking after benefits and favors agreeable to their senses, and in sleeplessly striving to avert from themselves, that which is painful or includes any hardship or trouble. It would be to their greatest benefit to seek tribulations diligently even when it is unmerited, yet they strive by all means to avoid them even when merited, though they cannot be happy and blest without having undergone such sufferings.

"When gold is untouched by the heat of the furnace, iron by the file, grain by the grinding stone or flail, and grapes by the winepress, they are all useless and will not attain the end for which they are created. Why then will mortals continue to deceive themselves, by expecting, in spite of their sins, to become pure and worthy of enjoying God, without the furnace or the file of sorrows? If they were incapable and unworthy of attaining the crown and reward when innocent, how can they attain it when they are in darkness and in disgrace before Almighty God?

"In addition to this, the sons of perdition are exerting all their powers to remain unworthy and hostile to God, avoiding crosses and afflictions which are the paths left open for returning to God. They reject the light of the intellect, which is the means of recognizing the deceptiveness of visible things, refuse the nourishment of the just, which is the only means of grace, the price of glory; they reject the legitimate inheritance, selected by My Son for Himself and for all His elect, since He was born and lived continually in afflictions and died upon the cross.

"By such standards you must measure the value of suffering, which worldly souls will not understand. Since they are unworthy of heavenly knowledge, they despise it in proportion to their ignorance. Rejoice and congratulate yourself in your sufferings, and whenever the Almighty deigns to send you any, hasten to meet them and welcome them as His blessings and pledges of His glorious Love.

"Furnish your heart with magnanimity and constancy, so that when occasions of suffering are given to you, you may bear them with the same equanimity as you would for agreeable things. Do not be sad in executing that which you have promised in gladness, for the Lord loves those who are equally as ready to give, as to receive. Sacrifice your heart and all your faculties as a holocaust of patience. Chant in new hymns of praise and joy, the justification of the Most High God, whenever in the place of your pilgrimage, He signalizes and distinguishes you as His own with the signs of His friendship, which are no other than the trials and tribulations of sufferings.

Holy Mary our Teacher: "Take notice that My most Holy Son Jesus and I are trying to find among those who have arrived at the Way of the Cross, some souls whom We can instruct systematically in the divine science of suffering, and whom We can withdraw from the worldly and diabolical wisdom. Enter into this School, in which alone are taught the lessons of the Cross and the manner of reaching true peace and delights.

"With this wisdom, the earthly love of sensible pleasures and riches are not compatible, nor the vain ostentation and pomp, which fascinates the bleary-eyed worldlings who are so covetous of passing honors, and so full of ignorant admiration for costly grandeur. You, My child, choose for yourself the better part of being among the lowly and the forgotten ones of this world. I was the Mother of the God-Man, and, on that account, Queen of all creation, yet I was little known; My Son Jesus was very much despised by mortals. If this lesson were not most valuable and secure, We would not have taught it by word and example. This is the Light, which shines in the darkness, loved by the elect, and abhorred by the reprobate."   Suffering 3*

*

"Be not dismayed that you were conceived in sin, and as an earthly creature feel within yourself earthly inclinations, but strive against your passions to the finish of your life."

*

"The greatest happiness which can befall you or any soul in this mortal life, is that Almighty God calls you to His House, consecrated to His holy service. By this benefit He rescues you from a dangerous slavery and relieves you of the vile servitude of the world, where, deprived of true liberty, you eat your bread in the sweat of your brow. Who is so dull as not to know the dangers of a worldly life, which is hampered by all the abominable and most wicked laws and customs introduced by the astuteness of the devils and the perversity of mortals? The better part is Religious Life and retirement; in it is found security; outside is a torment and stormy sea, full of sorrow and unhappiness. O soul, be not deaf to the voice of the Most High God; attend and correspond to it in all your actions. Remember that one of the greatest snares of the demon is to counteract the call of the Lord, whenever He seeks to attract and incline a soul to a life of perfection in His holy service."

*

"You, O soul, who have received more should consider yourself more needy, since your debt becomes so much the greater. You should humiliate yourself since you are nothing, nor can you do anything by your own power. You who are raised up by the Hand of the Almighty, should humiliate yourself as mere dust, for, since you are nothingness and unworthiness, you should esteem yourself so much the more indebted and bound to thankfulness for that which by yourself you can never repay. No one cay say: 'I have made myself, I preserve myself in existence, I can prolong my life or postpone death.' All your being and preservation is in the Hands of the Lord; humble yourself in His presence, and do not forget these truths."

*

Guardian Angels

Holy Mary our Teacher: "My dear child, by incessant praise and acknowledgment, show yourself thankful for the favor which God gave you in appointing Angels to assist you, teach you, and guide you through your tribulations. Mortals ordinarily forget this blessing. They do not consider what great mercy and condescension of the Most High it is to have ordained these Holy Princes as helpers, guardians, and defenders of mortals, their earthly fellow creatures, so full of miseries and sins. In forgetting how exalted in glory, dignity, and beauty these Spirits are, many souls deprive themselves of numerous blessings, which they would otherwise obtain from the Angels.

"In every place and at all times, love and revere these Holy Spirits, as if you saw them with your corporal eyes. Don't do before them what you would not do in public. Cease not to exert yourself in the service of God, even as they do and as they require of you. Remember that the Angels, being of the Blessed, continually see the Face of God. Since they at the same time see you, let there be nothing indecent in you. Show yourself grateful to them for their vigilance, defense, and protection. Be attentive to the calls, urgings, and aspirations, by which these Angels move and excite you to the recollection of the Most High and to the exercise of all the virtues. Be mindful how often they have responded to your calls, how often they have solicited from you sighs of love for your Spouse, and also kindly telling you of your carelessness and remissness.

"When, in your troubles and weariness, you lost the guiding star of God's Light, the Holy Angels renewed your hope, and patiently corrected you, directing your footsteps again into the narrow path of the Lord. Do not forget, My child, the greatness of the benefits bestowed upon you by these Holy Angels; strive to be grateful to your Lord, and to the Angels, His ministers.

"Admirable is the love, fidelity, and solicitude with which the Angelic Spirits assist mortals in their necessities, and most horrible is the forgetfulness and ingratitude on the part of mortals in failing to acknowledge this debt. In the Most High God, whose Face the Holy Angels see in beatific clearness, these heavenly Spirits perceive the infinite paternal Love of the Father in Heaven for mankind. They appreciate and estimate worthily the Blood of the Lamb by which souls were rescued, and they know the value of the souls purchased with the treasures of the Divinity. The Angels are watchful and attentive in securing the interests of the souls, which on account of the value set upon them by the Most High, have been given into their charge. I wish you to understand how, by the ministry of these Holy Angels, mortals could receive great enlightenment and favors from the Lord, if only they did not hinder them by their sins and by their forgetfulness of this inestimable blessing.

"Since God has dealt with you liberally in appointing Angels to guard you, be attentive to their instruction, and listen to their injunctions with reverence."

Gratitude

Holy Mary our Teacher: "Through the whole course of My life on earth, I gratefully kept in mind the words of the redemption, the Passion and Death of Jesus My Divine Son, especially after I had actually seen Him sacrificed on the cross for the salvation of mankind. I desire that this knowledge should cause you and all souls to be sorry for your monstrous forgetfulness of the incomprehensible benefit of the redemption. O what a shameful, horrible, and dangerous ingratitude of mankind is this! Forgetfulness is a sign of indifference. One does not easily forget what is treasured in the heart. What reason or excuse can there be for mortals to forget the eternal blessings they have received? Why do they despise the Love of the Eternal Father who has delivered over to Death His Only-Begotten Son?

"The insensible earth responds to the efforts of those persons who cultivate it; wild beasts become tame in return for benefits. Mortals among themselves are grateful to their benefactors; when such thankfulness is not forthcoming, the benefactors resent it, condemn it, and call it a great offense. What is the reason, then, that only toward their God and Redeemer, mortals should be so ungrateful and forget that He suffered in order to rescue them from eternal damnation? Besides being ungrateful, they even complain of not receiving His assistance as they want or desire.

"In order that mankind may understand what fearful guilt they load upon themselves by their ingratitude, I remind you that lucifer and his demons, seeing so many souls oblivious of the sufferings of Christ, say of such souls: 'These souls do not remember or esteem the benefit of God's Redemption, therefore, we are certain of gaining them over to our side; the souls who are so foolish as not to remember such a blessing, will certainly not detect our wiles.'

"As you have been so highly favored and distinguished by the blessings of the Lord, it is just that you give thanks with incessant praises, glorifying God for what He has condescended to do for you. Since ingratitude is so vile and reprehensible in creatures who owe Him little and forget the benefits of the Lord, greater will your guilt be in falling short of your obligations. Remember that the Lord often shows great favors to the unworthy, in order to manifest His Goodness. Do not become inflated, but acknowledge so much the more your unworthiness, for humility is a medicine and antidote against the poison of presumption. You must acknowledge that every good gift comes from the Father and cannot ever be merited. All have their source only in His Goodness, binding us and obliging us to be grateful.

"Meditate how God has waited upon you and consoled you, assured you in your doubts, quieted you in your fears, ignored and pardoned your faults, multiplied favors, caresses, and blessings. Confess in your heart that God has done such things; you of yourself can do nothing; you are poor and more useless than others. Let then your thanks be greater than that of all creatures."

Holy Mary our Teacher: "You must remember that no occupation, no matter how lowly it may be, can, if it is well-ordered, impede the worship, reverence, and exaltation of the Creator of all things. Occupations and acts of virtue do not exclude one another, but they are compatible with one another. I lived in the continual presence of the Highest Good without ever losing It from My sight by exterior activity. I adored and remembered God in all My actions, referring them all to His greater Honor and Glory; the Lord who orders and creates all things, despises none of them, nor is He offended or irritated by their smallness. The soul that loves God, is not disconcerted by any of these little things in His divine presence, for it seeks and finds Him as the beginning and end of all creatures. Because terrestrial creatures cannot exist without these humble occupations, and without others that are inseparable from their lowly condition and the preservation of human nature, it is necessary to understand this lesson well, in order that you may be governed by it.

"If you are engaged in thoughts and occupations without referring them to our Creator, they will cause many and great interruptions in the practice of virtue. Your whole life will be blameworthy and full of reprehensible defects, little removed from the sinfulness of creatures.

"According to this lesson, you must so regulate your terrestrial occupations, whatever they may be, that you do not lose your time, since it can never be recovered. Whether you eat, labor, rest, sleep, or watch, at all times, in all places, and in all occupations, adore, reverence, and look upon Your Great and Powerful Lord, who fills all things and conserves all things.

"Before the Incarnation, I pleaded for the coming of the Savior, so that the souls created by God could serve Him, love Him, and praise Him for all eternity.

"You also must pray and sigh for the eternal salvation of your brethren, so that the Name of My Son may be extolled by all mortals throughout the world. You must establish the habit of this kind of prayer, by a constant resolve, founded upon firm faith and unshaken confidence, never losing sight of your misery in profound humility and self-abasement. Thus prepared, you must battle with the Divine Love for the good of your people, firmly convinced that the most glorious triumphs of Divine Love may especially be looked for in His dealings with the humble, who love God. Give thanks for the special blessings conferred upon you and for those conferred upon the human race. Transformed by this Divine Love, you will merit other gifts, both for yourself and for your brethren. Whenever you find yourself in His Divine Presence, ask for His benediction.

"Enter into God's Eucharistic Presence with prayer and petitions. Since human frailty cannot remain constant, seek assistance, such as will help you to find your God. Ask Me and the Angels and Saints to help you praise your God."

Mary and Joseph find the Child Jesus in the Temple

Holy Mary our Teacher: "The Child Jesus absented Himself from Me in order that, seeking Him in sorrow and tears, I might find Him again in joy with abundant grace for My Soul. I desire that you imitate Me in this mystery, and seek Him with such earnestness as to be consumed with a continual ardent desire, without ever in your whole life coming to any rest until you hold Him and can lose Him no more. Love Him with all the powers of your heart and soul."

*

"Christ is Eternal Life, the True Light and the Pathway to Eternal Life; those who follow Him, He loves with an imperishable Love, and He offers them His Life and His company. He also offers Eternal Happiness, such as neither eyes have seen, nor ears have heard, nor ever can enter into the mind of any mortal."

*

"In obeying the Lord, it is only necessary that the Lord Creator commands and disposes. You must accustom yourself to look for this motive alone, and to learn solely to please the Lord, without distinguishing between fortunate or unfortunate events. Receive prosperity or adversity in this mortal life with peace of mind. Grieve not, nor vainly rejoice, but attend only to all that which the Almighty ordains according to His pleasure."

*

"Our Lord wished to have a Wound in His Heart: the Source of Love, in order that through this port, souls could enter and receive refuge and relief."

357

"Since you have for your Spouse the Supreme and Mighty Lord, who is the King of kings, consider it beneath your dignity to turn your eyes or your heart toward human creatures, for even the Angels love and respect you for your dignity as spouse of the Most High God."

*

"The three kings from the East offered the Newborn Infant, gifts of gold, frankincense, and myrrh. Your ceaseless offering of love is gold; your continual prayer is incense; your patient acceptance of labor and mortification is myrrh."

*

"Jesus is watching you so closely that not more than a slight screen intervenes between your soul and its vision of the Lord. Drawn onward, He approaches closely to you souls who love and serve Him in all things, while He withdraws from the lukewarm and negligent ones, or deals with them only according to the general rules of His Divine Providence. Aspire continually to be most pure and perfect in the practice of virtues, and study and invent new schemes and projects of love, so that all the forces of your faculties continue to be zealously occupied in what is most exalted and excellent in the service of the Lord."

*

"Why should you not love those who insult and offend you, thus giving you occasions to practice the highest perfection? Why not thank them for this benefit, and hold them, not as enemies, but as benefactors, who afford you a chance to obtain what is of so much importance for your welfare?"

*

The devil!

Holy Mary our Teacher: "The surest way of fighting the demon is to despise him, looking upon him as the enemy of the Most High God, who has lost all fear of God and all hope of good. In his stubbornness, he has deprived himself of all means of recovery and is without sorrow for his wickedness. Relying on this truth, you should show yourself far superior to him, exalted and unflinching in your thoughts. Treat him as a contemner of the honor and worship of his God. Knowing that you are defending so just a cause, do not let your courage decrease, but resist and counteract him with great strength and valor in all his attempts, as you are fighting at the side of the Lord. His Majesty assists all those that enter loyally into His battles. You are truly on the right way to Eternal Life, as long as you labor faithfully for your Lord and God.

"Remember that the demons detest what you desire and love, namely the Honor of God and your Eternal Happiness. The devils are striving to deprive you of Heaven which they cannot restore to themselves.

"The arrogance of the dragon is great, yet he is very weak; he does not represent more than a weak atom in the face of the Divine Power. As his cunning and malice far exceed that of mortals, it is not advisable to allow your soul to bandy words with him. From him, as from a smoking furnace, come the shadows of confusion, obscuring the judgments of mortals. If you listen to the dragon, he will fill your mind

The devil 1

359

with deceit and darkness, so that you will neither recognize the truth and beauty of virtue, nor the vileness of his poisonous falsehoods. Thus you, O soul, will be unable to distinguish the precious from the worthless, life from death, truth from error, and you will easily fall into the clutches of this fierce and wicked dragon.

"Whenever the Lord sends to you, or places in your way a needy soul, making you aware of its state, labor faithfully to assist it. Pray and weep with heartfelt and fervent love, that God may furnish the remedy for such great and dangerous evil, and do not neglect any means, divine or human, in order to obtain Eternal Life for the souls entrusted to you. By means of prudence, you must not become weary in admonishing, nor in praying for that which will benefit souls, and in all secrecy continue your labor on their behalf.

"I wish that when it is necessary, you command the demons in the powerful name of Jesus, and My own name, Mary, to depart and leave in peace the souls oppressed by them. As all this is to be done in secret, you can, in all propriety, animate and encourage yourself to this kind of work. The Lord will place you in a position to exercise this lesson. Do not forget it, nor fail to understand, how much you are indebted to His Majesty to use care and solicitude in extending the possession of your Father's House. Fear not, for you can do all in Him who strengthens you; His Power will strengthen you to do great things.

"The silence which you should maintain when

the devils advance their specious reasonings, should not prevent you from imposing silence upon them in the name of Jesus, and from commanding them to leave your presence in confusion. I desire this to be your prudent behavior when they assault you. There is no other defense so powerful against the dragon than to be conscious of the power which we possess as children of God, and to use the advantage which this confidence gives us, by exercising our superiority over the infernal spirits.

"The whole aim of lucifer, after he fell from Heaven, consists in enticing souls from their Creator, in sowing the seed of discord by which he hopes to separate from the Heavenly Father His adopted children, and the spouses of Christ from their Bridegroom. When lucifer perceives that a soul is united to its Creator and in living Communion with Christ, he tries to surpass himself in his furious attempts at persecuting it; his envy arouses the utmost exertion of his deceitfulness and malice for its destruction. As soon as he sees that he cannot succeed in his attempts, because the soul takes refuge in the unfailing and unassailable protection of the Most High, he weakens in his attempts and begins to writhe in torments. If the soul, thus strengthened with the authority of God's Truth, despises and casts him out, there is no creeping worm or ant so weak, as that giant of iniquitous pride.

"Darkness is lucifer; he is error, unhappiness, deceit, and death; he hates his followers and forces them into evil as far as possible, and finally, he inflicts upon them eternal fire."

The devil 3*

361

"Remember your earthly and corruptible nature, and be not ignorant of the fact that the Most High God has providentially formed mankind in such a way that their existence and formation remind them of the important lesson of humility, never allowing them to be without this salutary teaching. On this account God has not formed them of the most excellent material; He has concealed the noblest part of their being in the sanctuary of their interior, teaching them to weigh as on a balance, on the one side the infinite and eternal existence of the Lord, and on the other, their own ignoble existence. It is proper and just that all mortals give unto God what belongs to Him."

*

"Let your conversation be in Heaven with the Most High God, with Me, who am your Mother, and with the Angels and Saints of God."

*

"One reason why mortals should call Me: 'Mother of Mercy' is the knowledge of My loving desire, that all be satiated with grace, and taste the sweetness of the Lord with Me. I invite all to come with Me, for I am a Fountain of Grace. Let the poor and afflicted approach, for if they respond and follow Me, I will offer them My protection and help. I will intercede for them with My Son and obtain for them hidden Manna, which will give to them nourishment and Life. By the true Light, which you have received concerning the works of My Son and My own, contemplate and study yourself in this Mirror, in order to arrive at that beauty, which the Highest King seeks in you."

*

Holy Communion

Holy Mary our Teacher: "If I, the Mother of Jesus whom I was to receive, deemed Myself unworthy of Holy Communion, and by so many means sought the purity necessary for such a Sacrament, consider what you must do, so poor and subject to so many miseries and imperfections! Purify the temple of your interior, scrutinizing it by the Divine Light and adorning it with great virtues, since it is the Eternal God whom you are to receive: God, of whom nobody but Himself is worthy.

"I exhort you to call upon Me and ask Me to help you; I am the special Advocate and Protectress of those who desire to arrive at great purity for receiving Holy Communion. Whenever you invoke Me for this purpose, I present Myself before the Most High, and, as one knowing the dispositions required for harboring God Himself, I ask His favor and grace for those who are about to receive Him in the Holy Sacrament. I have not lost in Heaven the solicitude and zeal which I exhibited upon earth.

"I have given Jesus human form in order that He might converse with mortals and become the 'Property' of each one. He conceals Himself under the appearances of bread and wine in order to accommodate Himself to your needs, so that you may consider Him as your 'Personal Property', fit to offer to the Eternal Father. In this way He furnishes to each one an Oblation which no one else can offer, and the Most High God is satisfied with It, since there is nothing more acceptable nor anything more precious in the possession of creatures.

"Learn from My example the reverence, fear, and respect, with which you must treat Jesus, recalling how I acted, when I held Him in My arms. Follow My example whenever you receive Him in your heart in the venerable Sacrament of the Holy Eucharist, wherein is contained the same God-Man, who was born of My Womb. In this Holy Sacrament you receive Him and possess Him just as really as I did, and He remains in you just as truly as I possessed Him and conversed with Him, although in another manner.

"Receive Jesus in Holy Communion with as much humility, reverence, and worship as is possible to your combined powers and faculties. Even though your powers and faculties be exerted to the utmost limits, they will always fall short of what you owe to God, and of what He deserves.

"In order that you may, as far as possible, make up for your deficiencies, offer up what My most Holy Son and I have done. Unite your spirit and your affections in union with the Church Triumphant and the Church Militant, offering at the same time your life as a sacrifice. Pray that all nations may know, confess, and adore their true God who became Man for all.

"After asking Me, ask the Angels and Saints for their intercession, for they also are very anxious to see souls approach the Holy Eucharist with great devotion and purity."

*   Holy Communion 2*

†

Litany of the Sacred Heart of Jesus

Lord, have Mercy on us.
Lord, have Mercy on us.
Christ, have Mercy on us.
Christ, have Mercy on us.
Lord, have Mercy on us.
Lord, have Mercy on us.
Christ, hear us. Christ, graciously hear us.
God the Father of Heaven, have Mercy on us.
God the Son, Redeemer of the world,
God the Holy Spirit,
Holy Trinity, One God,
Heart of Jesus, Son of the Eternal Father,
            have Mercy on us. (we love You.)
Heart of Jesus, formed by the Holy Spirit in the Womb of the Virgin Mother,
Heart of Jesus, substantially united to the Word of God,
Heart of Jesus, of infinite Majesty,
Heart of Jesus, Sacred Temple of God,
Heart of Jesus, Tabernacle of the Most High,
Heart of Jesus, House of God and Gate of Heaven,
Heart of Jesus, Burning Furnace of Charity,
Heart of Jesus, Abode of Justice and Love,
Heart of Jesus, Abyss of all Virtues,
Heart of Jesus, most Worthy of all Praise,
Heart of Jesus, King and Center of all hearts,
Heart of Jesus, in whom are all the treasures of Wisdom and Knowledge,
Heart of Jesus, in whom dwells the Fullness of the Divinity,
Heart of Jesus, in whom the Father is well pleased,
Heart of Jesus, of whose Fullness we have all received, have Mercy on us.

Heart of Jesus, Desire of the Everlasting Hills,
Heart of Jesus, Patient and most Merciful,
Heart of Jesus, enriching all who invoke You,
Heart of Jesus, Fountain of Life and Holiness,
Heart of Jesus, Propitiation for our sins,
Heart of Jesus, loaded down with abuse,
Heart of Jesus, bruised for our offenses,
Heart of Jesus, Obedient unto Death,
Heart of Jesus, pierced with a lance,
Heart of Jesus, Source of all Consolation,
Heart of Jesus, our Life and Resurrection,
Heart of Jesus, our Peace and Reconciliation,
Heart of Jesus, Victim of sin,
Heart of Jesus, Salvation of those who trust in You,
Heart of Jesus, Hope of those who die in You,
Heart of Jesus, Delight of all the Saints,
    have Mercy on us.

Lamb of God, You take away the sins of the world, spare us, O Lord.
Lamb of God, You take away the sins of the world, graciously hear us, O Lord.
Lamb of God, You take away the sins of the world, have Mercy on us.

Jesus, Meek and Humble of Heart,
Make our hearts as unto Yours.

O Almighty and Eternal God, look upon the Heart of Your dearly Beloved Son Jesus, and upon the praise and satisfaction He offers You in the name of sinners and for those who seek Your Mercy. Graciously grant pardon, in the name of Jesus Your Son, who lives and reigns with You, in the unity of the Holy Spirit, world without end. Amen.

Benediction of the Most Blessed Sacrament

O Saving Victim opening wide,
The Gate of Heaven to man below!
Our foes press on from every side:
Thine aid supply, Thy strength bestow.

To Thy Great Name be endless Praise
Immortal Godhead, One in Three:
O grant us endless length of days
In our true Native Land with Thee. Amen

*

O Salutaris Hostia,   Uni trinoque Domino
Que caeli pandis ostium   Sit sempiterna gloria
Bella premunt hostilia,   Qui vitam sine termino
Da robur; fer auxilium   Nobis donet in patria.
                               Amen.

Tantum ergo Sacramentum
Veneremur cernui;
Et antiquum documentum
Novo cedat ritui;
Praestet fides supplementum
Sensuum defectui.

Genitori, Genitoque
Laus et jubilatio,
Salus, honor, virtus quoque
Sit et benedictio:
Procedenti ab utroque
Compar sit laudatio. Amen.

*

Panem de caelo praestitisti eis.
Omne delectamentum in se habentem.

*

Bowing low, then offer homage
To a Sacrament so great!

Here is new and perfect worship;
All the old must terminate.
Senses cannot grasp this Marvel:
Faith must serve to compensate.

Praise and glorify the Father,
Bless His Son's Life-giving Name,
Singing their Eternal Godhead,
Power, Majesty, and Fame,
Offering their Holy Spirit
Equal worship and acclaim. Amen.

*

Lord Jesus, You gave us the Eucharist as the memorial of Your Suffering and Death. May our worship of this Sacrament of Your Body and Blood bring us to the glory of Your Resurrection, for You live and reign forever and ever. Amen.

*

The Divine Praises

Blessed be God.
Blessed be His Holy Name.
Blessed be Jesus Christ, True God and True Man.
Blessed be the name of Jesus.
Blessed be His most Sacred Heart.
Blessed be His most Precious Blood.
Blessed be Jesus in the most Holy Sacrament of
        the altar.
Blessed be the Holy Spirit, the Consoler.
Blessed be the Great Mother of God, Mary most
        Holy.
Blessed be Her Holy and Immaculate Conception.
Blessed be Her Glorious Assumption.
Blessed be the name of Mary, Virgin and Mother.
Blessed be St. Joseph, Her most chaste spouse.
Blessed be God in His Angels and in His Saints.

Sing, my tongue, acclaim Christ present,
Veiled within this Sacred Sign:
Precious Blood and Risen Body,
Under forms of bread and wine:
Blood once shed for man's Redemption,
By his King, of David's Line.

Heaven's promised Gift to mankind,
Born to Virgin full of Grace,
Plants the seed of faith securely,
While He dwells with Adam's race,
Ends His Mission, leaves a symbol
Of the death He will embrace.

Dining with His twelve Apostles
On the night before He died,
Taking for the Paschal Supper
Foods the Law had specified,
Lo, He sets new Bread before them,
Handing each: Christ Crucified!

Word-made-Flesh makes bread His Body,
Consecrates it by His Word.
Wine becomes the Blood of Jesus:
He it is whose voice is heard.
Minds in doubt need faith's assurance:
God who spoke cannot have erred.

Bowing low, then, offer homage
To a Sacrament so great!
Here is new and perfect worship;
All the old must terminate.
Senses cannot grasp this Marvel:
Faith must serve to compensate.

Praise and glorify the Father,
Bless His Son's Life-giving Name,
Singing their Eternal Godhead,
Power, Majesty and Fame,
Offering their Holy Spirit
Equal Worship and acclaim. Amen.

O Sacred Heart! O Love Divine
Do keep us near to Thee;
And make our hearts as unto Thine,
That we may holy be.
Heart of Jesus, hear, O Heart of Love Divine!
Listen to our prayer, make us always Thine.

O Temple Pure! O House of Gold,
Our Heaven here below!
What sweet delights, what wealth untold,
From Thee do ever flow!
Heart of Jesus, hear, O Heart of Love Divine!
Listen to our prayer, make us always Thine.

*   *   *

The Eucharist

The Tabernacle is the Home of Jesus on earth. It is the place where I love to repose. There I find a Life which I cannot define, a Joy which I cannot comprehend, a Peace which is not found even under the most hospitable roofs of the dearest friends. The Eucharist is a Shelter to me against my enemies, against the devil, against the world, against my passions, and against my ill-regulated inclinations. The Eucharist is a Support to me in my weakness, a Consolation in sorrow, a Weapon in conflict, a Refreshment in heat, a Nourishment in hunger, a Recreation in fatigue, and a Heaven upon earth. The Eucharist is the Source of my Riches in poverty, my Treasure in want, my Clothing in nakedness, and my Crown in affliction. The Eucharist is my God and my All, my Jesus and my Beloved.

*

O Sacrament most Holy, O Sacrament Divine, all praise and all thanksgiving, be every moment Thine!

Litany of the Blessed Sacrament

Lord, have Mercy on us. Lord, have Mercy on us.
Christ, have Mercy on us. Christ, have Mercy on us.
Lord, have Mercy on us. Lord, have Mercy on us.
Christ, hear us. Christ, graciously hear us.
God, the Father of Heaven, have Mercy on us.
God, the Son, Redeemer of the world,
God, the Holy Spirit,
Holy Trinity, One God,
Living Bread, that came down from Heaven,
  we love You, O Jesus.
Hidden God and Savior,
Wheat of the elect, and Vine bearing virgins,
Perpetual Sacrifice and Clean Oblation,
Lamb without spot, Immaculate Feast,
Food of Angels, and hidden Manna,
Word-made-Flesh dwelling in us,
Sacred Host and Chalice of Benediction,
Mystery of Faith, most Excellent and Venerable
  Sacrament,
Atonement of the living and the dead,
Heavenly Antidote against the poison of sin,
Most Wonderful of all Miracles,
Most Holy Commemoration of the Passion of Jesus,
Plenitude of all gifts,
Special Memorial of Divine Love,
Overflowing Fountain of Divine Goodness,
Most High and Holy Mystery,
Life-giving Sacrifice,
Bread-made-Flesh by the Omnipotence of the
  Incarnate Word,
Sacrament of Piety, Sign of Unity, and Bond of
  Charity,
Priest and Victim,
Viaticum for those who die in the Lord,
Pledge of future Glory, we love You, O Jesus.

From an unworthy reception of Your Body and
Blood,   deliver us, O Lord.
From every occasion of sin, deliver us, O Lord.
Through the desire You had to eat this Pasch with
Your disciples,   we beseech You, hear us.
Through Your Precious Blood, shed for us on the
Cross, and really present on our altars,
Through the Five Wounds You received in Your
Sacred Body,   we beseech You, hear us.
May You preserve and increase our faith,
reverence, and devotion towards this Admirable
Sacrament,   we beseech You, hear us.
May we by frequent and sincere confession be
disposed for worthy Communion,
Deliver us from all tepidity, coldness, and hardness
of heart,   we beseech You, hear us.
Impart to us the Precious Fruit of this most Holy
Sacrament,   we beseech You, hear us.
At the hour of death, strengthen and defend us
with this most Holy Viaticum,
                                we beseech You, hear us.

Lamb of God, You take away the sins of the
world, spare us, O Lord.
Lamb of God, You take away the sins of the
world, graciously hear us, O Lord.
Lamb of God, You take away the sins of the
world, have Mercy on us.

O God, in this wonderful Sacrament, You have
left us a memorial of Your Passion and Death.
Grant, we beseech You, that we may so worthily
revere the Holy Mysteries of Your Sacred Body
and Blood, as continually to preserve in our
souls the Fruit of Your Redemption.
Amen.

Litany of the Holy Name of Jesus

Lord, have Mercy on us. Lord, have Mercy on us.
Christ, have Mercy on us. Christ, have Mercy on us.
Lord, have Mercy on us. Lord have Mercy on us.
Christ, hear us. Christ graciously hear us.
God, the Father of Heaven, have Mercy on us.
God, the Son, Redeemer of the world,
God, the Holy Spirit,
Holy Trinity, One God,
Jesus, Son of the Living God, have Mercy on us.
Jesus, Splendor of the Father,   (we love You!)
Jesus, Brightness of Eternal Light,
Jesus, King of Glory,
Jesus, Sun of Justice,
Jesus, Son of the Virgin Mary,
Jesus, most Amiable,
Jesus, Mighty God,
Jesus, Father of the world to come,
Jesus, Angel of Great Counsel,
Jesus, most Powerful,
Jesus, most Patient,
Jesus, most Obedient,
Jesus, Meek and Humble of Heart,
Jesus, Lover of Chastity,
Jesus, Lover of us,
Jesus, God of Peace,
Jesus, Author of Life,
Jesus, Example of Virtue,
Jesus, Zealous Lover of souls,
Jesus, our God,
Jesus, our Refuge,
Jesus, Father of the poor,
Jesus, Treasure of the faithful,
Jesus, Good Shepherd,
Jesus, True Light,
Jesus, Eternal Wisdom,
Jesus, Infinite Goodness,
Jesus, our Way and our Life,
Jesus, King of Patriarchs, have Mercy on us.

Jesus, Master of the Apostles,   have Mercy on us.
Jesus, Teacher of the Evangelists, (we love You!)
Jesus, Strength of Martyrs,
Jesus, Light of Confessors,
Jesus, Purity of Virgins,
Jesus, Crown of all Saints, have Mercy on us.

Lamb of God, You take away the sins of the world, spare us, O Lord.
Lamb of God, You take away the sins of the world, graciously hear us, O Lord.
Lamb of God, You take away the sins of the world, have Mercy on us.

O Jesus, You said: "Ask, and you shall receive; seek, and you shall find; knock, and it shall be opened to you." We ask You; we seek You; grant us the Grace of Your Divine Charity; may we love only You; may we praise You forever! Amen.

*

The Name of Jesus

"The name of Jesus is most powerful. Pronounce it often, let it be constantly in your thoughts. It will be strength to you in weakness, courage in timidity, love in hatred, health in sickness, joy in sorrow, wisdom in ignorance, and aid in trouble. If you will say My name, all things that you need will be given to you. You cannot repeat it often enough. Thousands of times a day would not be too often. Say My name; be at peace."

*

Holy God, we praise Thy Name.
Lord of all, we bow before Thee.
All on earth Thy scepter claim,
All in heaven above adore Thee;
Infinite Thy vast domain, Everlasting is Thy reign.
Hark the loud celestial hymn,
Angel choirs above are raising;
Cherubim and Seraphim
In unceasing chorus praising,
Fill the heavens with sweet accord: Holy, Holy, Holy, Lord!

†

IN HONOR OF MOST HOLY MARY

*   *   *   *   *   *   *

The Eternal Father instructs us about our duties towards Holy Mary

"It is My Will that during your pilgrimage in your mortal body, you place Holy Mary as the beginning of your joy, and that you follow Her through the desert of renunciation and abnegation of all that is human and visible. Follow Her by a perfect imitation according to your strength, and the light which you receive.

"Let Holy Mary be your guiding Star and your Directress: She will manifest to you My Will and you will find My Holy Law which is written in Her by My Power.

"Meditate upon it day and night. She, by Her intercession, will strike the Rock of Christ's Humanity, in order that in this desert may abound the Waters of Divine Grace and Light, so that your thirst may be quenched, your understanding enlightened, and your will inflamed. She will be a Light to illumine your path, and a Cloud to afford you shade and refreshment against the ardors of your passions and the fierceness of your enemies.

"You will have in Holy Mary, an Angel to guard and guide you, and lead you away from the dangers of Babylon and Sodom, so that My punishment shall not reach you.

"You will have in Holy Mary, a Mother to Love you, a Friend to counsel you, a Teacher to instruct you, a Protectress to shield you, and

Duties toward Holy Mary 1

375

a Queen whom you can serve and obey.

"In the Virtues which the Blessed Mother of the Only-Begotten exercised in the Temple, you will find a summary of all the highest perfections according to which you should arrange your life; an exact and reliable copy of all Her Sanctity; the beauty of virginity, the loveliness of humility, the utmost promptness in devotion and obedience, the steadfastness of faith, the certitude of hope, the fire of Love, and the most complete outline map of all My wonders.

"According to this Rule, you must regulate your life; by this Mirror, you must arrange and adorn yourself with the beauty and grace of a bride that wishes to enter into the chamber of her Spouse and Lord.

"If the nobility and condition of the teacher are a spur to the disciple and tend to make the lesson more acceptable, who can attract you more powerfully than your Instructress? She is the Mother of your Spouse, chosen as the most Pure and Holy among women! She is without blemish of sin, being at the same time a Virgin and the Mother of the Only-Begotten of the Eternal Father.

"Hear then, this Sovereign Virgin; follow Her in close imitation, and meditate without ceasing upon Her admirable excellence and virtues. Remember, that the life Holy Mary led in the Temple, is the original, which all souls that consecrate themselves after Her as spouses of Christ, must copy within themselves."

Duties toward Holy Mary 2*

Jesus: "Never leave your Immaculate Mother. She won't leave you either. Since suffering increases love, just imagine the tenderness She feels for you. Nothing could ever diminish Her Love for you, not even your ingratitude. Love the Virgin Mary; thank Her. Speak to Her about your Love, and this will draw you nearer to Me, your Savior. Where else would She lead you, if not to Me? Ask My Mother to teach you to live for Me. Put all your trust in Her. She will help you on your uphill climb; it is strenuous work climbing the mountain of perfection. Just when you think you are going up, you find that you are slipping back. Who will purify you? Who will put Light into your mind? Light can only come from those who possess it: the Saints and Holy Mary, the Queen of all Saints."

*

"Pray to My Mother in this manner:

O most sweet and amiable Virgin Mary, most Beloved Daughter of the Eternal Father, most tender Mother of the Eternal Son, most Holy Spouse of the Eternal Spirit, I come to You, O most loving Mother, to consecrate myself entirely to You.

You, Holy Mary, are all Pure, all Beautiful; You are the Immaculate, and have always been the delight of the most Holy Trinity; You have ravished the Heart of God Your Father, God Your Son, and God Your Holy Spouse, with Your Immaculate and Holy Soul.

O most Compassionate Mother, cast a glance of pity on these poor souls, made the target of many fierce temptations. By Your power, put to flight

377

the infernal enemy. I come to take refuge in Your Immaculate Heart. O most Merciful Queen of Virgins, preserve me pure and present me to my Lord and Spouse, Jesus.

I expect You, Holy Mary, at the hour of my death; until that hour I shall thank You and implore You to watch over me, so that I may please my Jesus in all things."

*

Sweetest Jesus, I beseech You, by the Love which caused You to take flesh of the most Pure Virgin, to supply for our defects in the service and honor of Your most Benign Mother, who is ever ready to assist us with maternal tenderness, in all our necessities. Offer Holy Mary the superabundant beatitude of Your sweetest Heart; show Her Your divine predilection. You chose Her from all eternity to be Your Mother, adorning Her with every Grace and Virtue. Remind Her of all the tenderness You manifested to Her in all things. Remind Her of the joys and glory of Her Assumption, when She was exalted above all the choirs of Angels, and constituted Queen of Heaven and earth.

*

I honor and greet You, O Virgin surpassingly sweet, in the intimate union in which You are united to God above all creatures. To make amends for all the negligences I have committed in Your service, I offer You, O Tender Mother, the most glorious and adorable Heart of Jesus Christ, with all that true, faithful, and filial Love He showed You in such perfection on earth, and will forever show You in Heaven. Amen.

*

A Consecration of myself to Jesus the Incarnate Wisdom, through the Hands of the Virgin Mary, the Mother of God and Queen of Heaven.

O Eternal and Incarnate Wisdom! O sweetest and most adorable Jesus, You are True God and True Man, only Son of the Eternal Father and of Mary ever Virgin! I adore You profoundly in the bosom and splendors of Your Father during eternity; I adore You also in the Virgin Mary, Your most worthy Mother, at the time of Your Incarnation.

I give You thanks for annihilating Yourself, in taking the form of a slave in order to rescue me from the cruel slavery of the devil. I praise and glorify You for submitting Yourself to Mary, Your Holy Mother, in all things, in order to make me Your faithful slave through Her. Alas, ungrateful and faithless as I have been, I have not kept the promises which I made so solemnly to You in my Baptism; I have not fulfilled my obligations; I do not deserve to be called Your child, nor even Your slave. As there is nothing in me which does not merit Your anger and Your rejection, I dare no longer to come by myself before Your most Holy and August Majesty. It is on this account that I have recourse to the intercession of Your most Holy Mother, whom You have given me as Mediatrix with You. It is by Her means that I hope to obtain from You: the acquisition and the preservation of wisdom, contrition, and the pardon of my sins.

I salute You, O Immaculate Mary, living Tabernacle

Consecration 1

379

of the Divinity, where the Eternal Wisdom willed to be hidden, and be adored by Angels and mortals. I hail You, O Queen of Heaven and earth, to whose Empire everything is subject which is under God.

I salute You, O sure Refuge of sinners. Your mercy fails no one. Hear the desire which I have of the Divine Wisdom, and for that end receive the vows and offerings which I present to You. I, a faithless sinner, renew and ratify today in Your Hands the vows of my Baptism; I renounce forever satan, his ostentatious display of magnificence and his works; I give myself entirely to Jesus Christ, the Incarnate Wisdom, to carry my cross after Him all the days of my life, and to be more faithful to Him than I have ever been before.

In the presence of all the Angels and Saints, I choose You, Holy Mary, this day for my Mother. I give and consecrate to You, as Your slave, my body and soul, my goods, both interior and exterior, and even the value of all my good actions, past, present, and future; leaving to You the entire and full right of disposing of me, and all that belongs to me, without exception, according to Your good pleasure, for the greater honor and glory of God, in time and in eternity.

Receive, O Benign Virgin, this little offering of my slavery, in honor of, and in union with that subjection which the Eternal Wisdom deigned to have for Your Maternity, in honor of the power which You and Your Son have over this little and miserable sinner, and in thanksgiving for the

Consecration 2

380

privileges with which the Holy Trinity has favored You. I desire, henceforth, to be Your true slave, to seek Your honor, and to obey You in all things.

O admirable Mother Mary, present me to Your dear Son as His eternal slave, so that as He has redeemed me by You, by You He may receive me! O Mother of Mercy, obtain for me the grace to acquire true wisdom of God, and for that end put me in the number of those whom You Love, whom You teach, whom You conduct, and whom You nourish and protect, as Your children and Your slaves.

O Faithful Virgin, make me in all things so perfect a disciple, imitator, and slave of the Incarnate Wisdom, Jesus Christ Your Son, that I may attain, by Your intercession and by Your example, the happiness to serve my Master all the days of my life on earth, and glorify Him for all eternity. Amen. Consecration 3*

*   *   *   *   *

Instruction

You souls, who are thus voluntarily consecrated and sacrificed to Jesus through Holy Mary, can no longer dispose of the value of your good actions. All you suffer, all you think, and all the good you say or do, belongs to Mary, in order that She may dispose of it according to the Will of Her Son, and His greater glory. That dependence in no way prejudices the obligations of the state you may be in at present, or may be placed in for the future. For example: that dependence in no way prejudices the obligations of a priest, who, by his office, should apply the satisfactory value of the Holy Mass to some person. You make the offering only according to the order of God and the duties of your state. This practice does not hinder you from praying for others, whether living or dead. You have impoverished yourself to honor Holy Mary and She will honor your requests out of gratitude to you.

You consecrate yourself at one and the same time to most Holy Mary and to Jesus Christ. You consecrate yourself to the most Holy Virgin, as the perfect means which Jesus Christ has chosen to unite Himself to us, and us to Him. You consecrate yourself to our Lord, our Eternal Repose, to whom we owe all we are, as our Redeemer and our God.

*

Trust not the gold of your charity, the silver of your purity, the waters of your graces, nor the wines of your merits and virtues to a torn sack, an old and broken coffer, a spoiled and corrupted vessel, like yourselves. If you do so, you will be stripped by the demons, who are seeking and watching you night and day; you will infect by your own bad odor of self-love, self-confidence, and self-will, all which God has given you. Pour into the Heart of Holy Mary all your treasures, graces, and virtues. She is a Spiritual Vessel, a Vessel of Honor, the marvelous Vessel of Devotion!

*

You can call our Lord: "Jesus of Mary", and our Blessed Mother: "Mary of Jesus".

*

To Jesus through Mary!

*

382

O Mary, Mother of God, Your Name is full of all Graces and Divine Blessings. You have nourished Jesus who nourishes all living creatures. He who fills Heaven and earth, and is Lord of all, has chosen to have need of You, since You have clothed Him with that Garment of Flesh. Rejoice, O Mother and Handmaid of God, rejoice, rejoice! You have for a debtor Him to whom all creatures owe their being. We are all debtors to God, but God is a debtor to You. Hence it is, O most Holy Mother of God, that Your Goodness and Charity is greater than all the Saints. We desire to honor and celebrate Your Glories and Attributes. May we know how great is Your Goodness, since You are mindful of us and of our miseries.

*

O Immaculate and wholly Pure Virgin Mary, Mother of God, Queen of the universe, our most Excellent Lady! You are superior to all the Saints! You are the only Hope of the fathers, and the Joy of the Blessed. By You we have been reconciled to our God. You are the only Advocate of sinners, the secure Haven of the shipwrecked. You are the Consolation of all souls in the world, the Redemption of captives, the Joy of the sick, the Comfort of the afflicted; You are the Refuge and Salvation of all mankind.

O Mary, full of Grace, illumine my intellect, and loosen my tongue so that it may sing Your praises. I salute You, O Peace, O Joy, O greatest of all Miracles! You are a Paradise of Delight, a Secure Haven, and a Fountain of Grace! You are the Mediatrix between God and mankind!

*

Exhortation about "Mary our Help"

If you perceive yourself, during this mortal life, to be sinking in treacherous waters, at the mercy of the winds and the waves, rather than walking securely on the stable earth, turn your eyes towards the splendor of this guiding Star, so that you will not be submerged by the tempest! When the storms of temptation burst upon you, when you are driven upon the rocks of tribulation, look up at the Star, call upon Mary. When buffeted by the billows of pride, ambition, hatred, or jealousy, look at the Star, call upon Mary. Should anger, avarice, or carnal desires violently assail the little vessel of your soul, look up at the Star, call upon Mary. If you are troubled because of the heinousness of your sins, confounded at the filthy state of your conscience, and terrified at the thought of the awful judgment to come, if you begin to sink into the gulf of sadness and to be absorbed in the abyss of despair, oh, then think of Mary! In dangers, in difficulties, and in doubts, think of Mary, call upon Mary!

Let not Mary's name depart from your lips, never let it leave your heart. That you may more surely obtain the assistance of Her prayer, walk in Her footsteps. With Mary for a Guide, you shall never go astray. Invoking Her, you shall never lose heart. As long as She is in your mind, you are safe from deception. While She holds your hand, you cannot fall. Under Her protection, you have nothing to fear. Since Mary walks with you, you will not grow weary; since She shows you Her favor, you will reach the Goal.

*

Prayer to the Immaculate Heart of Mary

O Heart of Mary, Mother of God and our Mother; Heart most worthy of love, in which the Adorable Trinity is ever pleased, worthy of the veneration and love of all the Angels and mankind; Heart full of goodness, ever compassionate toward our miseries. As Your Heart is one with the Heart of Jesus, melt our icy hearts and grant that they may also be changed into the Heart of Jesus. Pour into them the love of Your virtues, enkindle in them that Divine Fire with which You are inflamed. In You let Holy Church find a safe shelter; protect Her and be Her Refuge, Her Tower of Strength, impregnable against every assualt, of Her enemies. Be the Way which leads to Jesus, and the Channel through which we receive all the graces needed for our salvation. Be our Refuge in time of trouble, our Solace in the midst of trial, our Strength against temptation, our Haven in persecution, our present Help in every danger, especially at the hour of death, when all hell shall try to possess our souls. At that hour, O most tender Virgin, make us feel the sweetness of Your Heart, and the might of Your intercession with Jesus; open to us a safe refuge in that Fountain of Mercy, where we may come to praise Him with You in Paradise, world without end.

*

O Virgin Mary

O Virgin Mary, Queen of all creation, I am Your servant; I wish to be faithful for all eternity. Forever will I praise the Omnipotence of the Most High, because He chose to exalt You above all creation. Since You are so fortunate and so powerful with the Almighty, I ask You to look with Mercy on me, Your poor and miserable servant. Make me a partaker of the gifts which the Lord has placed in Your Hands for distribution among the needy; raise me from my abject state; enrich my nakedness and poverty. As a Queen, compel me to desire and do what is most perfect, helping me to find grace in Your most Holy Son and my Lord. I have nothing to oblige You as I am unworthy, but as a substitute I offer You, most Holy Mary, Your own Sanctity and Clemency.

*

Prayer to Mary Help of Christians

O Mary, Powerful Virgin, You are the Mighty and Glorious Protector of Holy Church, You are the marvelous Help of Christians. You are more powerful than an army in battle array. You alone have destroyed every heresy in the whole world. In the midst of our anguish, our struggles, and our distress, defend us from the enemy, and, at the hour of our death receive our souls into Heaven. Amen.

*

Hail, Holy Queen of the Heavens
(Ave, Regina Caelorum)

Hail, Holy Queen of the Heavens! Hail, Holy Queen of the Angels! Hail, Root of Jesse! Hail, Gate of Heaven! By You the Light has entered the world. Rejoice, glorious Virgin, beautiful among all women! Hail, radiant Splendor, intercede with Christ for us.

*

Holy Mary is our tainted nature's solitary Boast.

*

Prayers to Our Mother of Perpetual Help

Behold at Your Feet, O Mother of Perpetual Help, us wretched sinners who have recourse to You, and confide in You. We do not even merit that You should look on us, but we know that having seen Your Son die to save sinners, You also desire to aid us. O Mother of Mercy, look on our miseries, and have pity on us. We hear You called by all: "The Refuge of sinners, the Hope of the desperate, the Help of the abandoned." Be then, our Refuge, our Hope, and our Help. Assist us for the Love of Jesus Christ; stretch forth Your Hand to us miserably fallen creatures, for we recommend ourselves to You, and we devote ourselves to You in Your service forever.

We bless and thank Almighty God, who in His Mercy has given us this confidence in You, which we hold as a pledge of our eternal Salvation. Dearest Mother, in the past we have miserably fallen into sin because we have not had recourse to You. The danger is not over, our enemies do not sleep. We know that with Your Help, we shall conquer. We know that You will assist us, if we recommend ourselves to You. This grace we ask of You, and this we beg with all the fervor of our souls: that in all the attacks of hell, we may ever have recourse to You. O Mary help us; O Mother of Perpetual Help, never permit us to lose our God.

O Mother of Perpetual Help, grant that we may ever invoke Your most Powerful Name, which is the Safeguard of the living and the Salvation of the dying. O Purest Mary, O sweetest Mary, let Your Name henceforth be ever on our lips. In all our temptations and in all our needs, we shall never cease to call on You, ever repeating Your Sacred Name: Mary, Mary! O what consolation, what sweetness, what confidence fills our souls, when we pronounce Your Sacred Name, or even only think of You. We thank the Lord for having given You, for our good, so sweet, so powerful, so lovely a Name. We will not be content with merely pronouncing Your Name, let our love for You prompt us ever to greet You: O Mother of Perpetual Help.

O Mother of Perpetual Help, You are the Dispenser of all Gifts which God grants to us miserable sinners, and for this reason He has made You so powerful, so rich, and so bountiful, in order that You may help us in our misery. You are the Advocate of the most wretched and abandoned sinners who have recourse to You. Come to our aid, dearest Mother, for we recommend ourselves to You. In Your Hands, we place our eternal salvation, and to You we entrust our souls. Count us among Your most devoted servants; take us under Your Protection, and it is enough for us. Since You will protect us dear Mother, we will fear nothing; not from our sins, because You will obtain for us the pardon of them; not from the devils, because You are more powerful than all hell together. We do not even fear Jesus our Judge, because, by one prayer from You, He will be appeased. Obtain for us the pardon of our sins, love for Jesus, the grace to have recourse to You, a holy life, a good death, and finally Paradise. We trust in You; in You we hope, rest, and live; in You we wish to die. Into Your Hands we intrust our souls, O Mother of Perpetual Help.

Litany of the Blessed Virgin Mary

Lord, have Mercy on us. Lord, have Mercy on us.
Christ, have Mercy on us. Christ, have Mercy on us.
Lord, have Mercy on us. Lord, have Mercy on us.
Christ, hear us. Christ, graciously hear us.
God the Father of Heaven, have Mercy on us.
God the Son, Redeemer of the world,
God the Holy Spirit,
Holy Trinity, One God,
Holy Mary, pray for us.   (we love You.)
Holy Mother of God,
Holy Virgin of virgins,
Mother of Christ,
Mother of Divine Grace,
Mother most Pure,
Mother most Chaste,
Mother Inviolate,
Mother Undefiled,
Mother most Amiable,
Mother most Admirable,
Mother of Good Counsel,
Mother of our Creator,
Mother of our Savior,
Virgin most Prudent,
Virgin most Venerable,
Virgin most Renowned,
Virgin most Powerful,
Virgin most Merciful,
Virgin most Faithful,
Mirror of Justice,
Seat of Wisdom,
Cause of our Joy,
Spiritual Vessel,
Singular Vessel of Devotion,
Mystical Rose,
Tower of David,
Tower of Ivory,
House of Gold,
Ark of the Covenant, pray for us. (we love You.)

Gate of Heaven, pray for us.   (we love You.)
Morning Star,
Health of the sick,
Refuge of sinners,
Comforter of the afflicted,
Help of Christians,
Queen of Angels,
Queen of Patriarchs,
Queen of Prophets,
Queen of Apostles,
Queen of Martyrs,
Queen of Confessors,
Queen of Virgins,
Queen of all Saints,
Queen conceived without original sin,
Queen assumed into Heaven,
Queen of the most Holy Rosary,
Queen of Peace, pray for us.   (we love You.)

Lamb of God, You take away the sins of the world, spare us, O Lord.
Lamb of God, You take away the sins of the world, graciously hear us, O Lord.
Lamb of God, You take away the sins of the world, have Mercy on us.

We fly to Your Patronage, O Holy Mother of God; despise not our petitions in our necessities, but deliver us always from all danger, O Glorious and ever Blessed Virgin. Amen.

Pray for us, O Holy Mother of God,   that we may be worthy of the promises of Christ.

Grant, we beseech You, O Lord God, that we Your servants may rejoice in continual health of mind and body; by the glorious intercession of the Blessed Mary ever Virgin, may we be delivered from present sorrow and enjoy eternal gladness, through Christ our Lord. Amen.

†

THOUGHTS FOR A HOLY DEATH

"Do you think that I will abandon you at the moment of death, you who are so miserable that you cannot live without Me? As a mother embraces her newborn child, so will I enfold you in My Love, because you are My tiny child, and I know that you cannot live without Me."

*

"How can you make progress all by yourself? Let yourself be carried in stronger arms, just as you did when you were little. Don't be ashamed of being weak and imperfect. Be smaller still; I will Love you even more. Don't lose sight of the path of spiritual childhood. Cultivate your confidence; let it blossom as a flower. You can trust Me, can't you? Look back, don't you find that I am worthy of it? My friend, don't put any limit to your feelings for Me. I put no limit to My feelings for you.

"Come to Me, little by little, your heart will be on fire at the moment of death. Find a sweeter name for death. Call it: the 'meeting' and even now, though you can scarcely see Me in the twilight of time, you will stretch out your arms to Me. Oh, the charm of an impatient heart longing to be enfolded in Mine."

*

"Picture Me as a Living Being, who Loves you more than you could ever imagine, even in your greatest desires. Keep before you the thought that I, who gave My Life for you, am waiting with infinite yearning for the moment of our 'meeting'."

"My child, remember this: as one lives, so one dies. If during these moments before our 'meeting,' your heart is full of Me, if zeal for My Kingdom consumes it, if you are thirsty for My Glory, you will pass on to our 'meeting' with a thought of love. It will be your true birthday: born to Life Everlasting. I am your Life, your Jesus."

*

"Isn't your life on earth drawing to a close? Don't you need to warm your heart more often in the secret place of the Most High God? When someone is about to make a last voyage to a particular country, doesn't he live through it in anticipation, holding the far horizons to his heart?

"Look forward to your departure to Heaven, since it is to take you to your Beloved. Say to Him: 'It is time we saw one another. When will You unveil the sweetness of Your Face for me? Have I not been traveling long enough in the desert? May I not leave this cold and barren earth to throw myself into Your arms? Enliven my desires. Hasten my steps. No longer can any earthly tie hold me back. Let my soul escape from its body as a bird from its cage, so that the breath You have given me may be lost in Your Divine Being.' I will listen to your voice, for I too am at work in you, preparing for our 'meeting'. You will ask: 'Where is my Beloved?' I will be there all the time, since I am everywhere."

*

"Thank Me for your nature, even with all its faults and failings, for this can be a source of merit for you."

*

Jesus, Mary, I love You! Save souls!

"Instead of wounding My Heart with distrust, you should give a little more thought to the Heaven which awaits you! I did not create you for hell but for Heaven, not as a companion for the devil but to enjoy Me in everlasting Love! Only those go to hell who want to go there. How foolish is your fear of being damned! After having shed My Blood in order to save your soul, after having surrounded your soul with graces upon graces all through your entire existence, would I permit satan, My worst enemy, to rob Me of your soul at the last moment of your life, just when I am ready to gather in the fruit of the Redemption and when your soul is about to see Me and love Me in Heaven forever? Would I do that, when in the Holy Gospel I have promised to give souls Eternal Life and that no one can snatch them from My Hands? How is it possible to believe such a monstrosity?

"Final impenitence is found only in a soul who purposely wishes to go to hell and therefore obstinately refuses My Mercy, for I never refuse to pardon anyone! I offer the gift of My immense compassion to all, for My Blood was shed for all! No, it is not the multiplicity of sins which condemns a soul, since I forgive everything if one repents, but it is the obstinacy of not wishing to be pardoned, of wishing to be damned. Dismas on the cross had only one act of faith in Me, but many, many sins; he was pardoned in an instant however, and on the very day of his repentance he entered into My Kingdom and is a saint! Behold the triumph of My Mercy and of faith in Me!"

"You lose yourself in so many trifles, and you do not give to Me the one thing that I ask for: love. In your last hour you will desire in vain to live longer and perform one more act of love. It will then be too late!"

*

Lord Jesus, I thank You. You seem to go to all lengths to fill my cup of joy to the brim at the end of my life, don't You?

"Isn't My special task to give you joy? I am Fullness! Everything exists in Me, and those who possess faith drink deep. You must believe and hope. Oh, this great virtue of hope! Practice it often, so that it will increase in you. The more you expect, the more you receive. Then expect even the impossible and you will have it."

*

"Say: My Father, I offer You the Heart of Jesus in each one of my heartbeats."

*

My Jesus, I desire that You would be happy in my heart.

"Your desire pleases Me and gives Me great honor. You make reparation for yourself and you make reparation for the ingratitude of so many others. Do souls think of Me with a little affection even once a year? Do they accept the thought of My Love for each one of them? When will they realize that time, the span of earthly life, is too short, that I need all eternity to Love them? When will they realize that this present life of theirs is not their goal? When will they realize that this present life is only a means given to them to earn Heaven?"

"You are worried about the passage from this life to the next? Since it is the greatest proof of love that you can give Me, be glad. Offer your death to Me now with complete detachment, ready even for heroism. Say: 'Even if I did not have to suffer death, I would choose it in order to be more one with You.' In this way you will give Me the greatest glory a creature can give the Creator. O precious death of the Saints, that echoes even in the heavenly courts of the Father's Home!"

*

"Do you think of yourself as one not yet born? Your real birth is your entrance into heavenly glory. Prepare for it; make everything ready. Recall the life of the humble caterpillar crawling on the earth, then its secret, hidden life within the chrysalis, and at last, the butterfly with its magic-colored wings is flying free.

"O rejoice at the thought that you will soon be born to fullness of life."

*

"When the moment of death comes for My friends, I come gently, with all the delicate touches that you know, to take souls into My Kingdom? You would do the same if you were taking someone into one of your beautiful homes. You would want to feel the joy of their surprise, wouldn't you? I, your God, who Love more and possess more, how could I fail to be interested in the passing of My friends from time?"

*

St. Gertrude made a donation of all her merits and good works to the souls in purgatory. The demon appeared to her at the moment of death, and mocked her saying: "How vain you are and how cruel you have been to yourself. What greater pride can there be than to wish to pay the debts of others without paying one's own? Now we will see the result; when you are dead, you will pay for yourself in the fires of purgatory, and we will laugh at your folly while you weep for your pride." Then Sr. Gertrude saw her Divine Spouse approaching her, who consoled her with these words: "In order that you may know how agreeable your charity for the souls of the departed has been to Me, I remit all the pains of purgatory which you might have suffered; I promised to return to you a hundred for one, now I will further increase your celestial glory abundantly, giving you a special recompense for the charity which you have exercised towards My beloved souls in purgatory, by renouncing in their favor your works of satisfaction."

*

Holy Mary: "Jesus, my sweetest Love, highest Good and Treasure of my soul, draw me now after the sweetness of Your anointing, which You have permitted Your handmaid and Mother to taste in this world. My will always found its rest entirely in You, the highest Truth; never have I loved anyone but You! O my Hope and Glory, let not my course on earth be prolonged, let not the beginning of that much desired freedom of Heaven be postponed! Let the term of my life be fulfilled. Let that end come which I tended toward from the first instant in which I received my being from You. All the powers of my soul and all my faculties look towards You, the Sun which gives Life, desiring the Good they are awaiting in Heaven."

An Exercise of Preparation for Death

Jesus: "O religious soul, I instruct you that when you would perform the Exercise of Preparation for Death you should do it in this manner:

"Kneeling in spirit before God, acknowledge your nothingness; then you shall give your hand to Love, who will introduce you into the most Sweet, most Lovable, and most Tender Heart of your Jesus.

"Having entered this Heart, put yourself into a corner as a little atom of dirt, and say with faith these words: 'My Jesus, at the entrance of great palaces, carpets are laid in order that those who enter may cleanse their shoes from the dirt and mud; I am a little grain of dirt that does not merit to enter into the Palace of Your Heart.'

"After this 'Act of Humility,' Love will come to take you, and you will follow wherever He wishes to conduct you.

"In the Light of Love, examine the use you have made of the faculties of your soul and the senses of your body. Then you shall make an act of contrition and a firm purpose of amendment.

"You will conclude with this formula, which Love places on your lips: O Jesus, during this month I have abused so many of Your most precious graces and have failed in fidelity in the resolutions with which You in Your Goodness inspired me. My Jesus, Pardon and Mercy! If in You there were only Justice, I would have everything to fear, but since Your Heart is the Source of Mercy, I come to You with renewed confidence. O Jesus, since You have borne with me so long a time without any merit of mine, continue to be Merciful to me. O Jesus, I ask still more. Render me always faithful, and grant that I may begin again, a life altogether new, in You, for You, and with You. Amen. Blest be God."

*

Holy Mary our Teacher: "God has providentially formed mankind in such a way that their existence and formation indicate and rehearse the important lesson of humility, never allowing them to be without this salutary teaching. On this account He has not formed them of the most excellent material; He has concealed the noblest part of their being in the sanctuary of their interior."

*

"Die often during your lifetime, so that it will not be hard to die when the time comes."

*

"Have I asked you to merit the graces I give you? What I ask is that you should accept them. Always remember that I Love you because you are little, not because you are good.

"What would you do if you had not My Heart? The more feeble you are, the more tenderly I Love you."

*

How did Saint Aloysius rise to such a height of sanctity; in what time, and by what works?
"He rose to sanctity on the wings of great desires."

With Jesus, even the cross is delightful, but without Jesus all delights are but a cross.

Lord, show Your Mercy to me at the hour of my death.

"How can I fail to accomplish what I have already commenced?"

Lord, if You had taken me out of the world when I thought my death was near, I would have been better prepared to die than I am now, for my negligences have rendered me less worthy.

"All things are ordered by the Wisdom of My Providence; whatever you have once done is always before Me, and whatever you may add will not be lost.

"Preparation for death may be made long before the event, as a prince prepares for a long time in advance for his nuptials. In the preceding harvest, the grain and the grapes are stored up in his cellars, so that there may be an abundant supply when it is needed; the nuptials may not be spoken of again until the time approaches, although the preparations are made."

*

"When I behold mortals in their last agony who have thought of Me with pleasure, or who have performed any works deserving of reward, I appear to them at the moment of death with a countenance so full of Love and Mercy, that they repent from their inmost hearts for having ever offended Me, and they are saved by that repentance."

*

"Whenever you desire with all your heart to be delivered from the prison of the body, and at the same time are perfectly willing to remain as long as it shall please Me, I unite the Merits of My adorable Life to yours, which renders you marvelously perfect in the sight of My Eternal Father."

*

"I inclined your will to desire death, and, consequently you wanted to receive Extreme Unction. I have preserved in the depth of My Heart, for your eternal salvation, all that you have done in thought or act to prepare yourself for this Sacrament.

"If you were deprived of this Sacrament by sudden death, or if you receive It after having lost consciousness, which often happens to My elect, you would not suffer any loss thereby, because all the preparation for death which you have made is preserved in My Divinity, where, by My cooperation, it always remains for your Eternal Salvation."

*

"When any prayers, sacrifices, or desires are offered to Me for the faithful departed, I use them immediately according to My inclination to show Mercy and Pardon, either for the remission of their sins, for their consolation, or for the increase of their eternal Happiness, according to the condition of those for whom the offering is made. When a similar offering is made for the living, I keep it for their benefit, because they can still increase their merit by their good works, by their good desires, and by their good will; they should endeavor to acquire by their labor, what they desire to obtain through the intercession of others."

*

"As you desire in all your actions the glory of God, and not your own, the fervor of your zeal increases a hundredfold the gifts which you offer your Spouse, not only by the pious works which you actually accomplish, but even by those which you desire to do yourself or to see done by others, although it is not in your power to perform them. I will supply before My Heavenly Father your needs and your defects, and those of others for whom you are solicitous; therefore do not doubt that I will equally regard all you desire to do as if you had accomplished it. Know that the whole Court of Heaven rejoices in your advancement and returns thanks and praise to God for love of you."

*

"I beg the love of My creatures, who refuse it to Me and squander it upon things which pass away. They do not even think of giving it to Me. If you knew how painful it is to Love so much and not to be loved! I do not become weary; I am always seeking love but few give it to Me. Not only do some not love Me, but they even hate Me. Do you know what hinders Me from striking sinners? It is the prayers of the just; they disarm My Divine Justice."

*

O my Savior, why have I not a fire sufficiently strong to melt my heart, so that I might pour it forth entirely into You?

"Your desire is the fire which you will."

*

"When you confide in the prayers of another, with a firm confidence that through their intercession you will receive grace from God, I will pour forth on you My benedictions according to the measure of your desires and your faith, even when the person to whom you have recommended yourself, neglects to pray for you."

*

"When you wish to honor any particular Saint, and give Me thanks for all the graces I have bestowed on that Saint, I increase grace in your soul through the merits of that Saint.

"When you commit the end of your life to any of the Saints by special prayers, those prayers are borne up before the Judge, and I appoint those Saints to be your advocates and to provide whatever you need at that hour.

"If you say an 'Our Father' to honor all the Saints, with the intention, were it possible, of saying one for each of the Saints, your intention is accepted by them as though you had really done so.

"It is likewise most pleasant to the Saints to greet them in and through the Sacred Heart of Jesus, especially if you offer them My Divine Heart, because through It and from It they receive the greatest delights."

*

St. Gertrude offered Holy Mary one hundred and fifty Ave Marias, beseeching Her to assist her at the hour of her death by Her Maternal Tenderness. Each word which Sr. Gertrude repeated appeared like a piece of gold, which our Lord offered to His Mother, who used them for her help and consolation at the hour of her death.

*

Jesus, Mary, I love You! Save souls!

Lord, in one instant You can raise me to the height of sanctity as You did Paul the Apostle. Even though my sins are many, they are still finite, and You, My God, are infinite in Mercy and in Love. Since my soul was created by You to know You, to love, praise, thank, and serve You, surely You would not want the devil to gloat over one more soul in his power which would not love You for all eternity. I know that You have granted me graces beyond my greatest expectation, but this will redound for all eternity to Your honor and glory, for we truly cannot earn Eternal Salvation, which is Your gift to us mortals who try to observe Your Law, and desire to love You beyond the capacity of our fallen nature.

*

How cold, how terribly cold I am! My heart is a glacier. I beg You, Jesus, to permit the warm rays of Your blessings to transform this glacier into a furnace of love. How is it, that in spite of all my prayers, I do not love You as much as I desire? One thing comforts me: the desire to love is, in fact, love. Though my heart is all ice, my will is all on fire. How often I should like to repeat: "If You will, O Jesus, You may consume me!"

*

"If you do your share of penance in your life, I shall not have to send you the sicknesses which takes the place of neglected mortification."

*

"Consider how agreeable your concert of praise is, not only to My ears, but even to My most loving Heart. Do not urgently desire to be separated from the body, merely for the sake of being delivered from the flesh, in which I pour forth so freely the gifts of My grace, for the

more unworthy you are to whom I condescend,
the more I merit to be glorified for it by all
creatures."

*

"I grant you by My authority, a full remission of
all your sins and negligences. Do you think that I
possess less power than I have bestowed on My
creatures? Since I have given to the material sun
such virtue, that if a discolored garment is exposed
to its rays, it will recover its former whiteness,
and even become brighter than before, how
much more can I, who am the Creator of the sun,
by directing My looks upon sinners, remove all
their stains, purifying them from every spot, by
the Fire of My Love."

*

"You cannot imagine the pleasure I experience
in remaining with My creatures! I am always in
search of hearts that love Me, but I find only a
small number. I lavish upon them the plenitude of
My grace, for I have so great a Love for the souls
who are faithful to Me and let Me do what I please
with them, that I am as ready to gratify them as
if it were a law to Me."

*

"The wicked triumph; few souls remain faithful;
they abandon Me to seek happiness where it is
not to be found. O My spouse, can they be happy
while violating a Law so holy, so good and easy
as Mine?"

*

"The farther you advance in the way of
mortification, the nearer you will draw to God;
it is only the first step that costs. Treat your
body as an enemy; give it only what you cannot
refuse."

A journey to hell

I saw in front of me the devil. Sister Josefa

"Tie her feet and bind her hands."

Instantly I lost sight of where I was, and felt myself tightly bound and being dragged away. Other voices screamed: "It doesn't do any good to bind her feet, it is her heart you must bind."

"It does not belong to me," came the devil's reply.

I was dragged along a very dark and lengthy passage, and on all sides resounded terrible cries. On opposite sides of the walls of this narrow corridor were niches out of which poured smoke, which emitted an intolerable stench. From these recesses came blaspheming voices, uttering impure words. Some cursed their bodies, others their parents. Others reproached themselves for refusing grace and not avoiding what they knew to be sinful. It was a medley of confused screams of rage and despair. I was dragged through a corridor which seemed endless. Then I received a violent punch which doubled me in two, and forced me into one of the niches. I felt as if I were being pressed between two burning planks and pierced through with scorching needles. Souls were blaspheming and cursing me. What caused me most suffering, and with which no torture can be compared, was the anguish of my soul to find myself separated from God. It seemed to me that I spent years in hell, yet it lasted only six hours. I was violently pulled out of the niche, and I found myself in a dark place; after striking

A journey to hell 1

me, the devil disappeared and left me free.

How can I describe my feelings on realizing that I was still alive, and could still love my God! I do not know what I am not ready to endure to avoid hell, in spite of my fear of pain. I see clearly that all the sufferings of earth are nothing in comparison with the horror of no longer being able to love, for in that place all breathe hatred and thirst to damn other souls.

On another occasion, on reaching that "abode of horror," I heard yells of rage and devilish exultation because another soul had fallen into everlasting torments.

It seemed, that I was to be in hell forever. What an agony it was for me, for I remembered that I once knew and loved our Lord, that I was a Religious, that He conferred great graces on me, and many means by which to save my soul. What was it, then, that I did? How did I come to lose so many good things? How could I have been so blind? Now all hope was gone. My Communions came back to my mind, and also my novitiate.

The most crushing and overwhelming grief of all, was the torturing memory that I once loved the Heart of Jesus so dearly. I knew Him and He was everything to me. I had lived for Him. How could I exist without Him? How could I live without Love, and with blasphemies and deadly malice on every side? It is impossible to put into words the distress of my broken and oppressed soul.

O Jesus, my Love, please let me love You forever!

A journey to hell 2*

Death

Holy Mary our Teacher: "At the hour of death, the souls of mortals incur the most incredible and dangerous attacks from the demons, as well as from their own frailty and from the creatures around them. That hour is the great trial of life, upon which depends the last sentence of eternal death, or Eternal Life, of eternal suffering or Eternal Glory. When the devil and his satellites of darkness perceive, by the course of natural events, that anyone falls a prey to a dangerous and mortal disease, they immediately prepare to assail the poor and unbewaring soul with all their malice and astuteness, in order to vanquish the soul if possible, by various temptations.

"The devils persuade souls that have a disorderly love of earthly life, that there is not such a great danger, and they prevent others from undeceiving them. Those that have been negligent in the reception of the Sacraments, they try to make still more careless, and they place obstacles and difficulties in the way in order that they may not confess their sins and open their consciences. Other souls, they confuse and try to prevent from making proper restitution and thus unburdening their consciences. Other souls who love vanity, they entangle, even at that last hour, in many vain and proud desires with regard to what is to be done for them after death. Those that have been avaricious or sensual, they seek to excite violently toward what they loved so blindly during life. The devils avail themselves of all the bad habits that the souls were associated with, in order to fill their minds with images of creatures

Death 1

and draw them away from their salvation.

"Generally these enemies cause a great damage to the souls in the hour of death, by exciting in them the vain hope of a longer life or, of being able to execute later on what God suggests to them by means of the Holy Angels. Giving way to this deceit, souls find themselves afterwards betrayed and lost. There are few souls among the just whom this ancient serpent does not furiously attack in their last agony.

"A good life gives hope of a good end; all other reliance is doubtful, and salvation resting upon a death-bed conversion is very rare. The best precaution is to take a good start from afar. I therefore admonish you, that, at the dawning of each day, when you look upon the light, you seriously consider whether it may not be the last of your life; place your soul in such a state as to be able to meet death with a smiling face.

"Do not delay even for one instant, sorrow for your sins and a firm purpose of confessing them as soon as you find yourself guilty of any. Do not delay amending the least of your imperfections. Be careful not to leave upon your conscience the smallest defect without being sorry for it and without cleansing yourself by the Blood of My most Holy Son. Place yourself in such a condition that you are ready to appear before the Just Judge, who is to examine and judge your thoughts, words, actions, omissions, desires, and love.

"In order that you may help those who are in

danger of an unprepared death, you should give them these same counsels that I have given you. Exhort souls to lead a careful life in order to secure a happy death. Say some prayers for this intention every day of your life, fervently asking Almighty God to disperse the deceits of the devils, to destroy the snares prepared for those souls who are in the agony of death, and by His Power to confound all the demons.

"Know that I directed My prayers to that end for mortals, and in this I wish you to imitate Me.

"I wish you to command the demons to depart from the sick and stop their persecutions. You can very efficaciously use this power, even when you are absent from the sick, for you are to command them in the name of the Lord Jesus, and you are to compel them to obey you for the greater honor and glory of God Almighty.

"Admonish souls and help them to receive the Holy Sacraments; make sure that they receive them frequently during life in preparation for a good end. Seek to encourage and console them, speaking to them of the things of God and His mysteries contained in the Holy Scriptures.

"Exhort them to awaken their good intentions and desires, and to prepare themselves to receive the light and graces of God. Excite souls to hope, strengthen them against temptations, and teach them how they are to resist and overcome them. You shall not work by your own strength alone, but by the power which God wishes to exercise in you for His own glory.

"It is necessary that we pass through the portal of death to the Eternal Life, which we expect; bitter and painful is the passage, but also very profitable. Death was instituted by the Divine Goodness as the beginning of our security and rest; death satisfies by itself for the negligences and shortcomings of creatures in fulfilling their duties. Accept death, and through it pay the common debt with joy of spirit, and depart in confidence to the God of Love and to the Angels and Saints.

"My children, remember the desire for sufferings and attempts to see God are to be such, that your suffering becomes real through your sorrow at not being able to encounter actual torments, and at not being found worthy of bearing all the martyrdom you desire. In your desire to arrive at the Beatific Vision, you must permit no other lower motive to intermingle, such as the relief afforded by the joy of God's vision, against the hardships of this life; to desire the vision of the Highest Good, is not love of God, but love of self and of one's own comfort, and cannot merit reward.

"If you do all these things sincerely and in all perfection, as a faithful servant and spouse of My Divine Son, desiring to see Him in order to love Him, praise Him, and never to offend Him eternally, if you covet all labors and sufferings only for these ends, believe Me and assure yourself, that you will draw Jesus and Myself to you, and that you will arrive at the love you continually desire, since precisely for this purpose, God is so liberal with you.

"Preserve your heart independent and riveted only on Divine Providence. Let the Will of the Lord be your only delight and joy. Let not your fears dishearten you, and seek lovingly and diligently to follow in My footsteps.

"Among the fallacies introduced by the demon into the world, none is greater nor more pernicious than the forgetfulness of the hour of death and of what is to happen at the court of the rigorous Judge. It was through the devil that sin entered into the world, when he sought to convince the first woman that she would not die. Many live without thought of death and die forgetful of the unhappy end that awaits them. Be convinced that you must die, that you have received much and paid little, that the account shall be so much the more rigorous, as the Judge has lavished His gifts and talents upon you. I ask only that you give what you owe to your Spouse. Enkindle your heart with the desire of seeing your God."

*   *

"My choosing to die was so pleasing to Jesus, My Son, and My prudent Love therein obliged Him to such an extent, that in return, He immediately conceded to Me a singular favor to benefit the children of the Church: 'All those persons devoted to Me, who call on Me at the hour of death, constituting Me as their Advocate in memory of My desiring to imitate Him in Death, and in memory of My Happy Transition, shall be under My special protection in their last hour, shall have Me as a Defense against the demons, as a Help and Protection, and shall be presented by Me before the tribunal of His Mercy and there experience My Intercession. Jesus promised to confer great help with His grace for a good death and for a purer life on all those who in veneration of this mystery of My Precious Death, should invoke My aid.'

"By this solicitude you will oblige the Lord and Me to come to your aid in your last hour. I desire you to keep in your inmost heart, a devout and loving memory of this mystery of My Holy Death and Happy Transition; to bless and praise the Omnipotent God, because He caused such sacred miracles for Me and for all mortals.

"Since death follows upon life and ordinarily corresponds with it, therefore the surest pledge of a good death is a good life; a life in which the heart is freed and detached from earthly love. A sinful life, in that last hour, afflicts and oppresses the soul, and is like a heavy chain, restraining its liberty and preventing it from rising above the things in this world."

*   *   Death 6*

Prayer to Holy Mary

Mother of my Lord Jesus, my Protectress, You are the Consolation of the afflicted and Refuge of the needy. In the hour of my death, bestow upon me Your blessing which I desire. Offer for me, to Your Son, the Redeemer of the world, the sacrifice of my life, since I am burning with desire to be a holocaust for Him. Let Your pure Hands be the altar of my sacrifice, in order that it may become acceptable in the eyes of Him, who died on the cross for me. A happy death is a holy death. Into Your Hands, and through them into the Hands of my Creator, I commend my spirit.

"I am Love! I am all Love!
I am Pure Love! I am a Fire of Love!
I am God! God is Love!
My Heart is a Flaming Furnace of Love!
To say Jesus and to say Love is to say the same
thing.
I am Mercy!
To say Jesus and to say Mercy is to say the same
thing.
To say Jesus and to say Compassion is to say the
same thing.
To say Jesus and to say Tenderness is to say the
same thing.
My Merits are Myself!
Grace is your Jesus!
I am Just!
I am Wisdom!
I am Beatitude!
I am Peace!
I am Heaven!
I am Holy!
I am Infinite Wealth, Infinite Treasure!
I am Strength and Power!
I am Food and Drink!
I am Repose! I am Eternal Rest!
I am Meek and Humble of Heart!
I am God the Creator, God the Liberator!
I am Good, I am Goodness!
I am Gentle, I am Gentleness!
I am Tender, I am Tenderness!
I am the Resurrection!
I am the Way, the Truth, and the Life!
I am the Redeemer, I am the Savior!
I am the Supreme and Eternal Purity!
I am the true Sun, I am Heat!
I am the Light of the world, I am Light!

"I am the Bread of Life! I am the Breath of Life!
I am the Real Presence!
I am the Good Shepherd!
I am the Lamb of God!
I am the Immaculate Lamb!
I am the God of Pity!
I am the Victim of sin!
I am the Church!
I am a Priest forever!
I am a Fountain of Living Water!
I am a Prisoner of Love!
I am full of Compassion!
I am your Father, your Brother!
I am your Beloved, your Spouse!
I am your All!
I am your Physician, your Surgeon!
I am your Medicine, your Remedy!
I am your Teacher, your Master!
I am your Shield!
I am your Consoler, your Consolation!
I am your Friend!
I am your Employer!
I am a King! I am the King of Martyrs!
My Kingdom is Myself!
My Love is your Strength and your Courage!
My Love is your Rest and your Comfort!
My Love is your Life and your Salvation!
My Love is your Happiness!
My Heart is a Book!
My Heart is a Sanctuary!
My Heart is a Crucible!
My Heart is a Fountain of Living Water!
I am your neighbor!
Your love is a spark from My Fire of Love!
Love Me with My Love!
Take great care of your love, since it is I."

"When you feel weak, give Me your weakness. I take it into My Power and unite it with all My weariness on earth. Even before My crucifixion, in My journeyings and My work, I suffered much physical fatigue and sadness in the midst of so much human misunderstanding. Come close to Me even though you are weak. Come close to Me as though you had chosen to be at the end of your resources, in order to reach Me. We will be praising the Father, and ardently desiring His coming.

"Be filled with joy at the thought of approaching the Heavenly City. My child, the One who is waiting for you is your Creator and Savior. Joyfully meet Him as if you were going to a festival. Lovingly prepare your going away habit of virtue. Give others your humble smile, the smile of a child happy to be going Home.

"How good it is for you, from time to time, to feel near the gate leading out of this life. Your vision of the past is so clear now, isn't it? Things have lost the gloss of the world's opinion. You can see the real motive now which usually is selfishness, indifference to the Glory of God, when that alone should be your goal; unconcern for the salvation of your brothers, when the desire for it should set your thoughts on fire. What sadness, My child, if you were to arrive alone! Provide yourself with a cortege of companion-souls: the souls whom you have helped, and the Angels and Saints to join you at our 'meeting'.

"Mention to Me the names of those for whom you want to pray and offer sacrifices: for your proteges, your unbelievers, your deaf-mutes. I will hide them beneath My seamless robe steeped in My Blood. Why not use this time of solitude in bed as though you were in adoration before the Blessed Sacrament? What is there to hinder you? It only takes a little effort. Since all sickness destroys your body a little, and brings your soul nearer to the Gate of Life, why not transmute these days in your earthly prison into days of joy? Why not offer the Eternal Father your steady decline, so that your words and writings may bear fruit and nourish your brothers and sisters?

"I take all sufferings, little and big, and place them in the Treasury of the Church, the Treasury used for making Saints. You forget your past sufferings, but they continue to bear results in My sight. You love to look at gifts which were given to you. They are only trifles, something that has not cost the donor much. You treasure these things because those who gave them to you wanted to please you. For the same reason I have found joy in all the little presents given to Me by My children."

*

"You will be judged according to the measure of your love — on that alone!"

*

Lord, I have loved You so long, but I still do not know how to love You.

"To love the Eternal Father and the Holy Spirit, borrow My Heart; to love your Jesus, offer Him His Passion."

*

"Understand this: When you say 'Lord, I love You,' you can go no farther, for you have said everything; you can only repeat."

To say that I am happy, is an understatement. I am supremely happy. One could not be happier. I never imagined that so much bliss could exist in religious life.

*

To become a saint one must take two definite steps: one toward abandonment, the other toward confidence. One must break all attachments, no matter how holy, and place the soul in Mary's Hands, confident that She will offer it to Jesus in a manner worthy of Him. Since God will not refuse His Mother anything, He will accept Her offering, and fashion the soul after His own Soul, which means that it will "become perfect as our Heavenly Father is Perfect."

*

My little way of confidence is complete trust in our Lady. It is being confident that all things, even those pin pricks, come to us from our Holy Mother for our sanctification. Whenever I begin my meditation, office, or any other spiritual exercise, I unite my soul with Holy Mary's and I say to Her: "Virgin Mother of God, Your weak child begs You to turn my distractions into Your own Holy Thoughts. I place all my confidence in You!" Then I go on with my prayer because I am confident that, if I fail, my Mother will take over. Thus God will be praised every moment.

*

Hide me in Your Immaculate Heart. Only in Your Heart, dearest Mother, will I have the courage to live a life of faithful observance of the Rule and of perfect charity. Only through Your Heart will my actions emerge sufficiently purified to bring

Sr. Maria Teresita of Jesus 1

glory to Your Divine Son. Only from Your Heart will I merit a transfer to the Carmel of Eternal Delights — the Carmel where Jesus awaits the virgin souls who, with a new canticle, will forever praise His unspeakable Mercies.

*

Sweet Lady, I am misery itself. I am holding Your mantle! If I were less miserable, You would not protect and care for me. Since my misery keeps me small and very much in need of Your sweet attentions, I do not regret being a miserable soul. I expect nothing from myself because I am as helpless as a new-born babe, but I expect everything from You, dear Mother Mary, even sanctity, which of myself I cannot attain.

*

Sister Maria Teresita, why are you so sure that our Lady is going to take you to Heaven?

I have complete confidence in my Mother Mary. She knows my desire to look at the radiant beauty of Her Face, to listen to the sweetness of Her voice, and to delight in being near to Her.

*

Sister Maria Teresita, don't you feel a bit sad when you think of leaving all you love on earth?

I am not leaving all I love. I am going to my Father in Heaven who is waiting for me. My Mother Mary will come to bring me to Jesus. I have always loved our Lady above everything and everyone; that is my greatest comfort now. If you love our Lord with your whole heart, with every fiber of your being, you would never suffer sadness, not even while looking death straight in the face.

Sr. Maria Teresita of Jesus 2

I have never earned Heaven. Jesus and Holy Mary are giving it to me. Since I have never deliberately separated myself from God and His Mother, They are going to seal my union with Them now in this wondrous gift of Religious Profession. They are the King and Queen of Heaven, and I am Their little servant.

*

All day I have been dwelling on God's Mercy. How Good our Lady has been to me! As soon as I get to Heaven, I shall take a place at Her side. Nothing will ever again separate me from Jesus and His adorable Mother!

*

Do you know what has given me the greatest comfort in this hour of need? My devotion to our Lady! My sins do not worry me at all. My love for the Blessed Virgin means everything to me now.

*

I am not going to die of this disease, thanks be to God! I am going to die of love.

*

Dearest Mother Mary, will You please supply for whatever I lack in order to do this work perfectly?

*

The lily in my garden symbolizes chastity; the white rose, charity; the red rose, mortification; the forget-me-not represents obedience, and the carnation, poverty. My precious violet signifies humility; I came here to become a saint, and sanctity is impossible without humility.

*

Doctor, give me only enough medication to fulfill your obligation as a physician. These antibotics are going to delay my trip to Heaven.

Sr. Maria Teresita of Jesus 3

In Heaven I will adore our God with our Lady. Every moment will be one of rejoicing, of love, of praise, and of glory. In Heaven nothing will separate me from Jesus and Holy Mary. I am of very little use here on earth, but from Heaven you will see how busy I shall be.

*

How much I suffer! All for You, Sweet Lady! All for Jesus through my Mother Mary! Sweet Lady, I am very sick. I offer You this illness. I trust in You, Mary, my Mother. O Mary, I obey You. I love You, Queen of my heart!

*

My dear Mother, now You will take me with You to Heaven. My Jesus, I love You for those who do not love You. My Mother, I would rather die a thousand times than offend You once. Jesus, I have loved only You and my dear Mother Mary.

*

I am all Yours, O my Mother. For You I was born, for You I die. What do You wish of me? I am all Yours, all Yours, all Yours! O Mother of Love, cover me with Your mantle of blue. O my God, send workers to the missions, more workers.

*

Go away from me, devil! Begone! Go back to hell!

*

O Mary, defend me against the snares of the devil.

*

Mary, Jesus . . . Love! I am very ill today. My Mother Mary, whatever You wish!

How Beautiful! O Mary, how Beautiful You are!

Sister Maria Teresita of Jesus, a Carmelite Sister of Charity, died on Easter Sunday, 1950, at 20 years of age, in Madrid Spain.
Sr. Maria Teresita of Jesus 4*

†

*   *   *   *   *   *   *

O Divine Heart of Jesus

O Lord, although I am but dust and ashes, speak to my soul and enlighten my mind. When You speak I listen; my soul rejoices at Your voice. I offer myself entirely to You. Accept me as a victim to be sacrificed to Your Divine Love. If the victim is unclean, purify it and make it acceptable and worthy of You.

O Divine and Sacred Heart of Jesus, enkindle in my heart the Fire of Your Love, that I may be consumed as a perfect holocaust for Your Love and Your Glory. I thank You for all the benefits and Mercies granted to me until now. I am unworthy of so many favors. Have pity on me! O Lord, through the Merits of Your Sacred Heart, and for the sake of Your Precious Blood shed for me, look upon my soul, and it will be healed. Touch my heart, and it will be made holy. Send a spark of Your Sacred Fire, and all my being will be aflame with Your Love. The blessing I ask for myself, grant also to all mankind; I desire that all souls may love and serve You as You deserve to be loved and served.

To Your Sacred Heart I commend our Pontiff, the hierarchy, all persons consecrated to Your holy service, and public officials. Have Pity on the poor, the sick, the dying, the souls in purgatory. Bless all who work for Your glory. Bless our relatives, and benefactors. Have Mercy on poor sinners, the infidels, and enemies of Your Holy Church, for they, too, have been redeemed by Your Precious Blood. Save them all, O Merciful Father, and grant them Your choicest blessings.

*

Almighty God

Almighty God, kneeling before Your Holy and Divine Majesty, I adore You, and because You command me, I dare approach Your Divine Heart. What shall I say if You do not enlighten me with a ray of Your Divine Light? Speak to me! O Lord, enlighten my mind to understand Your eternal Truths; touch my heart and strengthen my will to put them into practice. Pour Your grace into my heart; lift up my soul weighed down by my sins; raise my mind to heavenly things, so that earthly desires may no longer appeal to me. Speak to my soul with Your Divine Omnipotence, for You are my Salvation, my Life, and my Peace, in time and in eternity.

Fortify me with the grace of Your Holy Spirit and give Your Peace to my soul, so that I may be free from all needless anxiety, solicitude, and worry. Help me to desire always what is pleasing and acceptable to You, so that Your Holy Will may be my will. Grant that I may rid myself of all unholy desires. For Your Love, I desire to remain obscure and unknown in this world, to be known only to You. Do not permit me to attribute to myself the good that You perform in me and through me. May I refer all honor to Your Majesty; may I glory only in my infirmities, renouncing sincerely all vain glory which comes from the world. May I aspire to that true and lasting glory, which comes from You. Amen.

Prayer before a Crucifix

Behold, O Kind and most Sweet Jesus, I cast myself upon my knees in Your sight; with the most fervent desire of my soul, I pray and beseech You, to impress upon my heart, lively sentiments of faith, hope, and charity, true repentance for my sins, and a firm desire of amendment. With deep affection and grief of soul, I ponder within myself Your five most Precious Wounds; having before my eyes that which David spoke in prophecy of You, O Good Jesus: "They have pierced My Hands and My Feet; they have numbered all My Bones."

*   *   *

Anima Christi

Soul of Christ, sanctify me.
Body of Christ, save me.
Blood of Christ, inebriate me.
Water from the side of Christ, wash me.
Passion of Christ, strengthen me.
O Good Jesus, hear me.
Within Your Wounds, hide me.
Never let me be separated from You.
From the malignant enemy, defend me.
At the hour of death, call me.
Bid me to come close to You.
With Your Saints, may I praise You, forever and ever. Amen.

*   *   *

Jesus, Mary, and Joseph, I give You my heart and my soul. Jesus, Mary, and Joseph, assist me in my last agony. Jesus, Mary, and Joseph, may I breathe forth my soul in peace with You. Amen.

*

Prayer to Saint Joseph

In our tribulation we fly to you, O Blessed Joseph, and, after imploring the help of your most Holy Spouse, we ask also with confidence for your patronage. By the affection which united you to the Immaculate Virgin Mother of God, and the paternal love with which you embraced the Child Jesus, we beseech you to look kindly upon the inheritance which Jesus Christ acquired by His Precious Blood, and by your powerful aid to help us in our need.

Protect, most careful guardian of the Holy Family, the chosen people of Jesus Christ. Keep us, most loving father, from all pestilence of error and corruption. Be merciful to us, most powerful protector, from your place in Heaven, in this warfare with the powers of darkness. As you once removed the Child Jesus from the danger of death, so now defend the Holy Church of God from the snares of the enemy and from all adversity. Guard each of us by your perpetual patronage, so that, sustained by your example and help, we may live in holiness, die a holy death, and attain everlasting happiness in Heaven. Amen.

*

St. Joseph, father and guardian of Virgins, into your faithful keeping were entrusted Innocence Itself, Christ Jesus, and Holy Mary the Virgin of virgins. We pray and beseech you, through Jesus and Mary, to keep us from all uncleanness. Grant that our minds may be untainted, our hearts pure, and our bodies chaste. Help us always to serve Jesus and Mary in perfect chastity. Amen.

*

A Plea for Mercy

My Lord, look with Mercy on Your people. You will be more glorified if You pardon so many creatures and give them the light of knowledge, since all will render You praise when they see themselves escape from mortal sin and eternal damnation through Your infinite Goodness; You will then, not only be praised by my wretched self, who have so much offended You, but by all creation. I pray that Your eternal and Divine Love take revenge only on me, and be Merciful to Your people. Never will I depart from Your presence until You grant them Mercy. What does it matter if I have life, and Your people death? What does it matter if darkness covers Your spouse? I desire, and beg of You, by Your grace, that You have Mercy on Your people. I plead that You do this by Your uncreated Love which moved You to create mankind in Your image and likeness. You created us that we might participate in everything belonging to You, the Most High and Eternal Trinity.

You gave us memory, in order to receive Your benefits, by which we participate in Your Power, O Eternal Father; You gave us intellect, that we might see and know Your Goodness and participate in the Wisdom of Your Only-Begotten Son; You gave us will, that we might love that which our intellect has seen and known of Your Truth, thus participating in the clemency of Your Holy Spirit. Why did You create mankind in such dignity? Your inestimable Love was Your only reason: You saw Your creature in Yourself! You loved us, You created us through Love and destined us to enjoy Your eternal Good. Through our sin we lost this dignity in which You originally placed us.

You were moved by that same fire of Love with which You created us; You willingly gave us a means of reconciliation, so that we would have peace. You gave us the Only-Begotten Word, Your Son, to be the Mediator between us and Yourself. He is our Justice, for He took on Himself our humanity. O abyss of Love! What heart would not break when it sees such dignity as Yours descend to such lowliness as our humanity? We are Your image, and You have become ours by this union which You have accomplished with mankind, veiling the Eternal Deity with suffering in the corrupted clay of Adam. Why did You do this? Love! You, O God, have become man, and mankind has become God. By Your effable Love I constrain You and implore You to be Merciful to Your creatures.

A Plea for Mercy 2*

*

O Love, You are God Almighty, strengthen me in love. You are Wisdom, give me the spirit of wisdom to love You. You are the Spring and Source of all delight, let me taste Your ineffable Sweetness. You are dear to me above all things, let me live for You alone. You are ever true, console me in all my trials. You are the chosen Companion of my life, perform all my works in me. O Love, it is You who will be victorious, grant me perservance to the end. O God, You are Love; grant that I may love You with all my heart, with all my soul, and with all my strength.

*

A Child shall lead them!

"Dear child, you see how much I Love you. Draw near and ask Me whatever you will, for you have stolen My Heart."

To love You and to give You glory, O Sacred Heart.

"Yes my little child, I understand and bless your prayer, but have you no special grace to ask of Me? Speak, be not afraid, you can command My Heart."

To love You and to give You glory, O Sacred Heart.

"You speak as My Saints do. I wish to prove that if you are Mine, I also am yours. Ask what you will."

To love You and to give You glory, O Sacred Heart.

"You have forgotten everything for My glory. Here is My Heart. I give It to you. Dispose of It as you will with all Its treasures. In this hour of grace tell Me what miracle of love you desire."

To love You even unto folly and to make You loved with the irresistible power of Your own Sacred Heart. May Your Kingdom come!

* * * * * * *

Our Lord asked a little girl of seven:

"Would you like to be My missionary?"

A little thing like me a missionary! How could I be, dear Jesus?

"Yes, just because you are so little, My child, you can be My missionary. Would you like to try?"

Dear Jesus, I don't understand how.

"Little one, offer Me your daily Communions, your prayers, your sacrifices, and everything that hurts or vexes you all through the day. Offer them with great love to win souls for Me, and you will be My little missionary."

*   *   *   *   *   *   *

"Do you really love Me very much?"

Dear Jesus, You should not ask me that.

"Why not?"

You know that I have given You my heart and it belongs to You.

"Yes, I know, but I want you to tell Me so. Very few souls love Me."

Later

My Jesus, is it really true that You, who are God, can Love a little thing like me?

"You should not ask Me that."

Why not?

"You know that I Love you. You are only Mine, My little apostle, and My Heart belongs to you."

Well, dear Jesus, I knew that You Loved me, only I wanted You to tell me so Yourself.

A Child shall lead them! 2*

428

A little Game

"Let us play a little game."

Oh, yes, my dear Jesus.

"Whichever of us loves the most will be the winner."

I am ready.

"I created you, I endowed you with the gift of Faith from the earliest moment of your existence, I surrounded you and presented you with innumerable and precious graces, I redeemed you, I pardoned you and called you to Religious Life; this is My Love. How much do you love Me?"

Jesus, I love You as much as I can, and to prove my love, I wish to refuse You nothing, not even the most trifling sacrifices.

"I know, but My Love is infinite, and yours?"

My love, O Divine Child, is infinite like Yours, since I love You with the Love of Your own Heart.

"You are right! It is a tie! We have both won!"

*

Another morning, my Little Jesus desired to play the game of the cross.

"In this game, whichever of us carries the cross better for the other wins."

As you will, my dear Little Jesus.

Jesus enumerated His sufferings and humiliations from the Crib to Calvary, His humiliations of the Holy Eucharist and the outrages and sacrifices met within the Sacrament of His Love, ending with:

"What do you suffer for Me?"

My dearest Jesus, I am happy to accept all the little trials You are pleased to send me, and I thank You in advance for those that You hold in reserve.

"I bore all, I suffered all without complaint."

I too aim at bearing my crosses with joy.

"I chose what was most difficult and painful."

Good Master, You know my ardent desire, my sincere intention never to be unfaithful to the least of Your graces. I am weak, but You know my frame, of what clay I am made. I love Your cross passionately even when it offers that which is most contrary to nature.

"My sufferings have an infinite value, and yours?"

I saw mine as poor and empty of merit, but I turned to Holy Mary, begging Her to enlighten me. The inspiration came quickly; I answered joyfully.

My Jesus, since my sufferings are united to Yours, they also are of infinite value.

"Well, this time again the game is even."

A little Game 2*

430

Prayer for Holy Church

O Eternal God, O Light above every other light, from You issues all Light! O Fire above every fire, You are the only Fire which burns without consuming, and consumes all sin and self-love found in my soul. You do not afflict me, but fill me with Your Love. The more I have of You, the more I seek; the more I desire, the more I find and taste of You, O Supreme and Eternal Fire, Abyss of Charity. Who has moved You to illumine me, Your finite creature, with the Light of Your Truth? You, the Fire of Love are the cause! It is always Love which constrained and constrains You to create us in Your image and likeness, and to be Merciful, giving immeasurable and infinite graces to Your rational creature.

O Goodness above all goodness! You alone are supremely Good and You gave the Word, Your Only-Begotten Son to converse with us mortals who are filled with darkness. What was the cause of this? Love! You loved us before we existed. You make Yourself humble and small to make mankind great. Everywhere I find the fire of Your Charity. Can a wretch like me pay back to You the graces and the burning Charity that You have shown and show with so much burning Love? No! You alone will be thankful and grateful for me, for I am nothingness and know not how to respond to Your Greatness. You alone are my Being; every grace that You bestow on me, You give through Love.

O sweetest Father, when the human race lay sick through the sin of Adam, You sent it a Physician, the Word, Your Son; when I was infirmed with the sickness of negligence and ignorance, You, O Physician, gave me a medicine, that I may be cured. The medicine soothed me with Your Love and Gentleness; Your medicine was sweet above all sweetness. You illumine my intellect with the light of Holy Faith, with Your Light, in the Mystical Body of Your Holy Church. I know that we do not know how to ask or desire as much as You can give!

O Eternal Father, ineffable Fire of Love, I do not wish that my heart should ever become weary in desiring Your honor and the salvation of souls. You have invited me to offer You sweet and loving desires, with humble and continual prayer. I beg You to have Mercy on all souls in the world and on Your Holy Church. I pray that You fҮlfill my desires which You have instilled in my heart. Do not put off any longer Your merciful designs towards all souls, but descend and fulfill the desire of Your servants.

You cause us to cry in order to hear our voices! Your Truth told us to cry and we would be answered; to knock, and it would be opened to us; to beg, and it would be given to us. O Eternal Father, Your servants cry out to You for Mercy; answer us!

I know that Mercy is Your attribute. You cannot refuse It to those who ask for It. Your servants knock at the door of Your Truth, because in the Truth of Your Only-Begotten Son they know the ineffable Love which You have for mortals. The Fire of Your Love cannot refrain from opening to those who know and plead with perseverance.

Open, unlock, and break the hardened hearts of Your creatures. Grant the prayer of those who stand at the door of Your Truth and pray. We pray that the Blood of Jesus will wash away our iniquities and destroy the stain of Adam's sin. The Blood is ours. You cannot deny us what we ask. Place in a balance the price of the Blood of Your Son, so that the devils may not carry off Your lambs. You are the Good Shepherd; Your Son fulfilled Your obedience; He gave His Life for Your lambs.

The Blood is what Your servants beg of You, to cause Your Holy Church to bloom with the fragrant flowers of good and holy pastors, who by their sweet odor of virtue shall extinguish the stench of sin. Eternal Father, You have said that through the Love You have for Your rational creatures, and the prayers, virtues, and labors of Your servants, to grant Mercy to all souls in the world, reform to the Church. Do not delay!

Turn towards us and reply! Open the door of Your inestimable Love which You have given us through Your Word. We seek Your honor and the salvation of souls. Give us the Bread of Life. With You everything is possible. You have created us without our help; You will only save us with our help. I beg You to dispose their wills to desire You. Re-create the vessels which You have created in Your image and likeness. Re-create them to grace in Your Mercy and the Blood of Your Son Jesus.

What is your ideal of sanctity?
To live by love!

What is the quickest way to reach it?
To become very little!

Who is your favorite Saint?
John the Apostle who rested on the Heart of Jesus!

What is your favorite virtue?
Purity! "Blessed are the clean of heart, for they
shall see God."

Give a definition of prayer.
Union with God!

What is your favorite book?
The Soul of Christ! In It I learn all the secrets
of our Father in Heaven!

Have you an ardent desire for Heaven?
I sometimes feel homesick for Heaven; except for
the vision, I already possess It in my soul.

In what disposition would you wish to die?
I would like to die in an act of love, and thus
fall into the arms of Jesus whom I love.

What form of martyrdom would you prefer?
I love all forms, especially the martyrdom of love!

What name would you like to have in Heaven?
"The Will of God."

What is your motto?
"God in me and I in Him."

Act of Reparation to the Sacred Heart of Jesus

Pope Pius XI

O Sweet Jesus, whose overflowing Charity for mankind is requited by so much forgetfulness, negligence, and contempt, behold us prostrate before You, eager to repair by a special act of homage, the cruel indifference and injuries, to which Your Loving Heart is everywhere subject.

Mindful alas, that we have had a share in such great indignities, which we now deplore from the depths of our hearts, we humbly ask Your pardon. We declare our readiness to atone by voluntary expiation, not only for our own personal offenses, but also for the sins of those, who, straying far from the path of salvation, refuse in their obstinate infidelity to follow You, their Shepherd and Leader, or, renouncing the vows of their Baptism, have cast off the sweet yoke of Your Law.

We are now resolved to expiate each and every deplorable outrage committed against You; we are determined to make amends for the manifold offenses against Christian modesty in unbecoming dress and behavior, for all the foul seductions laid to ensnare the feet of the innocent, for the frequent violation of Sundays and holy days, and the shocking blasphemies uttered against You and Your Saints.

We wish also to make amends for the insults to which Your Vicar on earth and Your priests are subjected, for the profanation, for the conscious neglect, and for the terrible acts of sacrilege of the very Sacrament of Your Divine Love; lastly,

Act of Reparation 1

435

we wish to make amends for the public crimes of nations who resist the rights and the teaching authority of the Church which You have founded.

Would, O Divine Jesus, that we were able to wash away such abominations with our blood. We now offer, in reparation for these violations of Your divine honor, the satisfaction You once made to Your Eternal Father on the cross, and which You continue to renew daily on our altars; we offer it in union with the acts of atonement of Your Virgin Mother, of all the Saints, and of the pious faithful on earth.

We sincerely promise to make reparation, as far as we can, with the help of Your grace, for all the neglect of Your great Love, and for the sins we and others have committed in the past.

Henceforth, we will live a life of unwavering faith, of purity of conduct, of perfect observance of the precepts of the Gospel, and especially that of charity. We promise to the best of our power, to prevent others from offending You, and to bring as many as possible to follow You.

O Loving Jesus, through the intercession of the Blessed Virgin Mary, our Model in reparation, receive the voluntary offering we make of this act of expiation; by the crowning gift of perseverance, keep us faithful unto death in our duty and the allegiance we owe to You, so that we may all, one day, come to that happy Home, where You with the Father and the Holy Spirit, live and reign God, world without end. Amen.

Act of Reparation 2*

Visit to Jesus in the Blessed Sacrament

My Lord Jesus Christ, for the Love which You bear mankind, You remain night and day in this Sacrament, full of Compassion and Love, awaiting, calling, and welcoming all who come to visit You; I believe that You are present in the Sacrament of the Altar. I adore You from the abyss of my nothingness. I thank You for all the graces which You have bestowed upon me, and in particular for having given me Yourself in this Sacrament, for having given me Your most Holy Mother Mary as my Advocate, and for having called me to visit You in this church. I now salute Your most Loving Heart, and this for three purposes: first, in thanksgiving for this great Gift; secondly, to make amends to You for all the outrages which You receive in this Sacrament from all Your enemies; thirdly, I intend by this visit to adore You in all the places on earth, in which You are least adored and most abandoned.

My Jesus, I love You with my whole heart. I grieve for having in the past so many times offended Your infinite Goodness. I resolve by Your grace nevermore to offend You for the future, and now, miserable and unworthy though I am, I consecrate myself to You without reserve. I give You my entire will, my affections, my desires, and all that I possess. From this day forth, dispose of me and of all that I have as You please. I ask and desire only Your Holy Love, final perseverance, and the perfect accomplishment of Your Will. I recommend to You the souls in purgatory, especially those who had the greatest devotion to the most Blessed Sacrament and to the Blessed Virgin Mary. I also recommend to You all poor sinners. My dear Savior, I unite all my love and desires with the Love and desires of Your most Loving Heart, and I offer them thus united to Your Eternal Father, beseeching Him in Your Name, because of Your Love, to accept and grant them.

* * * * * * *

Act of Consecration of the Human Race to the Sacred Heart of Jesus

Pope Leo XIII

Most Sweet Jesus, Redeemer of the human race, look down upon us, humbly prostrate before You. We are Yours, and Yours we wish to be; but, to be more surely united with You, behold, we freely consecrate ourselves today to Your most Sacred Heart. Many indeed have never known You; many too, despising Your precepts, have rejected You. Have Mercy on them all, most Merciful Jesus. Be King, O Lord, not only of the faithful who have never forsaken You, but also of the prodigal children who have abandoned You; grant that they may quickly return to their Father's House, lest they die of wretchedness and hunger. Be King of those who are deceived by erroneous opinions, or whom discord keeps aloof, and call them back to the Harbor of Truth and Unity of Faith, so that soon there may be but one flock and One Shepherd. Grant, O Lord, to Your Church, assurance of freedom and immunity from harm; give peace and order to all nations, and make the earth resound from pole to pole with one cry: Praise to the Divine Heart that wrought our Salvation: to this Sacred Heart be glory and honor forever. Amen.

438

Consecration of Mankind to the
Immaculate Heart of Mary

Pope Pius XII

Queen of the most Holy Rosary, Refuge of the human race, Victress in all God's battles, we humbly prostrate ourselves before You, confident that we shall receive mercy, grace, bountiful assistance, and protection, not through our own inadequate merits, but solely through the great goodness of Your Maternal Heart.

To You, to Your Immaculate Heart, we consign and consecrate ourselves in union, not only with the Mystical Body of Your Son: Holy Mother Church, now in such suffering and agony, and sorely tried in so many ways, but also with the entire world, torn by fierce strife, consumed in a fire of hate, victim of its own wickedness. May the sight of the widespread moral destruction, of the souls in danger of being lost eternally, move You to compassion!

O Mother of Mercy, obtain peace for us from God, and above all procure for us those graces which prepare, establish, and assure peace!

Queen of Peace, pray for us! Give to the world, that peace which all people ardently desire, peace in the truth, justice, and charity of Christ. Give peace to the nations at war, and to the souls of mortals, that in the tranquillity of order, the Kingdom of God may prevail.

Extend Your protection to the infidels, and to all those still in the shadow of death; give them peace and grant that on them, too, may shine

Immaculate Heart 1

the Sun of Truth, that they may unite with us in proclaiming before the one and only Savior of the world: "Glory to God in the Highest, and peace among men of good will."

Obtain peace and complete freedom for the Holy Church of God; stay the spreading flood of modern paganism; enkindle in the faithful the love of purity, the practice of Christian virtue, and an apostolic zeal, so that the servants of God may increase in merit and in number.

Lastly, as the Church and the entire human race were consecrated to the Sacred Heart of Jesus, so that in reposing all hope in Him, He might become for them the sign and pledge of victory and salvation: so we in like manner, consecrate ourselves forever also to You and to Your Immaculate Heart, our Mother and Queen, that Your Love and patronage may hasten the triumph of the Kingdom of God.

O Mary, may all nations be at peace with one another and with God; may all proclaim You Blessed, and with You, may they raise their voice to resound from pole to pole, the chant of the everlasting magnificat of glory, love, and gratitude to the Heart of Jesus, where alone they can find truth and peace. Amen.

*

Immaculate Heart 2*

O Mary, You are fair, and the stain of original sin is not in You. You are the Glory of Jerusalem; You are the Joy of Israel; You are the Honor of our people. You are the Brightness of Eternal Light, the unspotted Mirror of God's Majesty, and the Image of His Goodness. We love You!

The Name of Mary

The Divine Trinity: "Our 'Chosen One' shall be called MARY; this name is to be powerful and magnificent.

"Those who shall invoke the name of MARY with devout affection, shall receive most abundant graces.

"Those that shall honor the name of MARY and pronounce it with reverence, shall be consoled and vivified; they will find in it the remedy of their evils, the treasures for their enrichment, the light which shall guide them to Heaven.

"The name of MARY shall be terrible against the power of hell, it shall crush the head of the serpent, and it shall win glorious Victories over the princes of hell."

      *   *   *

Holy Mary our Teacher: "Be very devout toward My most sweet name.

"I wish that you be convinced of the great prerogatives and privileges, which the Almighty grants as a privilege to My name, so that when I saw them in the Divinity, I felt most deeply obliged and solicitous to make a proper return.

"Whenever the name MARY occured to My Mind and whenever I heard Myself called by that name, I was moved to thankfulness and urged to new fervor in the service of the Lord, who gave this name to Me."

*

Hail Mary

Holy Mary: "No one can please Me more than by saying the Angelic Salutation which the most Adorable Trinity sent to Me, and by which He raised Me to the dignity of the Mother of God.

"By the word: 'Ave', I learned that God in His infinite Power had preserved Me from all sin and its attendant misery which the first woman had been subject to.

"The name: 'Mary', which means 'Lady of Light', shows that God had filled Me with Wisdom and Light, as a shining Star to light up Heaven and earth.

"The words: 'Full of Grace' remind Me that the Holy Spirit has showered so many graces upon Me, that I am able to give these graces in abundance to those souls who ask for them through Me as Mediatrix.

"When you say: 'The Lord is with Thee,' you renew the indescribable Joy that was Mine when the Eternal Word became Incarnate in My Womb.

"When you say to Me: 'Blessed art Thou among women,' I praise Almighty God's Divine Mercy, which lifted Me to this exalted Happiness.

"At the words: 'Blessed is the Fruit of Thy Womb, Jesus,' the whole of Heaven rejoices with Me, to see My Son Jesus adored and glorified for having saved mankind."

*

I believe in God, the Father Almighty, Creator of Heaven and earth; and in Jesus Christ, His Only Son our Lord; who was conceived by the Holy Spirit, born of the Virgin Mary, suffered under Pontius Pilate, was crucified, died and was buried. He descended into hell; on the third day He arose again from the dead; He ascended into Heaven, and sits at the right Hand of God, the Father Almighty; from there He shall come to judge the living and the dead. I believe in the Holy Spirit, the Holy Catholic Church, the Communion of Saints, the forgiveness of sins, the resurrection of the body, and Life Everlasting.

Our Father, who art in Heaven, Hallowed by Thy Name; Thy Kingdom come; Thy Will be done, on earth as it is in Heaven. Give us this day our daily Bread. Forgive us our trespasses, as we forgive those who trespass against us. Lead us not into temptation, but deliver us from evil. Amen.

Hail Mary, full of Grace, the Lord is with Thee. Blessed art Thou among women, and Blessed is the Fruit of Thy womb, Jesus. Holy Mary, Mother of God, pray for us sinners, now, and at the hour of our death. Amen.

Glory be to the Father, and to the Son, and to the Holy Spirit, as it was in the beginning, is now and ever shall be, world without end. Amen.

O my Jesus, forgive us our sins, save us from the fire of hell; lead all souls to Heaven, especially those who have most need of Your Mercy.

O Sacrament most Holy, O Sacrament Divine, all praise and all thanksgiving, be every moment Thine!

Remember O most Gracious Virgin Mary, that never was it known, that anyone who fled to Your protection, implored Your help, or sought Your intercession, was left unaided. Inspired by this confidence, I fly unto You, O Virgin of virgins, my Mother; to You I come; before You I stand, sinful and sorrowful. O Mother of the Word Incarnate, despise not my petitions, but in Your Mercy, hear and answer me. Amen.

*

On this day, O Beautiful Mother, on this day we give Thee our love. Near Thee, Madonna, fondly we hover, trusting Thy gentle care to prove.

On this day we ask to share, dearest Mother Thy sweet care; aid us ere our feet astray, wander from Thy guiding way.
On this day, O Beautiful Mother, . . .

Queen of Angels, deign to hear, lisping children's humble prayer; young hearts gain, O Virgin Pure, sweetly to Thyself allure.
On this day, O Beautiful Mother, . . .

*

Hail, Holy Queen enthroned above, O Maria!
Hail, Queen of Mercy, Queen of Love, O Maria!
Sing Her praise, ye Cherubim! Join our song, ye Seraphim! Heaven and earth resound the hymn:
Salve, Salve, Salve, Regina!

Our Life, our Sweetness here below, O Maria!
From You all grace and comfort flow, O Maria!
Sing Her praise, ye Cherubim! Join our song, ye Seraphim! Heaven and earth resound the hymn:
Salve, Salve, Salve, Regina!

*

Salve, Regina, Mater Misericordiae; Vita, Dulcedo et Spes nostra, salve. Ad Te clamamus, exsules filii Hevae. Ad Te suspiramus gementes et flentes in hac lacrimarum valle. Eja ergo, Advocata nostra, illos Tuos Misericordes oculos ad nos converte. Et Jesum, Benedictum Fructum ventris Tui, nobis post hoc Exsilium ostende. O Clemens, O Pia, O Dulcis Virgo Maria.

Hail, Holy Queen, Mother of Mercy, our Life, our Sweetness, and our Hope. To You do we cry poor banished children of Eve; to You do we send up our sighs, mourning and weeping in valley of tears. Turn then, most Gracious Advocate, Your eyes of Mercy towards us, and after this our exile, show unto us the Blessed Fruit of Your womb, Jesus. O Clement, O Loving, O Sweet Virgin Mary.

*

O God, Your Only-Begotten Son by His Life, Death, and Resurrection, has purchased for us the rewards of Eternal Life; grant, we beseech You, that meditating upon these mysteries of the most Holy Rosary of the Blessed Virgin Mary, we may imitate what they contain, and obtain what they promise, through the same Christ our Lord. Amen.

*

Immaculate Mary, Your praises we sing.
You reign now in splendor with Jesus our King.
Ave, Ave, Ave Maria! Ave, Ave Maria!
In Heaven the Blessed Your glory proclaim,
On earth we Your children invoke Your sweet name!
Ave, Ave, Ave Maria! Ave, Ave Maria!
We pray for the Church, our true Mother on earth,
and beg You to watch o'er the land of our birth.
Ave, Ave, Ave Maria! Ave, Ave Maria!

Holy Mary: My soul magnifies the Lord; my spirit rejoices in God my Savior, because He has regarded the humility of His handmaid. Behold, henceforth all generations shall call me Blessed. God who is Mighty has done great things for me; Holy is His Name. His Mercy is from generation to generation, to them that fear Him. He has shown strength in His arm, He has scattered the proud in the conceit of their heart. He has put down the mighty from their thrones and has exalted the humble. God has filled the hungry with good things, and the rich He has sent away empty handed. He has received Israel His servant, mindful of His Mercy, even as He spoke to our father Abraham, and to his children forever.

* * *

Zachary: Blessed be the Lord, the God of Israel; He has come to His people and set them free. He has raised up for us a mighty Savior, born in the house of His servant David. Through his holy prophets He promised of old, that He would save us from our enemies, from the hands of all who hate us. He promised to show Mercy to our fathers, and to remember His Holy Covenant. This was the oath He swore to our father Abraham: to set us free from the hands of our enemies, free to worship Him without fear, holy and righteous in His sight all the days of our life. You, my child, shall be called the prophet of the Most High; you will go before the Lord to prepare His way, to give His people knowledge of Salvation by the forgiveness of their sins. In the tender compassion of our God, the Dawn from on High shall come to us, to shine on those who dwell in darkness and the shadow of death, and to guide our feet into the way of peace.

THE JOYFUL MYSTERIES

The Annunciation

Archangel Gabriel: "Hail Mary, full of Grace, the Lord is with You. Fear not, for You have found favor with God. You shall conceive and bring forth a Son; You shall call Him Jesus. He shall be great, and shall be called the Son of the Most High; the Lord God shall give to Him the throne of David His father; He shall reign over the house of Jacob forever."

"How shall this happen, since I do not know man?"

"The Holy Spirit shall come upon You, and the Power of the Most High shall overshadow You. The Holy One shall be called the Son of God. Elizabeth, Your cousin, has conceived a son in her old age; she who was barren is now in her sixth month, for nothing is impossible with God."

"I am the handmaid of the Lord; be it done to me according to your word." †

* * *

The Visitation

Elizabeth: "Mary, You are blessed among women, and blessed is the Fruit of Your womb! Why has the Mother of my Lord come to visit me? When I heard Your salutation, the babe in my womb leaped with joy. Blessed are You who have believed, for what the Lord has promised You shall be accomplished."

447

Mary: "My soul magnifies the Lord; my spirit rejoices in God my Savior, because He has regarded the lowliness of His handmaid."   †

*   *   *

The Birth of Jesus

An edict from Caesar Agustus required the registration of the whole world. Joseph went to Bethlehem, for he was of the family of David, with Mary his wife, who was with Child. While they were there, She brought forth Her first-born Son; She wrapped Him in swaddling clothes and laid Him in a manger, because there was no place for them in the inn.

*

There were shepherds in the fields keeping the night watch over their flock. The Angel said to them: "Fear not! I bring you tidings of great joy. Today, there has been born to you, a Savior, who is Christ the Lord, in the town of David. This shall be a sign: you shall find a Babe wrapped in swaddling clothes and lying in a manger." Suddenly there appeared with the Angel, a multitude of the heavenly Host praising God and saying: "Glory to God in the highest; peace on earth among men of good will." The shepherds went in haste and found the Babe lying in a manger.

*

The Wise Men: "Where is the King of the Jews who has been born? We have seen His star in the East and have come to worship Him."

The three kings saw the Child with His Mother Mary. Kneeling, they worshipped Him, and offered Him gifts of gold, frankincense, and myrrh.   †

The Presentation

"Every first-born male shall be offered to the Lord."

*

The Child Jesus was taken to the Temple forty days after His birth, and placed in the arms of Simeon.

Simeon: "Now, O Lord, You can dismiss Your servant, according to Your word, in peace; because my eyes have seen Your Salvation which You have prepared for all people; a Light to the Gentiles, and glory for Your people Israel." †

* * *

The Finding of the Child Jesus in the Temple

When Jesus was twelve, the Holy Family went to the Temple to pray. Returning home, Jesus was separated from His parents. Mary and Joseph searched for three days, finding Him in the Temple, in the midst of the teachers, both listening to them and asking them questions. All who heard Him were amazed at His intelligence and His answers.

Mary: "My Child, why have You done so to us? Your father and I have been seeking You in sorrow."

"Why have you looked for Me? Did you not know that I must be at My Father's business." †

* * *

THE SORROWFUL MYSTERIES

The Agony in the Garden

Our Savior Jesus went into the garden to pray. "Father, all things are possible to You; let this cup pass, yet not My Will, but Yours."

449

Jesus: "Could you not watch one hour with Me? The spirit indeed is willing, but the flesh is weak."

"The hour has come; the Son of Man is to be betrayed into the hands of sinners. Arise, let us go; he who will betray Me is at hand."

*

Judas kissed Jesus saying: "Rabbi!".

*

"You come with swords and clubs to arrest Me as if I were a robber. I was with you in the Temple and you did not seize Me." †

*   *   *

The Scourging at the Pillar

Caiphas: "I adjure You by the Living God: tell us whether You are the Christ, the Son of God."

"I AM."

"He has blasphemed! What further need have we of witnesses?"

"Crucify Him."

Pilate: "Who shall I release: Barabbas or Jesus?"

"Barabbas!"

Pilate: "What shall I do with Jesus of Nazareth?"

"Crucify Him! Crucify Him!"

Pilate: "I shall chastise Him and release Him!"

Jesus was tied to a pillar and severely whipped. †

450

The Crowning with Thorns

Pilate: "Behold your King!"

"We have no king but Caesar! Crucify Him!"

A purple garment, which was worn, dirty, and torn, was placed over the shoulders of Jesus. On His Head they placed a crown of thorns. In His Hands they placed a reed. Blindfolding Him, they struck Him saying: "Tell us who struck You!"

Pilate then condemned Jesus to death on the cross.

*   *   *   †

The Carrying of the Cross

Jesus willingly accepts the cross of wood.

Jesus falls three times under the weight of the cross.

Jesus meets His sorrowful Mother Mary.

Jesus is aided by Simon of Cyrene.

Veronica wipes the Face of Jesus.

Jesus consoles the weeping women of Jerusalem.

Jesus is stripped of His garments and crucified. †

*   *   *

Jesus Dies on the Cross

"Father, forgive them, for they know not what they do.

"Today you shall be with Me in Paradise.

"Woman, behold Your son! Son, behold your Mother.

"My God, My God, why have You forsaken Me?

"I thirst!

"All is consummated!

"Into Your Hands, O Lord, I commend My Spirit."

*   *   *   †

THE GLORIOUS MYSTERIES

The Resurrection

An Angel to the pious women: "Be not frightened! You seek Jesus of Nazareth, who was crucified. He is Risen; He is not here. Behold the place where they laid Him! Go, tell His disciples and Peter that He goes before you into Galilee; there you shall see Him, as He told you."

The pious women told the disciples what they had seen and heard. Peter and John went to the garden; looking into the tomb, they saw that it was empty.

The Angel to Mary Magdalen: "Woman, why are you weeping?"

"They have taken away my Lord, and I do not know where they have laid Him."

Jesus to Mary Magdalen: "Why are you weeping?"

"Sir, if you have carried Jesus away, tell me where you have laid Him, and I will remove Him."

452

"Mary!"

"Master!"

"Go! Tell My brethren that I ascend to My Father and your Father, to My God and your God."

*

The doors being closed, Jesus stood in the midst of the disciples saying: "Peace be with you! As the Father has sent Me, I also send you. Receive the Holy Spirit, whose sins you shall forgive, they are forgiven them; whose sins you shall retain, they are retained."

"Come Thomas, place your finger in the wound of My Hand, and place your hand in the wound of My Side."

Thomas: "My Lord and my God." †

*   *   *

The Ascension

Jesus to Simon Peter: "Do you love Me?"

Peter: "Lord, You know that I love You!"

Jesus: "Feed My lambs, feed My sheep!"

*

Jesus: "Go and preach the Gospel to every creature. Those who believe and are baptized, will be saved."

Jesus ascended before their eyes, and a cloud received Him out of their sight.

"Men of Galilee, why are you looking into heaven? Jesus has ascended; He will come again." †

453

The Descent of the Holy Spirit

There came a noise from Heaven, as of the rushing of wind, with thunder and lightning, which filled the whole house where they were praying. There appeared to them a fire, which parted into tongues of fire, and was seen over the head of each one of them. They were all filled with the Holy Spirit. There were in Jerusalem devout Jews from every country; when they heard the thunder, the multitude gathered and were amazed.

Peter: "Men of Israel, God sent Jesus to you with miracles, wonders, and signs as His credentials. He was crucified! He is Risen!"

"Are not all these who speak Galileens? How is it that we hear them in our own language?" †

* * *

The Assumption of the Blessed Virgin Mary

"Arise My Love!"

A great sign was seen in Heaven; a Woman clothed with the sun, and the moon under Her feet. †

* * *

The Coronation of the Blessed Virgin Mary

Upon Her Head was a crown of twelve stars.

"I am the Alpha and the Omega. To those that thirst, I will give Water from the Fountain of Life. I shall be their God, and they shall be My children."

"I am your Recompense, your Happiness, your All."

†

"I am the Resurrection!"

"I was Begotten from all eternity in My Father. I am the Word which utters eternally to God, My Father, the glories of My eternal Generation.

"I was Begotten in time in the womb of the Glorious Virgin Mary; on that day the Angels came down to earth to sing: 'Glory to God in the Highest, and peace on earth to men of good will.'

"I was Begotten also on earth to the Life of Glory. The sepulchre was the maternal womb which gave Me new Life. On the third day of the Pasch, (Easter), I received My Birth to the Life of Glory: the Godhead. Angels, mortals, and all nature celebrated this third Birth of God by the power with which I rose from the sepulchre; Angels, who came to act as witnesses to My Resurrection; mortals, those who had been dead, by rising with Me; those who would have prevented My rising; others, again, by beholding Me Risen from the dead; nature, by keeping silence before Me, and forgetting its laws to acknowledge only the might of My Divinity.

"O Life of the Son of Man! Death of the Son of Man! Resurrection of the Son of Man! Eternal Life of the Son of God! Admirable union of the Life of the Son of God with that of the Son of Man! Eternal Life of the Son of God with the Glorious Life of the Son of Man! Marvelous Lives of a God, of a God made Man, of a God made Man Risen again! Life Eternal and Life Mortal; Life Eternal and Life Immortal; Life without beginning or end; Life which began and has ended; Life which began and will never end; Life Glorious and henceforth Impassible! Consider the mystery of these Lives; do not seek to understand them, but seek therein your repose.

"Make Me a sepulchre in your heart. I desire to enclose in your heart these three Lives: My Divine Life, My mortal and suffering Life as Redeemer, My Life of Triumph and of Glory; the first, to make you a child of God; the second, to sanctify you; the third, to plant in you the germ of the Glorious Life which awaits you in eternity. I can die no more. I desire to be in you as One dead, who has command over life, as One buried, who bursts asunder the stone of his sepulchre, as One immolated, as a Victim offered in Sacrifice, who saves those who struck Him. I found death in Life, but in death I was able to take Life up again which will never end.

"You also are alive with the Life of God, which can no more be taken from you than My Divine Life can be taken from Me; you are alive with natural life, the life which is proper and personal to you: this life can be taken from you. You must make a sacrifice of your life. You must die to your inclinations, your desires, your thoughts, your affections, everything which is you; you must commit everything into the Hands of God, this day as well as the moment when He will call you to Himself; the sepulchre shall give you birth into My Glorious Life, My Impassible Life, which you will share with Me.

"I am the Resurrection!"

*

AFTERWORD

Jesus: "In order to labor for the salvation of your neighbor, make the saving Sign of the Cross upon your heart; utter My Name once before you speak, and after that you shall say all that My grace shall inspire you."

I make the Sign of the Cross upon my heart, pronouncing the name of Jesus.

Often I found myself in the church, not knowing what to say to Jesus, nor how to listen to Him. My delight was to read the lives of Saints and of Religious Souls to whom our Lord chose to reveal His Secrets.

Jesus: "What I tell one soul, I tell all souls."

Jesus: "As a flame needs to be fed, if it is not to be extinguished, so souls need constant fresh urging to make them advance, and new warmth to renew their fervor."

I decided to take notes, so that I also could stimulate and nourish my love for Jesus and His Mother Mary, taking advantage of the lessons taught to others by the Master in His School of Love. The reason our Lord asked St. Gertrude, St. Catherine of Siena and others to write His words, was precisely for weak, forgetful souls like me who need a constant source to enliven "prayer-time".

Consider the years of study needed to acquire a doctorate, and then consider the many years we poor souls have lived within the shelter of the Catholic Church, some of us even in Religious Life! What "degree" have we attained in the only Science that matters?

Why did our Lord choose hidden souls like Saint Margaret Mary, Sister Josefa, Sister Benigna Consolata and Saint Gertrude, to earn a "doctorate" in the Science of the Sacred Heart? Jesus chose these souls because they desired to love Him more! The Teacher is truly the Master of Love, the Supreme Architect and Master Builder. St. Teresa of Avila and St. Catherine of Siena were proclaimed Doctors of the Church by the Supreme Pontiff.

Our Lord does not speak audibly to most souls, nor does He appear to most of us. If one wants to make an in-depth study of ancient Greece, that person will need to research the works of others who have studied and written about ancient Greece.

If we wish to learn how to love Jesus, we must study the lessons our Master gave to former students. The substance is still available, for "those who seek shall find."

For those souls who believe, no explanation is necessary, for those who do not believe, no explanation is possible.

We, as Catholics, are required to believe that there are Three Persons in One God; that Holy Mary was conceived without sin; that She was a Virgin before Childbirth, in Childbirth, and after Childbirth; that She was assumed into Heaven, Body and Soul, etc. I must admit that I do not understand these Truths, nevertheless, I believe them.

Today, as in the past, some say: "Unless I put my finger into the wound of His Hand, and my hand into the wound of His side, I will not believe." Some say: "Unless I understand, I will not believe."

For many years my heart has been circulating blood through my system, second after second, minute after minute, hour after hour. I do not understand how my heart functions, yet, the lack of understanding does not have any bearing on the fact that the heart still performs a task that the intellect does not comprehend. Belief does not "hinge" upon understanding.

I have worked as an electrician for many years, yet I do not understand electricity. I know how to distribute it and use it. It does not frighten me in any way. If I were to say that electricity does not exist because I do not understand it, certainly the times that I received a 120 or 240 volt shock, and my hair stood on end while I was seeing many mini stars, at least then my senses would have been "enlightened" to inform me what my "great wisdom" was denying!

If it were necessary that I should understand how God is willing and even desirous to give His own Body and Blood to mortals, and to go so far as to dwell in my heart, then I would never be able to receive Holy Communion. It is beyond my comprehension. Holy Mother the Church asks only of Her children, even those eight-year-olds, who receive Holy Communion for the first time: "Do you believe?"

Our Lord asked Peter: "Do you love Me?" It seems to me that Peter's love was the only basis that Jesus used in choosing him as His Vicar.

Children accept what is said to them, without analyzing and without understanding. Theirs is a world of faith and love. This is what our Lord is asking from you, from me.

Holy Mary and St. Joseph were the first students at the Crib of the Infant Jesus. The poor ignorant shepherds followed, and the rich Wise Men were next.

The learned scribes and priests at the Temple of Jerusalem told Herod that according to the Prophecies of Old, they expected the King to be born in Bethlehem, but they did not go themselves. The shepherds and the Wise Men responded to the "call", and at the Crib they were taught by the Master in the "School of Love".

"A Child will lead them!" Where did the Child lead the shepherds and the Wise Men? Where will the Child lead us? The Child led them and will lead us to His Sacred Heart and to the Immaculate Heart of His Virgin Mother Mary.

To be good students in the School of Love, requires only that we be children of Love. Love is the only "degree" that will be conferred upon us.

Jesus conversed with and dictated prayers to Sister Benigna Consolata. He told her to be His little secretary. These conversations and prayers were approved by Holy Church for publication, so that they may benefit other souls.

Afterword 3

iii

Though I have finished compiling and setting the type for this book, I would even now destroy it, if I knew it to be the Will of God. Many times I was discouraged with setbacks; many times I wanted to give up. I feel that Jesus chose the least intelligent, the least cooperative soul, in choosing me. At times I wondered why our Lord didn't choose someone else who was a master of the language, who had a memory like St. Thomas Aquinas, and had a heart aglow with love as St. John the Apostle, to accomplish this work. O Lord, may Your Will be done!

Jesus: "You are the least worthy, the least capable, the least courageous, and the least cooperative soul that I could have chosen for this work. You are as nothing in My sight. Why, then, do you think that I have bestowed this grace upon you? In using you to confound satan I am more honored than if I used someone suited to the task. By My working with you and in you, satan is more humiliated than he would be were I using a proper instrument. For this reason he despises you and detests you. . ."

Jesus: "You are nothing but dust. I am your God and I have created you to give Me honor and glory. Have you never seen a ray of brilliant sunlight streaming through a haze of dust, and noticed that the minute particles, reflecting the light of the sun, sparkle like tiny gems? Similarly, when a soul is bathed in the brilliant Light of My Grace, it gives out a brilliance that is not its own. So it is with you. Why should you be proud? You are still dust. The only cause for any goodness you have, is the fact that you reflect the Glory of Him who sheds the sunlight of His Love upon you."

The pen of a nimble scribe cannot claim credit for a manuscript, nor the brush of a painter take credit for the masterpiece. I am only a poor instrument in God's Hands. I cannot take credit for this work. At most I can be called a "collector for Love," a "collector of Love."

Afterword 4*
Easter Sunday, 1979

Brother James, S.D.B.

iv

BIBLIOGRAPHY

The Way of Divine Love

(The Message of the Sacred Heart to the World)
Jesus speaks to Sister Josefa Menendez
Sister of the Congregation of the Sacred Heart
1890 - 1923
Imprimatur: E. Morrough Bernard
  Vicar General, Westmonasterii, Sep. 24, 1948
(Newman Press, Westminster and Maryland:
  copyright 1949.)

Sister Benigna Consolata Ferrero

(The Tenderness of the Love of Jesus for a Little Soul)
Religious of the Visitation Order   1885 - 1916
Imprimatur: James Cardinal Gibbons
  Archbishop of Baltimore, Maryland, Jan. 2, 1921
(John P. Daleiden Company, Chicago, Ill.:
  copyright 1925.)

Vademecum proposed to Religious Souls

Jesus dictated this book of prayers to Sister Benigna
Consolata.
Imprimatur: O. B. Corrigan, D. D.
  Baltimore, Maryland, October 7, 1917
(Georgetown Visitation Convent, Wash., D.C.   1921.)

Life and Revelations of St. Gertrude, Virgin and Abbess

Nun of the Order of Saint Benedict
1256 - 1301
Imprimatur: D. Moriarty, Bishop of Killarney
  December 17, 1870
(The Newman Press, Westminster and Maryland:
  copyright 1949.)

v

Prayers of Saint Gertrude and Saint Mechtilde

The Great, Flaming Furnace of the Sacred Heart

Letters and Writings of Sister Marie Lastaste

Jesus Appeals to the World

He and I

Gems of Thought from Saint Margaret Mary

Visitation Nun of Paray le Monial, France, 1647 - 1690
Imprimatur: Patrick Cardinal Hayes
  Archbishop of New York, September 15, 1931
(Benziger Brothers, New York, N.Y.:   copyright 1931.)

Spiritual Legacy of Sister Mary of the Holy Trinity

Poor Clare Nun 1901 - 1942
Imprimatur: Francis P. Keough, D.D.
  Archbishop of Baltimore, March 8, 1950
(The Newman Press, Westminster   copyright 1954.)

Dialogue of Saint Catherine of Siena

Third Order Dominican Sister of Siena, Italy. 1347 - 1380
Imprimatur: Gulielmus Episcopus Arindelensis
  Vicar General, Westmonasterii, December 13, 1906
(Tan Books and Publishers, P.O. Box 424
  Rockford, Ill. 61105:   Copyright 1974.)

Story of a Soul

The Autobiography of Saint Therese of the Child Jesus
Carmelite Nun, Lisieux, France. 1873 - 1897
Imprimatur: Edm. Can. Surmont,
  Vicar General, Westmonasterii, December 7, 1926
(ICS Publications, 2131 Lincoln Road, Wash., D.C. 20002:
  Translated: Rev. John Clarke   Copyright 1975.)

The Mystical City of God

The Life of the Blessed Virgin Mary, as revealed to the
Franciscan Nun, Venerable Mary of Jesus, 1602 - 1666
Imprimatur: Edwin V. Byrne, D.D.
  Archbishop of Santa Fe, New Mexico, February 9, 1949
(Corcoran Pub. Co., Albuquerque, N.M.: copyright 1949.)

TABLE OF QUOTES

GENERAL INDEX

xvi

General Index continued